The Role of Death in Life

VERITAS
Series Introduction

"... the truth will set you free" (John 8:32)

In much contemporary discourse, Pilate's question has been taken to mark the absolute boundary of human thought. Beyond this boundary, it is often suggested, is an intellectual hinterland into which we must not venture. This terrain is an agnosticism of thought: because truth cannot be possessed, it must not be spoken. Thus, it is argued that the defenders of "truth" in our day are often traffickers in ideology, merchants of counterfeits, or anti-liberal. They are, because it is somewhat taken for granted that Nietzsche's word is final: truth is the domain of tyranny.

Is this indeed the case, or might another vision of truth offer itself? The ancient Greeks named the love of wisdom as *philia*, or friendship. The one who would become wise, they argued, would be a "friend of truth." For both philosophy and theology might be conceived as schools in the friendship of truth, as a kind of relation. For like friendship, truth is as much discovered as it is made. If truth is then so elusive, if its domain is *terra incognita*, perhaps this is because it arrives to us—unannounced—as gift, as a person, and not some thing.

The aim of the Veritas book series is to publish incisive and original current scholarly work that inhabits "the between" and "the beyond" of theology and philosophy. These volumes will all share a common aspiration to transcend the institutional divorce in which these two disciplines often find themselves, and to engage questions of pressing concern to both philosophers and theologians in such a way as to reinvigorate both disciplines with a kind of interdisciplinary desire, often so absent in contemporary academe. In a word, these volumes represent collective efforts in the befriending of truth, doing so beyond the simulacra of pretend tolerance, the violent, yet insipid reasoning of liberalism that asks with Pilate, "What is truth?"—expecting a consensus of non-commitment; one that encourages the commodification of the mind, now sedated by the civil service of career, ministered by the frightened patrons of position.

The series will therefore consist of two "wings": (1) original monographs; and (2) essay collections on a range of topics in theology and philosophy. The latter will principally be the products of the annual conferences of the Centre of Theology and Philosophy (www.theologyphilosophycentre .co.uk).

Conor Cunningham and Eric Austin Lee, *Series editors*

The Role of Death in Life

A Multidisciplinary Examination
of the Relationship between Life and Death

edited by

JOHN BEHR *and*
CONOR CUNNINGHAM

CASCADE *Books* · Eugene, Oregon

THE ROLE OF DEATH IN LIFE
A Multidisciplinary Examination of the Relationship between Life and Death

Veritas 15

Cascade Books
A Division of Wipf and Stock Publishers
199 W. 8th Ave., Suite 3
Eugene, OR 97401

www.wipfandstock.com

ISBN 13: 978-1-4982-0958-8

Cataloging-in-Publication data:

The role of death in life : a multidisciplinary examination of the relationship between life and death / edited by John Behr and Conor Cunningham.

xvi + 190 p. ; 23 cm. Includes bibliographical references.

ISBN 13: 978-1-4982-0958-8

1. Death—Religious aspects—Christianity. 2. Death. 3. Life—Religious aspects—Christianity. I. Behr, John. II. Cunningham, Conor, 1972–. III. Series. IV. Title.

BS2545.D45 B44 2015

Manufactured in the U.S.A.

For Mary Ann Meyers, in whom there is Life in abundance

Table of Contents

List of Contributors

The Very Rev. Dr. John Behr is the Dean and Professor of Patristics at St. Vladimir's Orthodox Theological Seminary, New York, USA.

Dr. Jeffrey Paul Bishop is the Tenet Endowed Chair in Health Care Ethics and the Director of the Albert Gnaegi Center for Health Care Ethics at St. Louis University, USA.

Dr. Conor Cunningham is Associate Professor in Theology and Philosophy at The University of Nottingham, UK.

Dr. Douglas James Davies is Professor in the Study of Religion at Durham University, UK.

Dr. Emmanuel Falque is the Dean of the Faculty of Philosophy, Institut Catholique de Paris, France.

Dr. Alexei V. Filippenko is the Richard & Rhoda Goldman Distinguished Professor in the Physical Sciences and Professor of Astronomy at the University of California, Berkeley, USA.

Dr. Christina M. Gschwandtner is Professor of Philosophy, Fordham University, New York, USA.

Dr. Daniel B. Hinshaw is the Professor of Surgery at the University of Michigan, Medical School Palliative Care Program, Ann Arbor, USA.

Dr. Luc Jaeger is Professor of Chemistry and Biochemistry at the University of California, Santa Barbara, USA.

Dr. Henry L. Novello is an Honorary Research Fellow in the Department of Theology at Flinders University, South Australia

Preface

THE ESSAYS GATHERED IN this volume were originally delivered at a symposium with the same title, generously and graciously convened by the Humble Approach Initiative of the John Templeton Foundation, at Castel Gandolfo, June 2013. The subject, the relation between life and death, is one of perennial relevance for all human beings, and indeed, the whole world and the entire universe, in as much as, according to the dictum of ancient Greek philosophy, all things that come into being pass away. Yet it is also a topic of increasing complexity and urgency: complexity, in that life and death appear to be more intertwined than previously or commonly thought; and urgency, in that people living in the industrialized and post-industrialized Western world over the past century have, through the twin phenomena of an unprecedented increase in longevity and the rendering of death, dying, and the dead person all but invisible, lost touch with the reality of death, with implications—medical, ethical, economic, philosophical, and, not least, theological—that have barely begun to be addressed.

To begin this task, leading scholars from diverse disciplines were invited to reflect together, each from their own discipline, on the relationship between death and life. More specifically, the conveners of the symposium presented the participants with a particular "hypothesis" or "supposition," one that was self-consciously theological. The hypothesis of Christian theology, it was proposed, is that by his death, Christ has conquered death, and so life and death are reversed; that by dying, as human, Christ shows us what it is to be God, so offering us a way of participating in the life of God, and, in fact, becoming human. Death alone is common to all men and women throughout all time and space: thrown into this world without choice, our existence culminates inevitably in death. Yet, by showing us what it is to be God in the *way* in which he dies as a human being, Christ offers an alternative "use" of death: we now can actively "use" death, as a voluntary birth, completing God's project of creating living human beings by giving our own fiat, establishing our existence in the free self-sacrificial life that is the life of God himself.

Each participant was invited to consider whether this hypothesis has echoes in his or her own discipline, whether it elucidates, or is elucidated by, similar dynamics in the understanding of reality as approached by her or his own subject or whether it is at odds or incompatible with their findings. The goal was to be multi-disciplinary, with each discipline considering this hypothesis and speaking in the terms of their own disciplinary discourse, rather than the inter-disciplinary task of trying to relate each distinct discourse to each other directly, in some meta-discourse. So, with regard to the natural sciences, the question could be whether the relation between life and death on the human level is reflected in, and also informed by, similar phenomenon on macro-level (e.g., the death of stars) or on the micro-level (e.g., cell death)? In the field of anthropology, what impact do the varying patterns of death rituals have on our self-understanding? From a philosophical perspective, what do the insights of contemporary phenomenology offer to our understanding of the relation between life and death? For theology itself (for the hypothesis needs to be tested here as well), how has this supposition been articulated, or overlooked, in the history of theology? And then in the field of medicine, the care of the dying, and bioethics, how does the hypothesis relate to, or possibly inform, what is fast becoming the greatest medical (but also financial and legal) problem in the Western world: that the medical arts have become so focused on the perpetuation and extension of biological life that they no longer know the art of helping the dying to die and those around them to accept this passage? What insights do contemporary medical knowledge and the experience of those caring for the dying, in their turn, offer to the starting hypothesis?

The essays collected here are divided into these various fields. The first essays are given by an astrophysicist and a biochemist. In his contribution, "Made of Star-stuff: The Origin of the Chemical Elements in Life," Alex Filippenko demonstrates that life in fact only emerged in this universe through the death of stars, producing the necessary ingredients for life: such "death" lies, therefore, at the root of all life. In "A Biochemical Perspective on the Origin of Life and Death," Luc Jaeger argues that at the cellular level, as well, the process of life cannot be separated from death; it is the ability of informational polymers to degrade or "die" that facilitates the emergence of living systems.

Coming from the field of Anthropology, Douglas Davis, in his essay "Immortality," considers how death, and its interpretation, has been at work in the self-reflective construction of identity, with the cognitive dissonance created by the presence of a dead person becoming the occasion and means by which we imagine the unimaginable, our own death, and the hope for immortality undergirding our biological drive to survive.

In the field of philosophy, specifically that of the "theological-turn" of French phenomenology, Emmanuel Falque, in his essay "Suffering Death," considers the "passage" of Christ as he approaches his own death as both suffering and transformation, emphasizing that Christ does not do so already assured of the outcome, such that he would not truly inhabit our own darkness, but rather truly "suffers" the full weight and reality of death, to offer it to the Father who alone transforms it, and in this way fundamentally transforms the reality of the human condition of mortality. Christina Gschwandtner, in her essay "How Do We Become Fully Alive? The Role of Death in Henry's Phenomenology of Life," tackles the much discussed "death of the subject" in our contemporary technological culture of death, and turns to Michel Henry's "phenomenology of life," which finds that genuinely human life is not, in fact, to be found in the phenomena studied by biology and physiology, but in the transcendental affectivity of the subject, its suffering and joy, in which life is revealed to itself and becomes possible as life, and which, although radically distinct from "the world," turns out to be a material phenomenology, creating the very conditions for the body and the flesh.

Turning next to theology, John Behr, in "Life and Death in an Age of Martyrdom," looks at the way in which early Christian writers spoke of martyrdom as birth into life and "becoming human"; following Christ in voluntarily taking up the cross (as dying to oneself in living for others) is seen as an entry into a mode of life beyond death, for it is entered into through death, a mode of life that is shown to be God's own, and so the completion of God's own project, to create human beings in his own image and likeness. In his essay "New Life as Life out of Death: Sharing in the 'Exchange of Natures' in the Person of Christ," Henry Novello examines the way in which death has been treated in recent theology, and especially the shortcomings of the manner in which our death has been related to that of Christ, and argues, instead, that we should take seriously the application of the Christological principle of the "exchange of properties" (*communicatio idiomatum*) in its full application, not only as the imparting of divine properties on the human, but also the assumption human properties, in particular that most universal human property of mortality, in the divine, so that the assumption of death renders death, common to all human beings, salvific. The final essay in this section, that of Conor Cunningham, asks provocatively "Is There Life before Death?" If we take seriously the reductionism of much contemporary philosophy (and even some theology), can we even claim to be alive now, or even to be human beings? We must learn to rethink, the essay argues, our very understanding of ourselves, not as souls inhabiting bodies or as mere bodies (if we dispense with the idea of a soul), but rather as human beings, with the soul being the very form of the body, enabling this matter to be a living human being.

The final essays in this volume come from those who work in the field of palliative care and bioethics. Daniel Hinshaw, in "The Kenosis of the Dying: An Invitation to Healing," considers the dire implications of the profound demographic changes of the past century and the presuppositions of the medical profession, which views all illnesses and suffering as disorders that can be mechanistically understood and, in principle, cured. Looking at the rise of the hospice movement and palliative care as a response to the "denial of death" in the medical profession and society more broadly, the author turns to central tenets of Christian theology and anthropology to show how approaching death is a profoundly transformative experience both for the one entering this mystery and those ministering to them. And finally, Jeffrey Bishop, in his essay "Of Medical Corpses and Resurrected Bodies," traces the way in which current medical understanding and practice is based upon an approach that sees the body as an "anticipatory corpse," concentrating only on the material and efficient causes, in the Aristotelian framework, while neglecting formal and final causes: meaning and purpose are elided in order to understand the material and mechanisms of the world in a vacuum; the only "meaning" that remains is to be found in thinking of the (still living, but regarded as dead!) body as a source of parts for supporting the bare life of others. The predicaments that have arisen from regarding the corpse as epistemologically normative are profound and wide-ranging, but cannot be resolved within the discipline as it currently understands itself and puts its knowledge into practice. As such, the author raises the provocative question: "Might it not be that only theology can save medicine?"

The essays gathered here thus do indeed find considerable resonance with one another. Life and death are more intertwined than one might suppose, from the largest imaginable scale to the smallest discernable element. Moreover, what constitutes genuinely *human* life is more complex than we might have initially supposed: is it the perpetuating of the function of the material body, that is metaphysically and epistemologically regarded, paradoxically, as a corpse, or is it to be found, and lived, in a distinctively human manner, one that recognizes the fact of human mortality but "uses" this mortality to enter upon a different mode of living? And such questions, as many of these essays point out, have truly profound and urgent implications for us today. Can we afford to remain committed to a reductionist view of life? Is it possible to resolve the bioethical quandaries raised by modern medicine with the presuppositions and framework within which modern medical practice functions? Does the erasure of the visibility of the process of dying, the dead person, and death itself, from our contemporary Western culture also erase a vision of God who reveals himself through the human death of his Son, showing us thereby the means by which death is conquered? And does it in fact erase what is distinctively human about human life? This present collection of essays does not, of course, offer any definitive solution to these unsettling questions, but it does open up a space where scientists, philosophers, and theologians might creatively, constructively, and collaboratively discuss the perennial issues of life and death and what it is to be a living human being, who is, in the vivid words of Irenaeus of Lyons, "the glory of God."

I

PERSPECTIVES FROM ASTRONOMY, CHEMISTRY, AND BIOLOGY

1

Made of Star-stuff: The Origin of the Chemical Elements in Life

Alexei V. Filippenko

T‍HIS ESSAY DISCUSSES OUR present understanding of the origin of many of the ninety-two naturally occurring chemical elements in the Periodic Table of the Elements, of which the Solar System and all known forms of life consist.[1] We will see that the early Universe essentially contained only hydrogen and helium, the two lightest elements. The creation story of relatively heavy elements such as the carbon in our cells, the oxygen that we breathe, the calcium in our bones, and the iron in our blood, is arguably one of the most beautiful and profound realizations in the history of science. It is a powerful example, on grand scales, of the role of life in death and vice versa: without the birth of stars, and without their subsequent death, especially the violent final explosion that some of them experience, new stars and planetary systems having an enriched proportion of heavy elements would not have been created, the rocky and water-covered Earth

1. For a general overview of astronomy, including most of the astronomical concepts discussed here (and a very large number of beautiful photographs, including many of those shown in my oral presentation), see the introductory college textbook by Pasachoff and Filippenko, *The Cosmos*. This work also contains an extensive list of useful references and suggestions for further reading. A set of ninety-six richly illustrated video lectures covering much of introductory astronomy is that of Filippenko, *Understanding the Universe*. A higher-level college textbook that includes more advanced physics concepts is that of Carroll and Ostlie, *An Introduction to Modern Astrophysics*. For an older, but still relevant, classic, see Shu, *The Physical Universe*.

would not exist, and we would not be here discussing these issues. When we as sentient beings contemplate our cosmic origins, the following eloquent phrase provides a concise summary: "We are made of star-stuff."[2]

The Elements of Life

Let me first consider the main constituents of life on Earth, with humans (the focus of this collection of essays) being fairly representative. About 93 percent of our body mass (i.e., percent by weight) consists of only three chemical elements: oxygen (65 percent), carbon (18 percent), and hydrogen (10 percent).[3] Adding just three more brings the total to nearly 99 percent: nitrogen (3 percent), calcium (1.5 percent), and phosphorus (1.2 percent). (In plants and other organisms lacking skeletons, sulfur replaces calcium in the top six elements.) By number of atoms (i.e., atomic percent) instead of weight, the corresponding amounts in humans are even more impressive: hydrogen (63 percent), oxygen (24 percent), and carbon (12 percent) account for almost 99 percent, with small contributions from nitrogen (0.58 percent), calcium (0.24 percent), and phosphorus (0.14 percent). Hydrogen and oxygen are dominant because humans consist largely of water: 53 percent by weight for the average adult.

If we examine the relative abundances of elements by number in our Solar System, including the Sun, which has most of the mass, we see that hydrogen is by far the most common, as in humans. Helium is the second most abundant, but it doesn't combine with other atoms, so it is not surprising that humans don't contain helium. Oxygen and carbon are the next most abundant among the non-inert elements, and they are numbers two and three in humans as well. So we are made of the most common chemically active elements in the Solar System.

But life does not consist of just the top six elements listed above. About eighteen additional elements are of critical importance. Although five of them (sulfur, potassium, sodium, chlorine, and magnesium) constitute most of the remaining 0.1 percent by atomic percent, the others should not

2. This saying is often attributed to the astronomer and science advocate, Carl Sagan, *The Cosmic Connection*. However, Sagan certainly did not discover the concept, and it had long been stated in a similar way, or even nearly verbatim, e.g., Watson, "Astronomy"; W. E. Barton, quoted in an advertisement in the *Evening News* (Sault Ste. Marie, Michigan), January 24, 1921, 2, column 3; Garbedian "The Star Stuff that is Man," SM1, quoting astronomer Harlow Shapley.

3. Cf. Chang, *Chemistry*.

be forgotten. Iron, the most abundant of the "trace elements" in the human body, is necessary for the hemoglobin in red blood cells, while zinc and copper are needed in some proteins, and the thyroid gland uses iodine in the production of hormones that regulate the metabolism. There are some small differences between plants and animals; for example, some types of plants do not require sodium, yet all animals need it.

From where did all of these elements arise, so necessary for life as we know it? Were they present from the very birth of the Universe? The answer is no: various physical processes produced them, as I shall now describe.

In the Beginning

Modern cosmologists, who study of the structure and evolution of the Universe as a whole, now have a rather detailed, self-consistent, and observationally supported story regarding the past history of the Universe, starting from a tiny fraction of a second after the moment of creation. This "big-bang theory" postulates that the Universe began in a very hot, dense state about 13.8 billion years ago, and it has been expanding, cooling, and becoming less dense ever since. During the expansion, space itself is created, rather than material objects flying through a preexisting space; thus, the big bang was not really an "explosion" in the conventional sense, like a bomb, and there is no unique center within the spatial dimensions physically accessible to us.

When the Universe was less than one millionth of a second old and its temperature was higher than about ten trillion kelvin (10^{13} K), there was equilibrium between particles, antiparticles, and photons (packets or quanta of light): specifically, quarks and antiquarks annihilated each other, forming photons, and vice versa. But through a process not yet fully understood, a slight excess (one part per billion) of quarks over antiquarks was produced, and this eventually gave rise to neutrons and protons, "baryons" that each consist of three bound quarks. Initially there were somewhat more protons (simple hydrogen nuclei) than neutrons because protons are slightly less massive. Also, starting about one second after the big bang, neutrons began to systematically decay into protons and electrons, thereby producing a greater deficit of neutrons compared with protons. At this time, the temperature was about ten billion kelvin (10^{10} K), and collisions between baryons were too violent for them to stick together. Moreover, it was still so hot that electrons roamed freely, not bound to protons as in neutral atoms.

But by an age of one hundred seconds, the Universe had cooled to a temperature of "only" about one billion K (10^9 K).[4] Collisions between baryons were not as violent, sometimes resulting in particles bound together by the "strong nuclear force." As a first step, a proton and a neutron could bind together to form a deuteron, a heavy "isotope" or type of hydrogen.[5] Two deuterons could subsequently fuse together and form a light isotope of helium (He-3, with two protons and one neutron) plus a free neutron. He-3 and a deuteron could then fuse to produce the normal isotope, He-4 (with two protons and two neutrons), and a proton. Since protons outnumbered neutrons by a ratio of 7/1 at the time of such interactions, about 25 percent of the mass ended up as He-4, with most of the rest (75 percent) remaining as protons (H nuclei). A tiny bit of lithium, containing three protons and four neutrons (Li-7), was also produced.

Nuclei heavier than lithium (with the exception of a trace of beryllium-7) were not created during the big bang because the Universe was expanding and cooling rapidly; by an age of just ten minutes, the density and temperature had dropped so much that the process of "primordial nucleosynthesis" (the formation of the lightest nuclei through nuclear fusion) had ceased. In particular, the isotope of beryllium having four protons and four neutrons (Be-8) is unstable, decaying very shortly after its creation, and this caused a bottleneck in the fusion process; there was no easy way to reach carbon (with six protons and six neutrons). The Universe was left with plenty of H and He nuclei, a smidgen of Li, a trace quantity of Be-7, and no other nuclei. Eventually, when the Universe cooled to a temperature of about 3000 K around 380,000 years after the big bang, these nuclei combined with free electrons and formed neutral atoms, primarily of H and He. Although life on Earth relies on that primordial hydrogen, we need other mechanisms to produce the additional necessary elements. This is where stars and the way they generate their energy come into the picture.

---

4. If one thinks of hell as having ponds of boiling sulfur at a temperature of 718 K $\approx$ 1000 K, then the Universe was still about a million times hotter than hell at this time!

5. Cosmologists sometimes joke that the study of deuterons is known as Deuteronomy.

Star Formation and Energy Generation

We live in the Milky Way Galaxy, a gigantic, gravitationally bound collection of several hundred billion stars that might look similar to other large spiral galaxies. It is roughly one hundred thousand light years across and only about one thousand light years thick. If we were above the disk, we would easily see spiral arms. But the Sun is within the thin disk, about twenty-six thousand light years from the center of the Galaxy. An all-sky photograph clearly shows the disk, as well as the central bulge of stars. When we look along the plane of the disk, we see many stars compared with other directions; this forms the band of light called the Milky Way that can be viewed on a clear, dark night.

In the Milky Way Galaxy, we see many examples of giant clouds of gas and dust (tiny solid grains) in the "interstellar medium," the space between the stars; a good example is the beautiful Trifid nebula in the constellation Sagittarius. In the sword of Orion, the great hunter, one finds the Orion Nebula, another excellent example. If a cloud grows to a sufficiently large mass, or if it gets dense enough, it can become gravitationally unstable; its own self-gravity causes it to collapse inward, as has occurred in the Orion Nebula. During the collapse, it begins to fragment into many smaller subunits called protostars. As the density increases, collisions between the particles cause the gas to heat up and the pressure rises, thereby slowing each protostar's collapse.

Further contraction occurs more gradually, but gravitational energy is still being released and the temperature continues to rise. Eventually, when the central temperature of a protostar becomes sufficiently high (typically above four million K, but about fifteen million K in the Sun's core), nuclear reactions begin and we say that a star is born. In general, stars are produced in clusters that originated from the same initial cloud of gas and dust. Light from powerful, massive stars blows away excess gas; a star cluster remains. Presumably, our own Sun was formed in a cluster about 4.6 billion years ago, but the Sun and other stars gradually escaped from the cluster.

The energy released from a star is exactly balanced by nuclear reactions in its core; thus, there is no reason for further gravitational contraction and the star achieves mechanical equilibrium. A given star maintains roughly the same size and has a roughly constant intrinsic brightness (luminosity) for most of its normal life (technically, while it is a "main-sequence star"), though both the size and especially the luminosity are larger for more-massive stars. Typical stellar masses range from about 8 percent of the Sun's mass to roughly fifty solar masses, but most stars are less massive than the Sun and the very massive ones are extremely rare.

In the Sun, as in other main-sequence stars, the gases in the core are so hot that atoms are ionized; the electrons have been stripped away from the nuclei. Energy is produced by fusion of hydrogen nuclei to helium nuclei: four protons come together in a series of reactions, forming a single helium nucleus consisting of two protons and two neutrons (hence, two of the protons turned into neutrons along the way, though this detail need not concern us here). The specific sequence of reactions depends on the temperature of the core and therefore on the mass of the star, but the end result is the same: helium is produced, and it has a slightly lower mass (by 0.7 percent) than the original four protons that went into making it. That mass difference m, when multiplied by the square of the speed of light c^2, accounts for the energy release through Einstein's famous formula, $E = mc^2$. The Sun shines by fusing about six hundred billion kilograms of hydrogen to helium each *second*, yet there is so much hydrogen in the central region that this process can continue for a total of about ten billion years. The Sun is now a middle-aged star, about halfway through its normal main-sequence life.

What will happen as the Sun ages beyond about ten billion years, when the core consists mostly of helium nuclei? Over the next two billion years, the story will unfold as follows. Helium nuclei will be unable to undergo fusion because of the electric repulsion between them. Thus, the helium core will lose energy to surrounding layers and slowly contract under the force of gravity. But this contraction will heat up a surrounding layer of hydrogen that is still fusing to helium, thereby increasing the rate of fusion, eventually by a factor of one hundred or more. The Sun will become much more powerful (luminous), and its outer envelope of gases will expand outward and cool down. The Sun will be a "red giant" at this stage: a very luminous and bloated, but relatively cool and hence reddish-looking, star that will literally fry anything that remains on Earth's surface.

Stellar Nucleosynthesis beyond Helium

During the next stage of the Sun's life, heavier elements will be produced. As the helium core in the future red-giant Sun contracts, it will also gradually become hotter. When the temperature reaches about one hundred million K, a new process of nuclear fusion will begin: three helium nuclei can fuse together, forming a nucleus of carbon and releasing energy in the process. Moreover, a carbon nucleus can fuse with another helium nucleus, forming oxygen and releasing additional energy. This previously happened in other, similar stars as well. We are starting to see the creation of elements necessary for life on Earth!

After about a million years of helium fusion, a carbon-oxygen core will form in the Sun's center. It will not be sufficiently hot to undergo nuclear fusion; carbon and oxygen nuclei have so much positive charge that the electric repulsion is too great to overcome in a relatively low-mass star like the Sun. The carbon-oxygen core will thus contract, releasing energy and heating up the helium-fusing and hydrogen-fusing layers that surround it. This will accelerate fusion in these layers, causing the Sun to bloat into an even larger red giant.

At this point, the outer layers of gas will be only tenuously bound to the Sun, and atoms of gas will be blown outward in the form of a solar wind. More importantly, a recurring instability will abruptly eject parts of the outer envelope in what I like to call a "cosmic burp." High-energy light coming from the hot, exposed stellar surface will ionize the slowly expanding gases, causing them to glow. The result will a "planetary nebula," named this way because eighteenth- and nineteenth-century astronomers thought the disks of light resemble planets. They are very beautiful objects, but each one appears different in detail, so we don't know exactly what our own Sun's planetary nebula will look like.

The central star in a planetary nebula gradually becomes a dense carbon-oxygen "white dwarf"—a retired star that shines only because it radiates its life savings of stored energy, not because it is actively fusing light elements into heavier ones. A good example is Sirius B, the faint companion of the brightest star in the sky; it is roughly the size of Earth, but having a mass comparable to that of the Sun, it is very dense. For stars that are initially less massive than about 0.45 solar masses, the white dwarfs consist of helium, because carbon and oxygen were not formed. But for stars that are between about eight and ten solar masses, carbon can fuse to form a core of oxygen, neon, and magnesium, so that the corresponding white dwarf consists of these elements.

The gases in a planetary nebula are slightly enriched in heavy elements because part of the material from the core (mostly carbon and oxygen) mixed outward into the atmosphere of the star prior to the formation of the planetary nebula. Also, in somewhat more massive stars, nitrogen can be formed as a byproduct of H-to-He fusion. Finally, even heavier elements can be formed during the second red-giant stage through what is called the slow-neutron-capture process (the "s-process"), and they too can be ejected during the planetary nebula stage.

This s-process is quite interesting. It starts with an existing iron nucleus (twenty-six protons), or some other heavy nucleus from a previous supernova explosion (to be discussed below). This nucleus absorbs free neutrons from its surroundings one by one, though at a relatively slow rate. Between the capture of two consecutive neutrons, often (but not always) a neutron in the nucleus will decay into a proton and other particles (a process called "beta decay"), thereby creating the element having the next higher atomic number (number of protons). The process can continue all the way up to the element bismuth, which has eighty-three protons, and it is responsible for roughly half of the isotopes of elements between iron and bismuth. Strong evidence for the s-process was found in 1952, when the radioactive element technetium (which lasts roughly ten million years) was discovered in the outer atmospheres of certain types of stars that were billions of years old. The technetium could not have been present when the stars were born, and it was unlikely to have been produced deep in the cores where most of the fusion powering the stars was taking place.

In any case, the ejection of chemically enriched gases during the planetary nebula stage represents an important step in the process by which stellar death gradually increases the concentration of elements heavier than H and He in the interstellar medium.

Supernovae: A Key to Our Existence

Though normal stars produce some of the heavy elements in the Periodic Table, a crucial component comes from exploding stars (supernovae). Only a small minority of stars explode violently at the end of their lives, becoming millions or billions of times more powerful than the Sun, but those that do are crucial to our existence: they create many of the heavy elements and eject them into space, making them available as raw material for the formation of new stars, planetary systems, and ultimately life. This, again, illuminates the role of life in death and, more profoundly, the role of death in life.

There are two main types of supernovae. The progenitors of "core-collapse supernovae" (technically, Type II, Ib, and Ic supernovae based on observational distinctions) are stars more massive than about ten solar masses near the end of their lives. They bloat out to become red supergiants, a good example of which is Betelgeuse in the constellation Orion. They gradually build up successively heavier elements in their core. The ashes of one set of nuclear reactions become the fuel for the next set—H fuses to He; He fuses to C and O; C fuses to O, Ne, and Mg; O fuses to Si and S; Si and S fuse to Fe (iron). An iron core eventually forms, but it becomes too massive and collapses; protons combine with electrons to form neutrons, and the result is an extremely dense "neutron star." This core collapse initiates a titanic explosion of the surrounding layers, flinging out the previously made layers of C, O, Mg, and other "intermediate-mass elements." It also fuses and ejects additional elements such as calcium, and especially nickel which radioactively decays to cobalt and finally to iron.

Another breed is known as "thermonuclear supernovae," often referred to as Type Ia supernovae for historical reasons. Here, a carbon-oxygen white dwarf becomes unstable and undergoes a runaway chain of thermonuclear reactions, completely obliterating itself in the process. Carbon fuses to heavier elements, and about half the star's mass becomes radioactive nickel, which then decays to cobalt and eventually iron. Exactly how the white dwarf reaches the unstable mass is still unclear: either it steals gas from a relatively normal companion star, or perhaps two white dwarfs in a binary system spiral toward each other and merge. In any case, many elements up to iron are produced by such stellar deaths and ejected into the interstellar medium.

Let me also mention the heaviest elements, including most isotopes of gold, silver, and platinum. Though in general not necessary for life as we know it, they are still of interest, and they are much used by humans. Such elements form through the rapid-neutron-capture process (the "r-process"). In the r-process, there are so many available free neutrons that quite a few get captured in quick succession before any neutron in the nucleus decays to a proton. This can produce neutron-rich isotopes, as well as all elements heavier than bismuth, through uranium. The site of the r-process has not yet been definitively confirmed, though core-collapse supernovae produce a great number of free neutrons and are thus a good candidate. Also, recent calculations show that merging pairs of neutron stars might be prime candidates for the r-process. Again, stellar death is involved, directly or indirectly.

We have compelling evidence that supernovae do indeed produce heavy elements and eject them into space. Spectroscopic studies of supernova remnants, the expanding debris of fatal stellar explosions, reveal heavy elements in such great quantities that they could not have been present in the original stars; we know of no stars having similar abundances. Moreover, studies of the particularly nearby, spectacular Supernova 1987A (whose light was first detected in on February 23, 1987) revealed the presence of short-lived radioactive nuclei that could not have been present in the 10-millon-year-old star prior to the explosion. The explosion itself must have produced these nuclei!

The Chemical Evolution of Galaxies and the Formation of Life

So what happens when some stars violently explode, or when most others gently eject their outer envelopes of gases? Well, in both cases, but especially in supernovae, the gases are chemically enriched. They go flying out into space, becoming part of the interstellar medium. For example, we see supernova remnants at various stages of expansion and dilution: the relatively compact Crab Nebula is the remains of a supernova that was seen by Chinese astronomers in the year 1054 CE, whereas the Vela supernova remnant has an age of several tens of thousands of years. The rapidly moving gases are generally trapped within the galaxy by the galaxy's overall gravitational pull, so most of the newly formed heavy elements are retained.

Gradually the gases encounter other clouds of gas, either preexisting in the galaxy or the remnants of other dying stars, and they coalesce, forming progressively larger clouds. Some of these clouds eventually grow sufficiently big that they become gravitationally unstable and collapse, forming a new cluster of stars. In other cases, a nearby supernova explosion might compress the cloud, thereby initiating collapse and the formation of new stars. This is yet another example of how, in the cosmos, death can be an important precursor to life.

In any case, new generations of stars are born and die, and the chemical enrichment process continues. Over time, certain clouds of gas become so abundant in heavy elements that rocky, Earth-like planets can form in the disks of debris surrounding newborn stars. We have long known that this happened in our Solar System, and we now also know that such planets are common around other stars as well. In particular, the spectacular

Kepler mission has recently discovered a few thousand planets, most of which are just two or three times the size of Earth and many of which are probably rocky. Planetary systems broadly similar to ours abound.

On Earth, through a process not yet understood, molecules of ever-increasing complexity formed and eventually combined to create the simplest living cell, the common ancestor to bacteria and archaea at the beginning of the tree of life.[6] Gradually, again through a complex series of steps that are still not well explained, prokaryotes (cells without a nucleus) evolved to eukaryotes, and then to creatures of progressively greater complexity, culminating with humans—sentient beings who can think about and study the Universe, in a quest to understand their origins.

Studying the emergence and evolution of life on Earth is one of the greatest challenges of modern science. It is an exciting field, full of exploration and opportunity, and I'm confident that someday we will learn the answers. But at least we already know the origin of the raw materials for life, the chemical elements of which we consist: hydrogen came from the big bang, and stars produced the rest through a repeated process of life, death, and rebirth. Stellar life allows chemical elements to be created, and stellar death creates additional elements and liberates all of them into space, leading to the formation of new stars, planets, and ultimately life. We are, indeed, made of star-stuff.

6. Excellent books on the origin and evolution of life include those of Zubay, *Origins of Life on Earth*; Davies, *The Origin of Life*; and Cowan *History of Life*.

2

A Biochemical Perspective on the
Origin of Life and Death

Luc Jaeger

This paper is dedicated to Saint Albert the Great, patron saint of scientists and Saint Thomas Aquinas, patron saint of universities and students.

FROM A BIOCHEMICAL PERSPECTIVE, the process of life cannot be separated from the notion of death. As such, we can consider the origin of biological life to be at the origin of biological death. It is however necessary to clarify what life and death really mean at a biochemical level of integration. This essay will first explore the physico-chemical characteristics of the biopolymers on which life is presently based on. By considering cellular life as an informational process, we will then show that the process of life is intimately connected to the process of death through bottom-up and top-down causal effects. Top-down causation (TDC) by information control and adaptive selection are at the root of converging forces that shape the evolution of living bio-systems from the simplest to the most complex levels. Living systems can be defined as self-reproducing systems that function via TDC by information control and adaptive selection. Consequently, Darwinian evolutionary processes in cells are not only ruled from the bottom-up but also by organizational principles that impose necessary constraints from the top-down and determine the survival (life) or elimination (death) of cellular bio-systems. This can be seen as resulting from the ability of informational biopolymers to be eliminated (or die) and to be selected (or live).

Definitions of Life at an Organic Level

From a naturalistic, scientific point of view, there is presently a significant body of research suggesting the emergence of the properties of animate, living matter (or organic life) from inanimate, non-living matter.[1] The abiogenesis of life implies continuity between physics, chemistry, and biology and their natural laws. It also strongly suggests that the emergence and development of organic life are dependent on processes and conditions that are probably not unique to Earth. Despite agreements on the abiogenesis of life, an unequivocal definition of life at an organic level is still a matter of debate. Most scientists will agree that living systems are characterized by autonomous properties, homeostasis, self-organization, physical boundaries, the existence of a metabolism (anabolism and catabolism), growth, reproduction, and the ability to adapt in response of the environment (evolution).[2] What raises issues is the formulation of a minimalist definition of organic life that establishes a clear distinction between inanimate and animate matters. Among the abiogenic definitions of life, many share the notion that cellular life is associated to the emerging properties of a replicating informational molecular system able to mutate.[3] However, while informational self-replication is an essential property for life, this alone might not be sufficient. For instance, viruses, which seem to fit this notion, are not considered by many as truly alive because of their inability to fabricate by themselves their own proteins. More inclusive definitions attempt to define organic living systems as autopoietic systems (from the greek αὐτό *(auto)*, meaning "self", and ποίησις *(poiesis)*, meaning "creation") by emphasizing that: "a living system is a system capable of self-production

---

1. Cf. Benner, Kim, and Carrigan, "Asphalt, Water, and the Prebiotic Synthesis of Ribose, Ribonucleosides, and RNA"; Benner, Kim, and Yang, "Setting the Stage: The History, Chemistry, and Geobiology behind RNA"; Schrum, Zhu, and Szostak, "The Origins of Cellular Life"; Robertson, and Joyce, "The Origins of the RNA World"; Pino, Trifonov, and Mauro, "On the Observable Transition to Living Matter."

2. Cf. http://en.wikipedia.org/wiki/Life.

3. Cf. Damiano and Luisi, "Towards an Autopoietic Redefinition of Life"; Danchin, "Bacteria as Computers Making Computers"; Luisi, "About Various Definitions of Life"; Joyce, "RNA Evolution and the Origins of Life."

and self-maintenance through a regenerative network of processes which takes place within a boundary of its own making and regenerates itself through cognitive or adaptive interactions with the medium."[4]

An essential characteristic of organic life that is often overlooked in these definitions is regulation. The ability to control self-reproduction and self-maintenance through regulatory feedback loops is likely to be one of the most fundamental properties of life as it is through regulation that cognitive or adaptive interactions can take place within a network of processes. Albeit not explicitly stating it, the autopoietic definition of organic life is the only one to suggest implicitly the need of regulatory controls in life.

The scientific investigation of the origin of life does not necessarily have to settle on a specific definition of organic life.[5] A clear distinction between living and non-living matter becomes more and more elusive as researchers investigate the possible bridges that link chemistry to biology. For the chemist, it might never be possible to identify the specific point in time when the physico-chemical world led to the biological world. Moreover, it might also be extremely difficult to decipher at which stage a chemical system becomes truly alive. Nevertheless, identification of the set of properties that characterize modern day living-matter (life) from non-living matter is far from being useless. For instance, by looking at the properties of biological molecules, much can be learned to understand the necessary transitions and driving forces that led to the emergence of life.

One aspect that contributes to the difficulty in defining life at an organic level is that it is a process rather than a pure substance.[6] Life is a process out of thermodynamic equilibrium, and for death, the process can be seen as a return to thermodynamic equilibrium. As such, the life process has been described as a dynamic kinetics state of matter; the fitness of living systems is therefore "dynamic kinetics stability" rather than "thermodynamic stability."[7] This characteristic of life is particularly well emphasized by the universal chemical constituents of all modern living systems: nucleic acids (RNA and DNA), proteins, polysaccharides, and lipids.

---

4. Cf. Damiano and Luisi, "Towards an Autopoietic Redefinition of Life."

5. Cf. Szostak, "Attempts to Define Life Do Not Help to Understand the Origin of Life."

6. Cf. Mautner, "Directed Panspermia."

7. Cf. Pross, "On the Emergence of Biological Complexity."

Informational Biopolymers of Life (and Death)

All living systems on earth are essentially based on the chemical elements C, H, O, N, P, and S, which are among the most abundant elements produced by the stars (this is especially the case for C, H, O, N).[8] Because of their reactivity and abundance in the universe, these chemical elements are at the foundation of organic chemistry and are particularly suited for building up chemical compounds of greater structural complexity. Behind the fact that these elements are characterized by well-defined set of physical and chemical properties, one can see a probabilistic determinism for the genesis of a diversity of reactive compounds by combination of these fundamental elements. For instance, small compounds like hydrogen cyanide (HCN) and formaldehyde (HCHO) are able to form quite spontaneously from C, H, O, N, and have been detected even in the interstellar space.[9] Their chemical reactivity in prebiotic conditions can lead to the formation of amino-acids, bases, sugars, and polycarbon chains.[10] Polymerization of activated forms of these building blocks can potentially lead to the emergence of nucleic acids, proteins, polysaccharides, and lipids. Because RNA can carry functional information (recognition, catalytic, and regulatory functions) as well as genetic information (able to be replicated), RNA was proposed to be the key polymer on which life developed. This led to the notion of an old "RNA world" at the origin of the present modern RNA worlds.[11] While the prebiotic synthesis of the RNA building blocks, or nucleotides, have been considered much more challenging than the one of the protein building blocks, or amino acids,[12] recent developments in prebiotic chemistry

8. Cf. Filippenko, "Made of Star-stuff," in this volume.

9. Cf. Benner, Kim, and Carrigan, "Asphalt, Water, and the Prebiotic Synthesis of Ribose, Ribonucleosides, and RNA"; Matthews and Minard, "Hydrogen Cyanide Polymers, Comets and the Origin of Life."

10. Cf. Matthews and Minard, "Hydrogen Cyanide Polymers, Comets and the Origin of Life"; Ritson and Sutherland, "Synthesis of Aldehydic Ribonucleotide and Amino Acid Precursors by Photoredox Chemistry"; Hein and Blackmond, "On the Origin of Single Chirality of Amino Acids and Sugars in Biogenesis"; Lazcano and Miller, "The Origin and Early Evolution of Life"; Saladino, Crestini, Pino, Costanzo and Di Mauro, "Formamide and the Origin of Life."

11. Cf. Robertson and Joyce, "The Origins of the RNA World"; Cech, "The RNA Worlds in Context."

12. Cf. Joyce, "RNA Evolution and the Origins of Life"; Parker, Cleaves, Dworkin, Glavin, Callahan, Aubrey, Lazcano, and Bada, "Primordial Synthesis of Amines and

indicate highly plausible chemical routes towards the production of nucleo-tides and amino acids as well as their enrichment in prebiotic conditions.[13] Moreover, several plausible scenarii suggest that chemical polymerization of activated nucleotides can occur in water, in presence of mineral surfaces or lipid vesicles.[14] If the likelihood of generating informational and stable biopolymers is a key argument for sustaining the abiogenic origin of life, often overlooked is the fact that these biopolymers can also hydrolyze back to their building block units (Table 1).

Amino Acids in a 1958 Miller H2S-rich Spark Discharge Experiment."

13. Cf. Benner, Kim, and Carrigan, "Asphalt, Water, and the Prebiotic Synthesis of Ribose, Ribonucleosides, and RNA"; Ritson and Sutherland, "Synthesis of Aldehydic Ribonucleotide and Amino Acid Precursors by Photoredox Chemistry"; Powner, Gerland, and Sutherland, "Synthesis of Activated Pyrimidine Ribonucleotides in Prebiotically Plausible Conditions"; Bowler, Chan, Duffy, Gerland, Islam, Powner, Sutherland, and Xu, "Prebiotically Plausible Oligoribonucleotide Ligation Facilitated by Chemoselective Acetylation"; Joshi, Aldersley, Price, Zagorevski, and Ferris, "Progress in Studies on the RNA World"; Saladino, Botta, Pino, Costanzo, and Di Mauro, "From the One-Carbon Amide Formamide to RNA All the Steps are Prebiotically Possible."

14. Cf. Bowler, Chan, Duffy, Gerland, Islam, Powner, Sutherland, and Xu, "Prebiotically Plausible Oligoribonucleotide Ligation Facilitated by Chemoselective Acetylation"; Joshi, Aldersley, Price, Zagorevski, and Ferris, "Progress in Studies on the RNA World"; Pino, Costanzo, Giorgi, and Di Mauro, "Sequence Complementarity-Driven Nonenzymatic Ligation of RNA"; Meyer, Ellefson, and Ellington, "Abiotic Self-Replication"; Mansy, Schrum, Krishnamurthy, Tobe, Treco, and Szostak, "Template-Directed Synthesis of a Genetic Polymer in a Model Protocell"; Costanzo, Pino, Botta, Saladino, and Di Mauro, "May Cyclic Nucleotides be a Source for Abiotic RNA Synthesis?"; Engelhart, Powner, and Szostak, "Functional RNAs Exhibit Tolerance for Non-Heritable 2'-5' versus 3'-5' Backbone Heterogeneity"; Joshi, Aldersley, and Ferris, "Homochiral Selectivity in RNA Synthesis: Montmorillonite-Catalyzed Quaternary Reactions of D, L-purine with D, L-pyrimidine Nucleotides"; Huang and Ferris, "One-step, Regioselective Synthesis of up to 50-mers of RNA Oligomers by Montmorillonite Catalysis."

TABLE 1

reaction	bond $t_{1/2}$		number of bonds per polymer	$t_{1/2}$ per cleavage event
	25°C	100°C		25°C
RNA hydrolysis	4 years	1.3 weeks	27000 (*coronavirus PTGEV*)[a]	1.3 hours
protein hydrolysis	400 years	5.5 weeks	123 (RNase A)	4 years
DNA hydrolysis	140000 years	1144 weeks	35000 (DNA virus genome) 9200000 (*E. coli* genome)[b]	4 years 5.5 days
polysaccharide hydrolysis	4700000 years	8320 weeks	100000 (glycogen)	47 years

TABLE 1: **Half-life ($t_{1/2}$) of biopolymers at 25°C and 100°C.**[15] *The half-life of a molecule is a measure of the time for which half of the molecules still remain intact. It is also the time at which half of the molecules are degraded. On the right side the table, the stability ($t_{1/2}$ per cleavage event) is given for various biopolymers containing a specified number of bonds.* [a] *coronavirus PTGEV: porcine transmissible gastroenteritis virus;* [b] *E. coli genome is double stranded.*

Informational biopolymers result from a process of prebiotic chemical selection that likely favored the emergence of cyclic, dynamic chemical networks in aqueous medium. In order to build up dynamic kinetics stability, slow degradation of the first biopolymers into small building block units is therefore as important as the polymerization reactions leading to their formation. Theoretically, open systems that produce in a continuous fashion the chemical building blocks of the first biopolymers can potentially develop into self-replicating systems with exponential growth. However, if these polymers were to be based on very highly stable covalent bond linkages, these chemical systems would not be well suited for regulation (and

15. Adapted from Wolfenden and Snider, "The Depth of Chemical Time and the Power of Enzymes as Catalysts."

the emergence of metabolism[16]). Without continuous chemical supplies of building blocks, such type of chemical systems can quickly result in the formation of homogeneous thermodynamically stable materials rather than a kinetically stable state of matter. The ability of degradable biopolymers is therefore an important feature of kinetic stability and therefore, of living systems. Through their own hydrolytic degradation, old biopolymers can contribute to the supply of fresh building blocks that can be used for generating new biopolymers that allow the system to self-regenerate but also to evolve. Based on the chemical stability (towards hydrolysis) of the covalent linkage joining two adjacent biopolymer units, RNA is the biopolymer with the highest chemical instability of its backbone, followed by proteins, DNA and polysaccharides (Table 1).[17] As such, it is an ideal informational medium for enabling regulation. Interestingly, in modern day biology, the half-life of the RNA bond linkage is still compatible with the survival of RNA viral genome of up to ~30000 nucleotides (nts). In an RNA world taking advantage of RNA as the sole support of the genetic information and with catalytic functions performed by RNA molecules and small peptides, a genome of this length should have likely been able to encode most, if not all, basic functions necessary to sustain the first living cells. Additionally, it is also likely that the chemical stability of an RNA-based genome can be increased by additional molecular factors protecting the RNA from degradation, as is the case for viral RNA. Considering that a bacteria like *E. coli*, divides every twenty minutes with a genome one hundred times bigger, a primitive living cellular system based on a 30000 nts genome replicating one hundred times more slowly than the one of *E. coli* would still have a fairly high probability to survive intact and evolve. In summary, it is because of its ability to hydrolyze within a certain chemical regime that RNA is likely to be one of the best polymers for originating cyclic, kinetically stable networks, even in the absence of enzymatically-catalyzed reactions. With the fitness being "dynamic kinetics stability" rather than "thermodynamic stability,"[18] we can speculate that the establishment of cyclic kinetically stable networks based on RNA molecules would have favored kinetic coupling between RNA replication and the catabolic reactions associated to the primitive metabolism, responsible for the sustained production and

16. Cf. Wagner, Pross, and Tannenbaum, "Selection Advantage of Metabolic over Non-Metabolic Replicators."

17. Cf. Wolfenden and Snider, "The Depth of Chemical Time."

18. Cf. Pross, "On the Emergence of Biological Complexity."

regeneration of nucleotides building blocks. A key feature in the emergence of these networks was likely the emergence of regulatory feedback loops. It is only at a later stage that DNA would have become an alternative support of the genetic information,[19] offering not only an increased chemical stability of the backbone by substituting ribose by deoxyribose, but also an increased stability of the stored genetic information by substituting uracil by thymine: by contrast to RNA, substituting genomic uracil with genomic thymine at the level of DNA allowed repair of uracil resulting from the hydrolytic decay of cytosine.[20] Therefore, behind the emergence of DNA, one can see a complex set of enzymatic reactions that eliminated and repaired the two most likely hydrolytic reactions taking place in RNA polymers and limiting RNA as a universal support of the genetic information in living systems. This led to cyclic kinetically stable networks with greater informational contents. Nevertheless, in our modern biological world, RNA remains the support of the genetic information of many viruses. Moreover, RNA is still extensively used in all living organisms for carrying catalytic, regulatory and structural functions in cells. For instance, more than 90 percent of the human DNA genome is transcribed into RNA.[21] As such, eukaryotic (and bacterial) cells are presently being recognized as having genomes working as RNA rather than DNA.[22]

Based on the above considerations, it is because of the ability of informational polymers to degrade or "die" that living systems may have emerged from chemistry.

19. Cf. Jaeger and Calkins, "Downward Causation by Information Control in Micro-Organisms."

20. Cf. Jaeger and Calkins, "Downward Causation by Information Control in Micro-Organisms;" G. Auletta, G. F. Ellis, and L. Jaeger, "Top-Down Causation by Information Control: From a Philosophical Problem to a Scientific Research Programme"; Jogalekar http://wavefunction.fieldofscience.com/2011/03/how-college-student-can-derive-rna.html.

21. Cf. Amaral, Dinger, Mercer, and Mattick, "The Eukaryotic Genome as an RNA Machine"; Dinger, Amaral, Mercer, and Mattick, "Pervasive Transcription of the Eukaryotic Genome."

22. Cf. Amaral, Dinger, Mercer, and Mattick, "The Eukaryotic Genome as an RNA Machine"; Mercer, and Mattick, "Structure and Function of Long Noncoding RNAs in Epigenetic Regulation."; Brosius, "The Persistent Contributions of RNA to Eukaryotic Gen(om)e Architecture and Cellular Function."

From Informational Biopolymers to Cellular Life

Biopolymers are molecular information and as such, they have functional meanings. Interestingly, the regulation of the phenotypic expression of particular biopolymers (and consequently their meanings) becomes only possible through the controlled production and degradation of these bio-polymers. Therefore, it is because of the controlled half-life (or death) of a biopolymer that the functional meaning of the operations performed at the level of a cell can change in order to maintain dynamic kinetics stability with respect of changes and cues in the environment. As such, it is because of the degradation (or death) of specific biomolecules that a more global functional meaning can be reached by a cell or a "living" dynamic kinetics state. Therefore, living systems (objects) are built up from processes that involve an upward movement of matter leading to the regulated production of molecules of increasing complexity (anabolism) and that is associated to a downward movement of matter leading to the controlled degradation, elimination or destruction of these complex molecules into more elementary building blocks (catabolism).

Another important aspect is the process of selection of biomolecular and cellular information carried by informational biopolymers. Through natural selection, some kind of biological information present within a space of possibilities dies to the benefit of another kind of biological information that is retained (Table 2). Interestingly, information selection is defined by a semiotic relation, in which the selected element becomes a sign of the input.[23] While this is evidently true when the selected element is connected to the initial information, the selected element can also be a sign of things that are not obvious consequences of the input, especially when certain items are taken to be a sign of the needed element (able to satisfy the goal).[24] For example, when considering a continuous physico-chemical process from inanimate to animate matter, the animate matter resulting from the natural selection process says something about the input information, the inanimate matter, and becomes a sign for the initial non-selected information. In the context of evolution, the process of information selection led to a limited variety of biopolymers on which all living systems are based (Table 2). Analysis of these biopolymers and their properties is

---

23. Cf. Auletta, Ellis, and Jaeger, "Top-Down Causation by Information Control: From a Philosophical Problem to a Scientific Research Programme."

24. Ibid.

therefore indicative on possible chemical and biochemical constraints that led to their emergence. Furthermore, biochemical and biological investigations can offer possible explanations for the transitions from proto-cells to modern cells and cellular organisms.

TABLE 2

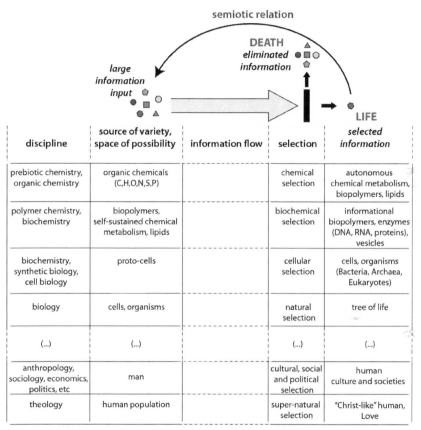

discipline	source of variety, space of possibility	information flow	selection	selected information
prebiotic chemistry, organic chemistry	organic chemicals (C,H,O,N,S,P)		chemical selection	autonomous chemical metabolism, biopolymers, lipids
polymer chemistry, biochemistry	biopolymers, self-sustained chemical metabolism, lipids		biochemical selection	informational biopolymers, enzymes (DNA, RNA, proteins), vesicles
biochemistry, synthetic biology, cell biology	proto-cells		cellular selection	cells, organisms (Bacteria, Archaea, Eukaryotes)
biology	cells, organisms		natural selection	tree of life
(...)	(...)		(...)	(...)
anthropology, sociology, economics, politics, etc	man		cultural, social and political selection	human culture and societies
theology	human population		super-natural selection	"Christ-like" human, Love

TABLE 2: **Information selection, life and death.**[25] *In the schematic on the top, large input information is a source of variety or a space of possibility that initiates an informational process that is concluded when selection is accomplished. During this process, while some informational elements are selected, others are eliminated. In any information exchange, the selection is at the end, not at the start. This selection delineates a semiotic relation in which the output says something about the input.*

25. Adapted from Figure 6 in Ibid.,

A living cell is an informational system able (i) to self-reproduce its cellular machinery (through both genetic and epigenetic information), (ii) to replicate its genome information and (iii) to undergo evolution. As such, a living cell is truly a system capable of information control and selection. As previously described in Jaeger and Calkins, the functions of reproduction and replication of the cell are the master functions delineating the functional, informational constraints that ultimately define the "boundaries" within which whether any information carried by informational biopolymers will be kept or not.[26] This process of top-down causation (TDC) by information control leads to the death of a certain kind of biological information to the benefit of another kind of biological information at the level of the cell (Table 2).[27] The selected biological information is typically the information that is said to allow survival of the fittest cell or population of cells to a particular medium or environment in which the cells develop. However, this also implies the elimination or "death" of the cells that contain biological information with a lower fitness to the environmental constraints. However, within the context of evolution, death as an outcome is an integral part of the process of natural selection. Considering for example a bacteria population, there are typically millions of cells that can proofread the quality of the information and function in parallel (like parallel processors of information). To be fully operational, cells therefore need to perform within a space of possibilities. The process of selection for valid information is operated "in a blind way" by multiple copies of identical (or quasi-identical) cells. The information that survives the selection process is the effective information that is transmitted by reproduction and replication from one cell into two daughter cells.

Therefore, bacteria cells can be defined as self-reproducing systems that function via TDC by information control and adaptive selection. Consequently, Darwinian evolutionary processes in cells are not only ruled from the bottom-up but also by organizational principles that impose necessary constraints from the top-down and determine the survival (life) or elimination (death) of cellular bio-systems. Any molecular information requires selection for its viability within the living system. As previously mentioned by Jaeger and Calkins:

26. Jaeger and Calkins, "Downward Causation by Information Control in Micro-Organisms."

27. Cf. Auletta, Ellis, and Jaeger, "Top-Down Causation by Information Control."

the new information is expressed and controlled for its ability to operate within the cell. The control of the "quality" of the information (through feedback control) is embedded within the replicating system and can be seen as a necessary underlying property associated to the function of replication. However, the issue here is not merely to replicate but to also properly segregate the new information resulting from replication so that what is essential to the system is kept while what is deleterious (lethal) to the system is disregarded. Therefore, the replicating system requires compartmentalization with selective reproduction of the molecular sub-functions responsible for DNA replication and cell reproduction, as well as the novel functions that are not detrimental to the cellular master functions.[28] While there is a drive here for perpetuating the informational master properties (reproduction and replication) within the cell through time (a drive for life that allows exploration of novelty), there is also a drive for eliminating parts of the molecular information that do not fulfill the master cellular functions (therefore a drive towards decay and death). The main selection drive behind perpetuation of the informational properties is to retain among others, the novel functions that allow intake of the sources of chemical energy, production of the molecular building blocks necessary for the synthesis of the biomolecules that support the master functions of the cell as well as their repair, etc. The main selection drive behind the elimination of undesirable information is to retain, for example, the functions that favor degradation processes and the segregation of undesirable molecules from the correct ones as well as elimination of the cellular systems that have aged, etc.[29]

Selective death of less adapted cells leads to the progressive elimination of the information content of these cells within a cellular population. During evolution, this has the consequence to enrich the overall population with the information content of the fittest cells. This enrichment does not result only from the reproductive advantage of the fittest cells, but also from the fact that a rather limited and overall constant amount of nutrients will lead to a continuous decrease in size of the population of less adapted cells with respect of the population of more adapted cells.

In summary, the process of natural, adaptive selection is a process based on the elimination (death) and conservation (life) of a certain kind of

28. Cf. Danchin, "Natural Selection and Immortality."

29. Jaeger and Calkins, "Downward Causation by Information Control in Micro-Organisms."

information (Table 2). Therefore, death can be seen as the process enabling TDC to operate in the evolution of micro-organisms. In other words, without death as a mean to eliminate some kind of information, TDC by information control and adaptive selection would not be able to operate at the level of cellular life and cellular evolution would not be possible. This framework is not limited to cellular life and can potentially be generalized to the tree of life and higher levels of complexity (Table 2).

Conclusion

In his *Summa Theologica*, commenting on the work of the sixth day, Thomas Aquinas writes about the possibility of "spontaneous" generation of living creatures from inanimate matter resulting from the corruption (death) of other living forms of lower complexity. Through time, his statement was often interpreted and presented in a fanciful way, leading many scientists to deride the idea of spontaneous generation as mere fantasy, lacking in solid scientific ground. The concept of spontaneous generation ended up to be fully rejected after the famous 1859 experiment of Louis Pasteur, which demonstrated that bio-organic inanimate matter (resulting from dead microorganisms) could not spontaneously originate life. While it might be difficult to fully comprehend the meaning of the words of Aquinas without immersion in the cultural and historical context of his time, Aquinas' statement on spontaneous generation can certainly be re-interpreted to fit the present abiogenesis hypothesis to the origin of organic life on Earth. No doubt that with our current scientific knowledge available to him, Aquinas would have agreed with it. Note that Aquinas recognizes that time is not the same for God as for humanity and as such, the time of God's creation as mentioned in the Bible does not have to be taken literally. This certainly offers the proper settings for the timeline of the evolutionary history of life presently accepted by a large portion of the scientific community. While modern science might never be able to unravel the origin of life on Earth per se, it nevertheless contributes to the understanding of the necessary transitions and driving forces that led to the emergence of organic life. For instance, with the recent progress in nanotechnology and synthetic biology,[30] we can anticipate that the creation of artificial biochemical

---

30. Cf. Gelfert, "Synthetic Biology between Technoscience and Thing Knowledge"; Lee and Na, "The Impact of Synthetic Biology"; Grabow and Jaeger, "RNA Modularity for Synthetic Biology."

systems mimicking the properties of natural living systems will be possible in a not too distant future.

From a purely naturalistic and materialistic point of view, death is an intimate part of natural selection. From this perspective alone, one could easily be prone to despair because "death" constrains from the top all the living systems that emerge from the bottom up. It is therefore not surprising that some atheists, such as Richard Dawkins, look at natural selection as something dreadful from which humanity needs to be freed by "creating the man of the future" through genetic engineering, eugenics practices, and trans-humanism.[31] Clearly, a naturalistic vision of the world falls short in providing answers on the ultimate cause (ultimate origin) of all things and the ultimate purpose of all things. As such, a purely naturalistic vision of the world falls short at explaining what humanity is and does not provide any clues on our position within the universe. By considering all things as mere organization of matter, a naturalistic vision of humanity will often tend to reduce man to a set of properties that do not go beyond describing man as a conscious animal. In this context, death can be truly dreadful and scary as the ultimate goal of all living systems, including human beings, ends up as dust. With a definition of life that is merely restricted to the natural world and does not set apart humans from the rest of the living creatures, the notion of death is clearly without hope and love. It is important to notice that Thomas Aquinas clearly distinguishes human beings from all other living creatures, humans being not only made of matter, but of spirit. Interestingly, evidences and facts provided by our modern scientific world support the vision of a transcendental nature of humanity. To recognize this, one can look at the life of the saints: Padre Pio and Giuseppe Moscati are two contemporary examples whose lives point at the supernatural reality of human beings.[32] Additionally, in support of the reality of a supernatural dimension of humanity, reproducible facts like Eucharistic miracles are well documented and have been investigated scientifically.[33] As living creatures, our physical body is rooted in the tree of life while our true human nature

31. Cf. Dawkins, "Darwin's Five Bridges" (Lecture delivered at the University of California, Santa Barbara, UCSB), http://www.youtube.com/watch?v=t1nuEbFvZ-8 (April 2012).

32. Cf. Derobert, *Padre Pio: Transparent de Dieu*; F. D'Onofrio, *Joseph Moscati: As Seen by a Medical Doctor*; Parrella sj, *St. Joseph Moscati: The Holy Doctor of Naples*.

33. Cf. Linoli, "Histological, Immunological and Biochemical Studies on the Flesh and Blood of the Eucharistic Miracle of Lanciano (8th century)"; Tesoriero and Han *Unseen*; Tesoriero, *Reason to Believe: A Personal Story*.

takes its root in the spiritual dimension. If one accepts this proposition, there is an evolutionary discontinuity between man, who originated both from matter and spirit, and the rest of the tree of life, which originated only from matter. In table 2, this is emphasized by the divide (or chiasm), which separates the various categories pertaining to the emergence of the tree life from those pertaining to human beings. Interestingly, Alfred Russell Wallace, who independently from Charles Darwin conceived the theory of evolution through natural selection, was inclined to this vision of the human.[34]

As seen from this essay, death can be seen as intimately connected to top-down causation. When biological information is selected, it is selected according to pressures that eliminate some type of information to the benefits of others. In other words, something needs to die so that something else emerges and lives. Death acts therefore more like a sieve, a filter that enables the selection and subsequent amplification of a specific kind of information, the effective information that would otherwise never be seen within the space of possible random information (or intrinsic information). Here, death becomes a passage, to reveal something else that was initially unseen or hidden. What survives the selection is the uninterrupted stream of life, the tree of life. The process of death is therefore directly linked to the process of emergence of meaningful information (or effective information). This vision of natural death is more suited to a Christian perspective. For human beings, death uplifts the veil that hides a greater truth, the truth of love and eternal life. As such, death can be seen as a new beginning, the beginning of our real spiritual journey.

---

34. Cf. Wallace, *My Life: A Record of Events and Opinions.*

II

PERSPECTIVE
FROM ANTHROPOLOGY

3

Immortality

Douglas J. Davies

T HIS ESSAY TAKES THE theme of immortality as an invitation to consider
death and the interpretation of death in terms of our human self-
reflective construction of identity, driven by the question of why human
beings so often conceive of life after death. While my dominant approach
will be largely anthropological, I will, at the outset, also present some
issues from a theological perspective, approaches that may, respectively, be
summarized as imagining eternity and intuiting eternity. The "imagining"
approach, grounded in a social scientific perspective, assumes that human
imagination has created the notion of immortality in response to a variety
of human needs expressed in a variety of cultural forms. By contrast, the
"intuiting" approach reflects a confessional theological assumption that
eternal life exists, that humans perceive this, that theology is its mode of
discourse, and that "religions" constitute the prime arena for its expression,
albeit in a variety of cultural forms. I take the intuiting view first before
spending more time on the imagined worlds of immortality

I: Intuiting Eternity

An intuition of eternity pervades many cultural traditions, intensifying
around what we tend to call "religion." Human animals adapt to their total
world and cosmic environment through an intuition of self that seems to
transcend self. This generates the idea of immortality, with people sensing

this experience to be a true reflection of the way things are, which confers a sense of being at home in the cosmos. This, in turn, engenders a confidence of purpose, and frees the self to explore the physical environment: fear of insignificance amidst immensity and complexity is allayed. When a theological frame is brought to bear upon the emotional and philosophical sense of things, especially if it asserts a deity possessing the capacity for relationship with humans, then such a confidence also fosters a sense of trust. Within the Christian tradition, for example, God is said to be eternal, to have made "time" as such, and to be the "Father" whose eternal home will be the destiny of mortal human beings once death has been transcended through a participation in a transformative resurrection already presaged in the narrative of the life of Jesus. In this sense of immortality the cosmos not only becomes intelligible as a "place" or state of interpersonal relationships, but also a moral-ethical process in which evil is ultimately transcended and injustices and wrongs are righted.

Often, this perspective identifies the self as intuiting eternity and participating in it through ideas of soul or life force, expressed philosophically, theologically, and ritually, as in Iranian, Egyptian, Tibetan, Indian, and other texts describing the process of dying, transmigration, resurrection, judgment, and the like. So, too, with recent ideas of psychical research, out of the body, near death, and mystical experiences, which speak of a timeless domain. The Jewish-Christian-Islamic tradition adopts the notion of resurrection as their mode of ongoing identity. I have explored some of these themes with lesser known Christian theologians in my book, *The Theology of Death*.

Two other, and quite different, scholars will suffice to illustrate the above sense of transcendence. First, we have John Bowker, whose *The Sense of God* and *The Religious Imagination and the Sense of God* pursued notions of "cues of meaning" by which humans respond to what are, in effect, divine messaging, all understood in terms of communication theory. Then, second, in Kevin Seybold's *Explorations in Neuroscience, Psychology, and Religion* we encounter an apologetic account of neuro-scientific developments on experiences involving a sense of timelessness, infinity, or of being close to God. He does not find this approach "a serious challenge to religious faith,"[1] because of his personal religious faith in the notion that "the truth revealed in nature will not and cannot conflict with the

1. Seybold, *Explorations*, 137.

truth revealed in scripture."[2] He discusses brain research associated with experiences of "innate spirituality," often allied with the practice of prayer and meditation, arguing that "if God exists and has created humans for the purpose of enjoying a relationship with him . . . there should be some physical mechanism to allow for the development of that relationship."[3] He aligns himself with the position that "brain structures and networks implicated in religious experience might have evolved because there is a spiritual world."[4] As already indicated, Seybold embeds this—"might"—in his personal experience of religious conversion whilst singing a hymn at a Christian gathering. Some other neuroscientists would, doubtless, offer non-religious interpretations, as below.

II: Imagining Eternity

In moving from that more theological world to a more anthropological-sociological perspective I will allude to some aspects of my own previous research alongside some speculative thoughts for future consideration.

Words against Death

I begin with "words against death," an idiom used in my *Death, Ritual and Belief* volume where I speculated on the emergent human animal using its new, powerful, capacity for language to engage with the impact death seems to make upon self-conscious social beings. As self-consciousness aligns the death of others with a potentially alarming sense of the death of one's self, so the power of language (and allied cultural creations) are deployed in defensive stratagems. In other words, ideas of immortality emerged in response to the problem dead people posed for how the living should view them, and for how living persons could also view themselves in the light of the death of others.

Cognitive Dissonance and Death

It is a philosophical commonplace to suggest that because the living "self" cannot imagine its own dead "self" one should not worry about "death"

2. Ibid., 142.
3. Ibid., 85.
4. Ibid., 81.

since one will not "be there" when it happens. The logical force of this argument is not, however, entirely persuasive because it is to the thinking and living person that the "dead," especially those known and loved, pose a problem in the here and now. The notion of cognitive dissonance might, itself, help in framing the idea that self-consciousness cannot, by definition, comprehend the idea of non-consciousness. Dissonance arises from this very inability. One response to this situation may lie in the way religions provide means of thinking about post-mortality, whether in the life of offspring and descendants who will perpetuate my identity, or in ideas of sleep prior to a resurrection awakening or, again, in an ongoing transmigratory journey of the soul. As for ideas of the soul, spirit, or life force, understood as breath or wind, the very symbolic nature of these terms encapsulates the fleeting and non-concrete nature of "life" to reduce the dissonance in and through the "mystery" inherent in the concepts.

Mysterium Vitae

At this point I invoke "mystery" as a notion that may host us within the domain of the unimaginable. The drive for meaning, not least in its combined emotional-intellectual "sense" of things, works on the basis of a culture possessing categories by which such "things" may be ordered. Some "things" are, intrinsically, hard to understand and are often placed in an appropriate category that somehow catches the idea of complexity or uncertainty, e.g., luck, fortune, fate, mystery. To have a general category for the inexplicable makes them less inexplicable; in emotional terms it reduces the fear of the unknown. Such categories include the divine will, providence, fate, destiny, and karma. The idea that God knows what he is doing even if I cannot see the sense in things helps me make some sense of them. It helps even more when God is said to view all things from the perspective of eternity: this is especially significant in relation to the death of those I love, for it enhances their own destiny and mine in relation to them. The idea of immortality, in this context, allows for a category of mystery that helps manage what is otherwise inexplicable and probably emotionally troubling.

As for evidential bases that create or sustain immortality we have the personal experience of living persons of those who are dead. Edward B. Tylor argued that dreams of the dead afford one basis for people coming to believe in the idea of the soul.[5] My research on contemporary beliefs

---

5. Tylor, *Primitive Culture*.

of death and afterlife in the UK reveals that somewhere around a third of the population have experienced a sense of presence of the dead.[6] Even without theological or philosophical underpinning such experiences prove influential, fostering that sense of mystery in life which, in itself, might possess adaptive significance in fostering both caution within and exploration of the world. This may be why the emotion of fear is sometimes invoked in connection with mystery as is discernible in Rudolph Otto's well-known study *The Idea of the Holy* and its descriptive use of the expression *mysterium tremendum et fascinans* to cover the Holy.[7]

Mirror-Neurons and the Uncanny

Let me for a moment offer one particular kind of distinctive argument that might, speculatively, be related to the paradox of death. I emphasize its speculative nature because I have no empirical basis for arguing it, though I think it might well be worth exploring in empirical ways. This concerns the cognitive science topic of what have been called mirror neurons.[8] Heralded by some as involving a potential paradigm shift in understanding some aspects of human relations, the mirror neuron theory describes how parts of the human brain are not only activated by a person performing an action but also by that person watching the action performed by another. Some have, taking the argument in a philosophical direction, seen this as one basis for "theory of mind," i.e., that I come to assume that others are like me, that they have a mind that works like mine, and that I must consider this in my relations with them. Some others take this in a different direction and see mirroring as the basis for empathy, and for interpreting the interaction of social life. Indeed, some scholars have used the idea when considering theatre, and the nature of empathy between audience and actors.

It is here that I add my own speculation regarding the death paradox, and do so in the form of the statement that we are so used to the process of mirroring the behavior of others that the sight of a corpse triggers a distinctive pattern of response that we call grief. My query here lies in whether grief is the emotional outcome of the dissonance experienced in the presence of the dead. Unlike a living person, and even unlike a deeply sleeping person, a corpse does not move, it does not breathe. These familiar factors,

---

6. Davies and Shaw, *Reusing Old Graves.*

7. Otto, *Idea of the Holy.*

8. Rizzolatti and Craighero, "Mirror Neuron."

ones that we have a deep capacity to mirror, are no longer present: and it is the very strangeness of this absence that contributes to a sense of grief. I had, in fact, written that before becoming aware of, for example, MacDorman and Ishiguro's paper, which includes the observation not simply that "our bodies are constantly moving," but the more particular notion that "the normal functioning of our visual system depends on this movement."[9] What is more, their work affords opportunity for me to press my speculation into the domain of robotics, android science, and the notion of "uncanny valley" responses, especially in terms of mortality salience that some have identified as part of human–android interaction. They suggest that "an uncanny robot elicits an innate fear of death and culturally supported defenses for coping with death's inevitability."[10] They speak of "disassembled androids" as potentially playing on our "unconscious fears of reduction, replacement, and annihilation."[11] Or again, Mori has proposed that "our impression of death can be explained by the movement . . . to the uncanny valley."[12] It is interesting to me that this reference to the uncanny, could, in some way, be related to Rudolph Otto's *tremendum et fascinans*, or to the anthropologist Malinowski's note on the attraction-repulsion factor of the dead body.[13] While these are all ideas for consideration and potential exploration, one reason for dwelling upon this speculation here is to pinpoint the significance of the emotional cluster of hope and despair, since it is widely observed that grief involves some degree of identity depletion and loss of some sense of reality. Here, of course, I do not invoke any stage-theory of grief, for we know there is little research evidence for such linear stages, rather I speak of the kaleidoscopic turns of emotions which may be intense and longer lasting close to a bereavement and more sporadic later.

Presence, Grief, and Immortality

In association with such emotional configurations let me now invoke a theory that has, as far as I am aware, not been used in connection with grief theory before, viz., that of Ernesto de Martino and his notion of "presence." His theory of self involves our sense of "presence," itself a potentially

9. MacDorman and Ishiguro, "Uncanny Advantage," 314.

10. Ibid., 313.

11. Ibid.

12. Mori, "Bukimi," 35.

13. Malinowski, *Magic, Science and Religion*, 49.

unstable state of being, yet one in which the world makes sense to us and we make sense of ourselves in the world. Theoretically speaking, this resembles various scholars who speak in terms of the sociology of knowledge and of the processes or structures of the "life-world" (as in Alfred Schutz, Peter Berger etc.). De Martino, however, is distinctive in stressing the fragility of this "presence." Accordingly, it is easy to deploy his approach in relation to grief when a crisis of presence causes our "world" to fall about us, and to amaze us that other people carry on with their lives while ours has become so strange and senseless.

I invoke this approach as a potential gloss on my assumption that the normal functioning of mirror neurons is part and parcel of our life-world and that a corpse ruptures that normalcy. In emotional terms, the triggering of grief prompts degrees of hopelessness, for hope is a notion that assumes the ongoing nature of fruitful relationships. Hope involves an imagination of the self in the future, a future world that involves significant others. It is the perceived absence of such a person, demonstrated in their corpse, that prompts a degree of hopelessness amidst the experience of grief.

Immortality Adaptive Significance

It is precisely here that the idea of immortality may serve to allay the anxiety of hopelessness. Immortality becomes an imaginative construct to offset emotional dis-ease. The "words against death" inherent in the notion of immortality thus become an adaptive response to the environment encountered as an ecology containing death. In evolutionary terms, immortality can then be regarded as a concept of positive adaptive significance within a world where many things die, from plants and other animals to the phases of the moon and change of seasons. In other words, the perception of change, and of the transience of things, comes to be set in opposition to an intuitive sense of the nature of self as enduring and not as ceasing to exist.

This line of argument can even benefit from the scene of changes in nature, for the rising and setting sun, waxing and waning moon, or the changes in seasons, may all serve as natural symbols of processes that extend to the human condition as one that changes and yet remains. This can even include the experience of ageing.

Hope

Continuing with the theme of immortality, one of the key orientations to the world that we may take from early anthropologists, especially from William Robertson Smith and his intellectual protégé in the sociology of religion, Emile Durkheim, is the phenomenon of hope. Robertson Smith's *Religion of the Semites* emphasized the sense of excitement and transcendence that accompanied sacrificial ritual, and in that sense emphasized how a rite involving death helped generate a sense of vitality within a community. That insight went on to spark Durkheim's imagination allowing his previous studies in both *Rules of Sociological Method* and his famous work on *Suicide* to flower in his subsequent *Elementary Forms of the Religious Life*.

Self as Society

The work of Durkheim's collaborators reinforced this perspective with his nephew, Robert Hertz, stressing the idea that "society" sensed itself to be immortal and addressed the death of individual members of society accordingly:

> Society imparts its own character of permanence to the individuals who compose it: because it feels itself immortal and wants to be so, it cannot normally believe that its members . . . in whom it incarnates itself should die.[14]

Here, we firmly encounter a sociological expression of "immortality" as an attribute of "society." The reification of "society" within this French school of sociology is well-known; it also pinpoints the fact of personal existence within an enduring community. Later scholars in the sociology of knowledge, especially in phenomenological thought, reiterated just such ideas in describing society as the matrix of individual life, one that truly existed before us, will continue to exist after us, and which gives us the very basis for thought itself. On such a view it is easy to understand why God and society could be equated in Durkheimian thought.

So it is that Arnold van Gennep, in his well-known work, would describe rites of passage as a process in which society takes us by the hand and

---

14. Hertz, "Contribution to the Study," 77

leads us through potentially perilous times of change in our social status, not least in association with funerals.

Ritual Reality Generation

It is, then, through funerary rites that the idea of immortality gains a significant part of its social force, with rituals of dying, death, and after-death giving new identity to the dead as also to the surviving kin. The ordinary social processes of life in society are, in a sense, extended to the afterlife. The dead become ancestors for the living and are initiated into afterlife worlds of their own. Prayers and gifts mark their new status and bind living and dead within a wider overarching world, which in traditional Christianity takes the form of the communion of saints. For groups without after-life beliefs, a sense of immortality is also feasible as ancestors are set in ongoing generations of descendants.

Over-World, Hope, and Immortality

The atmosphere of overarching worlds is one of hope, beckoning the living to pass through fear. Indeed, hope is a crucial concept in relation to the notion of immortality and I have devoted some time to considering it in my study of *Emotion, Identity, and Religion*, subtitled, *Hope, Reciprocity, and Otherness*. One useful way of approaching hope is to see it as the cultural expression of the biological drive to survive, striking as it does the positive emotional tone that opposes fear. We might even see "hope" as one over-arching cultural dimension lying beyond either the flight or fight response: hope resides in each. Hope also provides the emotional dynamic to the rational paradox of the incapacity to think of one's self as dead.

Intensive Living

As a kind of symbolic opposite of that impossibility, and as another way of depicting the bio-cultural nature of hope, lies the concept of intensive living, a notion pinpointed by Glaser and Strauss as one response of people diagnosed as terminally ill.[15] Despite a sense of life coming to an end, some folk gave themselves as strongly as possible to putting as much into and

15. Glaser and Strauss, *Awareness*, 131.

getting as much as possible out of life while they still had the strength to do so, all in a display of an embodied pragmatism of hope set against an awareness of mortality.

Superplausibility

From that more clinical context, let me now introduce a new concept, that of superplausibility, which may throw its own light on the rise and demise of the notion of immortality. This concept develops the notion of "plausibility" as described in the sociology of knowledge and in phenomenology, which I first explored in my *Meaning and Salvation in Religious Studies*.[16] Plausibility speaks of the sense we come to make of the world as we are socialized into it. Superplausibility refers to what some groups and individuals in a society may experience in and through some initiation rites, further education, processes of professionalization, and in such phenomena as religious conversion or near-death experiences.[17] It is a process in which earlier views of the world are transcended as new ways of understanding are taught. We might speak of this as individuals first coming to "see" or understand the world in one way and, later, coming to "see through" that previous scene as they adopt a new view. We might, accordingly, speak of the everyday life-world of people as the means by which they "see" the world, only for some to develop, later, another perspective. In speculative fashion we might then speak of the world as a place of death and termination becoming transcended as humanity saw through it into a scene of immortality, with the cultural eras of the growth of afterlife beliefs marking that precise, "seeing through" mortality into immortality. For yet other people, as time passed still further, they came to "see through" immortality, taking it as an untruth. Here the critical high tide of Schleiermacher and Freud enjoined the brave new world of mortality.

In theological worlds many maintain ideas of an afterlife in an overworld, even deploying new ideas of physics to affirm the feasibility of identity continued after death. Theologians such as N. T. Wright attempt a superplausibility of their own, arguing that Christian resurrection is a phenomenon quite unlike human ideas of an afterlife, but betokening a "life after life after death."[18] Some Christians even attempt science-like no-

16. Davies, *Meaning and Salvation,* 29–41.

17. Davies, *Emotion,* 240–44.

18. Wright, *Resurrection.*

tions that set the resurrection of Jesus as "the first instantiation of a new law of nature", or FINLON in its anagram form, as proposed by Robert John Russell from the Centre for Theology and the Natural Sciences at Berkeley's Graduate Theological Union.[19] In terms of anthropological theory one might also draw ideas from Maurice Bloch's notion of "rebounding conquest" in which ordinary life-experience is transformed into a new level of emotional-existential engagement through ritual activity.[20] Something similar could be derived from Harvey Whitehouse's dual-model of religion with its emphasis on the emotional impact of "imagistic" forms of ritual initiation, rather than the "doctrinal" embedding of religious learning.[21] In all of these we see attempts at describing experiences of transcendence, whether prompted by ritual acts or textual materials.

In conclusion, immortality can be seen to express an ideological form of hope, itself a cultural form of the drive to survive and a means of fostering human flourishing. Immortality also enhances human life by adding a sense of value to it. Indeed, we might even wonder whether the very idea of human rights had its origin in some notion of immortality, especially where theological ideas posited the worth of each self to God. In more archaeological terms, immortality may well have begun in giving heroes, inspiring leaders, or power-brokers, a funeral that marked their ongoing sense of a place in the afterlife, a recognition that later became increasingly democratized. Whatever else immortality may be, it has prompted the human animal to raise the notion of destiny to a prime place.

19. Russell, "Bodily Resurrection."
20. Bloch, *Prey into Hunter.*
21. Whitehouse, *Modes.*

III

PERSPECTIVES FROM PHILOSOPHY

4

Suffering Death[1]

Emmanuel Falque

(Translated by Christina M. Gschwandtner[2])

"JESUS KNEW THAT HIS hour had come to depart from this world and *pass to* the Father. . . . [Jesus] got up from the table, took off his outer robe, and tied a towel around himself" (John 13:1, 4). This "passing" at the time of the final meal (at the foot washing) is usually interpreted as a leap or as a "point of departure for moving beyond," to take up the celebrated phrase of Plato's dialectic (*Resp.* 6:511b). In fact, certainly in philosophy, but also in theology, it seems as if "passing from this world" would mean for Christ, and for us following him, to leave this world in order to join another world. While the "fatherland" (*patria*) seems assured, it apparently becomes necessary to spurn the "way" (*in via*) to it. Nevertheless, in Greek, "passing" [*passer*] from this world, while it certainly can refer to a "passage"

---

1. I here return to and synthesize certain results of the first volume of my triptych: *Le passeur de Gethsémani: Angoisse, souffrance et mort. Lecture existentielle et phénoménologique*, which is completed by *Métamorphose de la finitude: Essai philosophique sur naissance et la résurrection* and *Les noces de l'agneau: Essai philosophique sur le corps et l'eucharistie*. The middle volume appeared in English as *Metamorphosis of Finitude: An Essay on Birth and Resurrection*; the other volumes are in preparation for translation.

2. French words from Falque's original text have occasionally been given in [ ].

[*passage*], it also means "suffering" [*pâtir*] or "transformation": *metabe ek tou kosmou*—certainly "passing" to an other world (metabasis), but also "suffering," "passion," and "being transformed" by this world (metabolism). For a Christian understanding, therefore, death refers less to a Platonic leap toward another world (immortality of the soul) than it attests to the transformation of finitude (resurrection of the body).

Although, at least in the West, Christianity is not obvious, it is still fully justified in showing this passage to concern the entirety of the world rather than the flight into another world. Especially for the Christian philosopher, the "credibility" of Christianity, regardless of the implications for its "belief," hinges on the possibility of "presenting the doctrine in a manner that responds to the requirements of our age," to cite again John XXIII's celebrated phrase at the opening of the Second Vatican Council. As Thomas Aquinas in the Middle Ages deserves credit for welcoming what was new in his time (i.e., Aristotle) in order not only to assimilate it, but also to transform it in the light of Christianity, so we also must perform the same gesture in all modesty, namely to take up and to question Christ's death in light of modernity. Obviously we do so not in order to deny the tradition, but instead to dare to become its inheritor and to try to continue it: "modern man . . . is not possible except through the *form of finitude*," underlines Michel Foucault. "But, more fundamentally, our culture crossed the threshold beyond which we recognize our modernity when finitude was conceived in an interminable cross-reference with itself."[3]

It is consequently now advisable to consider that Christ's death could and should be read in the light of modern conceptions of human finitude and also in accordance with our simple created state of being, as Thomas Aquinas himself established the "limit," rather than the unlimited, as our most proper state. This way one would deny Martin Heidegger the false privilege of excluding Christians from finitude, as if they did not first of all belong to the rest of all of humanity. As Heidegger formulates it in a note to *Being and Time*: "The anthropology worked out in Christian theology—from Paul right up to Calvin's *meditatio futurae vitae*—has always *kept death in view in its interpretation of life*."[4] In other words, according to Heidegger, the anguish or anxiety before death in question here would be inaccessible to the Christian as such, and even more to Christ, inasmuch as "death scenarios" would be at work in Christianity (following the example

3. Foucault, *The Order of Things*.
4. Heidegger, *Being and Time*, §49, 249, n.6 (n.1 in German); italics added.

of Epicureanism or of Stoicism) in order to flee the reality of death, or at the very least to lighten its darkness. Even so, the "glory" (*kabod*) bestowed on the resurrection is measured by the "weight" we give to death, and hence to finitude. The guiding idea of my work *The Metamorphosis of Finitude* (chap. 5), which is that "the resurrection changes everything," requires measuring the weight of suffering and death Christ confronted in Gethsemane (*Le passeur de Gethsémani*), so that an eros capable of bearing and of displaying it would respond to the gift of the body in the Eucharist (*Les noces de l'agneau*).

1. Death Scenarios

It is well known that there are many ways to flee death—from Epicurus' version of death "about which one knows nothing," because one has not lived it and from which no one has ever returned, to Epictetus, who speaks of the "transformation of our opinion about death" rather than of death itself. According to Heidegger, three modalities of "being-toward-death" or of "being-toward-the-end" allow us to turn away from the anxiety before death (*Being and Time*, §42). In my opinion, a certain Christianity would not be absent from these modalities. (a) First, *resignation into disappearance.* "Sunshine follows rain," just as bread that has been consumed is said to be "finished." Appearing implies disappearing and it is proper to leave one's place for others. Even in certain Christian understandings the passing to another life is occasionally justified by this, not in order to save one's life, but in order to give life to others. Often believers do not fail to be resigned, more with a Stoic than a Christian attitude, taking a mysterious refuge in the place of such unknowing that they come to doubt that one could get off so lightly. (b) Second, *the certainty of resurrection* is a second way of fleeing death, in its sense as "diversion" or "passing." It is as if—and in this case this is any ordinary Christian's understanding—the road were "blocked" or "under construction" and it would be enough to bypass the obstacle or to follow the "detour" in order to arrive at last. Thus, no one would fear death, not even Christ, knowing that it contains the salvation of the beyond and hence not shrinking at all from the sufferings of the here and now. (c) Third, the *heroism of achievement* refers to a third and final way not to allow death to be death. Who has not dreamt of putting one's signature and finishing touch on life via an act of death, in such a way that the similarity of acts and of thoughts (an argument often evoked in theology) would be enough to turn a Christian's death into a sacrificial death. This becomes all the more justified when this death is offered to others, in an acknowledgment or gift in return, which will then justify its abandon. On this interpretation Christ's death would seem like Socrates' accomplishment: he would only have endured death because this action would give rise to life or begin a new life.

We know, or at the very least we sense, that such scenarios of flight before death would not be suitable for Christianity, and even less for Christ himself. A "silence about the end" is even called for in the four canonical Gospels, and in contrast to the apocryphal gospels. For example, the *Gospel of Peter* (5–6) stresses with a profusion of detail: "It was noon, and darkness came over all Judea. And they were troubled and distressed for fear the sun had set while Jesus was still alive. . . . And many went about with lamps, supposing that it was night, and fell down. . . . And in that hour the veil of the temple of Jerusalem was rent in two. And then they drew out the nails from the hands of the Lord and laid him upon the earth. The whole earth quaked and great fear arose." The soberness of the canonical Gospels hence forces us to have another look at the scene of Christ's death, in order to consider it in another way.

2. The Failure of the Setting [*la mise en scène*]

The tragic hero is not a hero. That is probably the first lesson to learn from Gethsemane, as also from Golgotha. It really will have been necessary that Christ die from "common death" or from "ordinary death"—"the death of the whole world . . . of the death of which your father died, my child, and the father of your father . . . ; the death to which your mother will one day succumb; and your wife, and your children, and your children's children; with yourself at the center." [5] This, so that *his* death would be of a piece with *my* death, and hence *his* resurrection with *mine*. The previously developed traits would thus be, if not thwarted, at least offset.

(a) *The resignation into disappearance* was largely developed by the Council of Trent in the *Decree on Justification* as a kind of sacrificial understanding of Christianity: "By his holy passion on the wood of the cross the Son has made satisfaction for us to God, his Father." [6] This understanding will find its counterbalance in the more Irenaean perspective of reca-

5. Cf. Péguy, *Dialogue de l'histoire et de l'âme charnelle* (Pléiade), vol. III, 743.

6. Denzinger, *Enchridion*, #1529.

pitulation, which is taken up during the Second Vatican Council by the pastoral constitution *Gaudium et spes*: "He has restored the divine likeness in Adam's descendents."[7] Here the "happy exchange" is not opposed to the "praiseworthy cause," far from it. Nevertheless this makes it possible not to think of ourselves, and even less of Christ, as resigned to our death in the name of a sacrificial understanding that is very often not understood properly. (b) *The certainty of resurrection*, inherited from the understanding of death as "passing" or "detour," certainly will be more difficult to question. The distinction between the two natures in the person of Christ makes it possible to bring about a division between his divine nature's complete vision of the resurrection and his human nature's absolute ignorance of the afterlife. Yet one may well wonder about the "knowledge" at stake in this aforesaid "certainty of resurrection." The theologian Karl Rahner emphasizes that "an authentically human consciousness must have an unknown future before itself."[8] One can speak with Hans Urs von Balthasar of the "certainty of faith," rather than of strict "intellectual knowledge," in regard to the consciousness of the resurrection in Christ's person. Knowing "neither the day nor the hour" for the end of time (Mark 13:32), maybe he knows no more about his own death, except in the trust (and even absolute certainty) in his Father's ability to raise him: "To explain in detail this ignorance of the Son and its place in the economy of salvation matters little; it is a reality and that is enough for us."[9] (c) *The heroism of achievement* also cannot stand up to a proper reading of Golgotha. According to an hypothesis that will certainly not fail to astonish us, one cannot and should not too quickly interpret Christ's cry "it is finished" on the cross as the cry of a super-human who would fulfill his life by his act of death. *Tetelestai*—"it is finished" (John 19:30). The expression has its roots in Greek tragedy, before being adapted by the New Testament text, though obviously in a different sense. In the verb *teleo*, the *telos* certainly means the achievement of a work, but it can also designate the end of a journey, or the completion of a race—"reaching the end of the rope" (to *come to one's end*),[10] following Aeschylus' libation bearer: "like a tyrant come to his ruin" (*oimoi despoton teloumenoun*).[11] We must hence also return to this obvious fact, that the death of the Son of Man

---

7. Ibid., #4517.

8. Rahner, *Traité fondamental de la foi*, 282.

9. Hans Urs von Balthasar, *La Foi du Christ*, 30.

10. [The italicized phrase is in English in the original.—Trans.]

11. Cf. Scott, *A Greek-English Lexicon*, s.v. "Teleo."

would also be, first and foremost, the death of the Son of God, in the non-rupture of his addressing his Father, as in the pangs of death. Yet, at least at the beginning and this in order to cut short any heroism of the subject, one must recognize that for the Son also "this is done with living," at least in order to raise and take up the question of the meaning of life, about which any human being on the verge of death wonders.

3. Dread and Anxiety[12]

It is thus understood that a proper reading of Christ's death today does not necessarily require raising doubts again about its rightly sacrificial character or focusing the reading unjustifiably on the existential character (anxiety before death) to the point of forgetting its redemptive feature (anguish over sin), but first of all getting rid of the scenarios that we ourselves have put together, which would forbid him to inhabit our own darkness. The brilliant distinction in Heidegger's *Being and Time* (§46–53) between "the fear (*Furcht*) of passing away" and the "anxiety (*Angst*) before death" surprisingly finds a trace, or rather a form of possible rereading, in the Synoptic Gospels themselves: "He took with him Peter and James and John, and began to be distressed (*ekthambesthai*) and agitated (*ademonein*)" (Mark 14:33). In order to show against Heidegger, while nevertheless relying on his analysis, that it is false to say that Christians cannot experience anxiety before death, because they have "always *kept death in view in [the] interpretation of life*" (see above), thus comes down to explaining how Christ himself has assumed its "suffering" and "passing," especially in the Gethsemane episode.

"Fear" (*Furcht*) is actually characterized by the fact that it (a) makes one draw back before something "determined," either "formidable" or "harmful," (b) opens onto a modality of our existence that displays its "precariousness," or even "abandonment," (c) and tries to "share" itself in the sense that one always wants to have fear "with" someone else, in such a way that above all one does not find oneself alone in this terror of someone who feels abandoned. Did Christ, then, have "fear" of death for the same reason any human being does on the verge of his end or of his demise, even

---

12. [*L'angoisse* is both "anxiety" and "anguish." Although the term is usually translated as "anxiety" when referring to Heidegger, Falque's use of the word is often closer to "anguish" than to "anxiety." Both senses should be kept in mind throughout the text.—Trans.]

if the episode in Gethsemane had no other meaning than the transition from "fear" to "anxiety," from recoiling before something to crushing and burying into the nothing?

If "what has not been assumed has not been redeemed," as Gregory of Nazianzus insists in the "Letter to Cledonius," then it comes down to the Son of God taking responsibility first for this existential and metaphysical part of our humanity, [of] "fear" (*Angst*) or "dread" (*ekthambesthai*), albeit to transform it. (a) Following the example of someone condemned to death, which ultimately applies to all of us, at least at first Christ resists his own imminent death. With Corneille in *Polyeucte* and Péguy following him (in the *Dialogue de l'histoire et de l'âme charnelle*), we must say that "even God fears death." This is what is going on in the Son's act of recoiling: "Abba, Father, for you all things are possible; *remove* this cup from me" (Mark 14:36). There is nothing more "determined" and more "formidable" here than the "cup," which he must drain to its dregs, namely the sentence of death by which one's self-consciousness and joy may well disappear with the annihilation of the "self." (b) The awaited demise, or the approach of imminent death, thus produces an act of precariousness or of abandonment, a feeling of transience, indeed of futility, of all of existence, a feeling which Christ himself was not spared, at least in regard to sharing the whole of our humanity: "I am *deeply grieved*, even to death; remain here, and keep awake" (Mark 14:34). (c) Finally, the fear of death calls for the aspiration of being able to be shared with another, as if what is first one's own and only one's own (death) could also become other or that of the other (dying with, even dying for): "'*Remain* here while I pray'; he took with him Peter and James and John. . . . '[R]emain here and *keep awake*. . . . Simon, are you asleep?'" (Mark 14:32–37). Following the example of those shipwrecked on the Titanic, the Son of Man looks for people to accompany him in his fight for survival, a final act of hope in order still to give meaning to life. We will come back to this: if the Son's death is really first the death of him who speaks to his Father in a specific, and for us salvific, relationship, this death remains no less, and from the beginning, a human death by which one tries to "live with" death, for lack of being able to "be exempted from living it."

The move from "fear" (*Furcht*) to "anxiety" (*Angst*), or—to say it in Greek or New Testament fashion—from "dread" (*ekthambesthai*) to "anguish" (*ademonein*), therefore happens in the crossing of Gethsemane in the back and forth undergone by the dying Christ, going three times from the Father to his disciples and vice versa. The Son of God as a "guide [*passeur*] of Gethsemane"[13] does not simply pass [*passe*] from death over to life, but he suffers [*pâtit*] the weight of death or, in other words, of our finitude, in order to offer it to his Father, who alone is capable of transforming or even of metamorphosing it. At the heart of this "finitude" as the horizon limiting our existence, which should in no way be identified with the "finite" as simple delimitation of the infinite, the traits of "anxiety" [or "anguish"] thus oppose those of "fear." It is no longer a question of *the end of life*, as it is the case for Christ's and for our "demise," but of "death," understood in this instance as a way of living, rather than as an achievement of existence. Ignatius of Loyola recommends as the final rule of discernment to "consider *as if I were at the point of death*, the form and measure which I would then want to have kept in the way of the present election, and regulating myself by that election, let me make *my decision* in everything."[14]

(a) Anxiety, contrary to fear, has no fear of anything [*de rien*]. Or rather, the "nothing" [*le rien*] that causes fear is no longer "some thing," understood here as a determined being (shipwreck or the condemnation to death), but our being-in-the-world as such, inasmuch as it loses and no longer finds meaning, not just solely at the moment of dying, but at the very idea of death while one is still living: "Anxiety does not know what it is anxious about" (*Being and Time*, §40). In anxiety, "there is nothing left to lean upon" and "nothing remains and only this nothing happens to us."[15] (b) Thus, entering into the "nothing," anxiety in this sense, and contrary to the fear that is attached to my own feeling of abandonment, "reveals the nothing," leaves me suspended between heaven and earth, without being able to decide regarding the sense or non-sense of life. Nothing in my life makes sense, even to the point of including the hypothesis of filling this "nothing" with "some thing." (c) In this way the anxiety before death forces us to enter into an "existential solipsism." Not in terms of the impossibility of sharing one's death with another, because the other would be incapable of receiving its weight, but by the fact that death "cannot be shared," remaining

13. [The author is here employing imagery impossible to recreate in English: *Passeur* means "ferryman" and *le gué* (in the previous sentence) is a ford, as in fording a stream or river. Christ is the guide who bears us across the river by first passing over its divide himself in the garden of Gethsemane. At the same time, Falque is playing on the connections between *passeur*, *passer*, and *pâtir* (suffering), which are all etymologically related.—Trans.]

14. Loyola, *Spiritual Exercises*, 186.

15. Heidegger, "What is Metaphysics?" 88 [English translation modified to catch nuances of Falque's reading].

"always mine" (*Jemeinigkeit*), regardless of the desire not to be or to remain alone in it. That is what it means to go beyond fear and to enter into anxiety. To deepen the human and the question of the meaning of life, without stopping short at the mere animal feeling of survival—that is the movement of the "back and forth" that defines the Gethsemane episode: "He came and found them sleeping . . . , and once more he found them sleeping. . . . He came a third time . . ." (Mark 14:37–42). Taking upon himself the traits of "anxiety," even more than those of "fear," Christ plunges into this "nothing" of the meaning of life in order to allow us metaphysically to remain a "being in question," and hence properly human, at the hour of dying, or better, of living in full consciousness of death.

(a) The "vagueness" of anxiety, contrary to the feature determined by fear, is shown precisely in the handing over of the "cup," in the crossing from the positive to the negative, of the total delivery of self to another. This causes Christ to relinquish the object of his fear (the simple condemnation to death) in order to enter into the questioning about life: [the move] from the "if it is possible (*si possibile est*), let this cup pass from me" (Matt 26:39) to the "if this cannot pass unless I drink it" (*si non possibile est*) (Matt 26:42). Renouncing any hanging on to the end of life, the Son of God himself at Gethsemane enters into the metaphysical quest for the meaning of life, making of the relinquishment of choice for meaning as also for meaninglessness a place of freedom by which the human will also have to be determined. "Not what *I* want, but what *you* want" (Mark 14:36). This is the admission, or rather the opinion, not that life has no meaning, but that we cannot and should not *ourselves* give it meaning. From the moment of the handing over of the "cup" to his Father, and hence of his fear, in order to enter into anxiety, Christ here definitely takes leave of Heideggerian *authentic Dasein* in its ambition to "overcome death," even as "possibility of life."[16] True abandonment for the Son does not solely come down to offering himself to another than his Father, but to dare to defer or let go of all the reasons for living as also for dying in order to stay in the call that will never be broken off, even if only a silence would be able to answer it, at least in the beginning: "'Eloi, eloi, lema sabachthani?' which means, 'My God, my God, why have you forsaken me?'" (Mark 15:34). No "battle between God and God" is going on here, as Jürgen Moltmann has falsely asserted (in *The Crucified God*), but the Son's unceasing addressing of the Father in the greatest abandonment, sure that the link could never be broken,

16. Heidegger, *Being and Time*, §53.

even in the absence of any "knowing" or "feeling" that would be able to believe in it. (b) Anxiety's reduction to nothing thus leads "to enter into the nothing." Nevertheless, in the mystery of the cross, the *nothing* [rien] *of kenosis* takes over from the nothingness [*néant*] of anxiety. Penetrating the nothing, Christ precisely attains our "nothing," not in order to make it "a" something, but in order to empty himself in it and not to abandon this creation, itself "subject to futility" (Rom 8:20). He, "though he was in the form of God, . . . *emptied* himself (*ekenosen*), taking on the form of a slave, being born in human likeness. . . . He *humbled himself* (*etapeinosen*) and became obedient to the point of death—even death on a cross" (Phil 2:6–8). (c) As for the impossible wish to "share" anxiety: "In his anguish [or agony (*en agonia*)] . . . his sweat became like great drops of blood falling down on the ground" (Luke 22:44). This comes to a head and is at play in the disciples' abandonment of the Son to himself and to his Father: "Simon, are you asleep? . . . Are you still sleeping and taking your rest? *Enough!*" (Mark 14:37, 41). What is accomplished here? Nothing, or at the very least nothing visible, except the passing over of the battle against the "fear of demise" to that of "anxiety before death." "It is finished," or, better, "it is done for" (*apaxei*), as one sometimes translates, indicating not that one has enough of life, as one would falsely believe, but that the combat is already won and that nothing human, especially our anxiety before death, would be able to escape the Son, and hence the Father, in order to be offered and radically transformed.

Conclusion: Passing to the Father

By *suffering* finitude, and hence the anxiety before death, the Son passes it to the Father in Gethsemane. There, still, the rest remains, for the Son certainly, but also this time for the Father. The interpretation of the Son's passion by way of "God's suffering" certainly contains something stimulating and even fascinating, although it cannot be supported as such. *Ipse pater non est impassibilis*—"the Father himself is not impassible," formulates Origen in a remarkable fashion in his *Homilies on Ezechiel* (6.6). He turns this "passion of charity" into the most proper mode of God as a whole, there where "One of the Trinity has suffered" (Second Council of Constantinople). Yet, one must correct "passion" with "compassion," [turn] the passibility of suffering into the activity of an elected sympathizing: *Pater est impassibilis, sed non est incompassibilis*—"the Father is impassible but not incompassible [or devoid of compassion]," Bernard of Clairvaux corrects with good reason in his own "Sermon on the Song of Songs" (26.3). *God's passion*, in fact, differs in this from *human passion*, that it shows itself in complete liberty and without ever being imposed. The Father "without flesh" chooses to share his Son's passion "in the flesh," to bear its weight and to raise the body from it even in the resurrection, in such a way that only the "force of the Spirit" will compete with the aspirations of a "super-humanity" yearning to take on everything. The celebrated "responsibility for the other" is prompted in my view in the Christian system and precisely in this figure of the Son in Gethsemane, by "supreme irresponsibility" or by a "childish spasm of lamentation." Being Christian is not to carry "even more" responsibility (according to Lévinas ["we are all the Messiah"]), but rather "less responsibility," certain of the conviction that "it is *greater* to *be able to do something by oneself and to give to another the power of doing it, than to do it by oneself only*."[17]

---

17. William of Auxerre, *Summa aurea*, 9.4 (absolute power and conditioned power).

5

How Do We Become Fully Alive?
The Role of Death in Henry's
Phenomenology of Life

Christina M. Gschwandtner

W**HAT DOES IT MEAN** to become truly human? Although this can be said to be the perennial philosophical question from Socrates onward,[1] twentieth-century philosophy has been preoccupied with it in a quite different fashion. The earlier part of the century celebrated the death of the subject and even thinkers who want to retrieve a sense of the human self as a viable and important notion are fairly critical of modern notions of subjectivity in a strong Cartesian sense, where the independent and powerful subject in control of all its objects is the assumed center of its world, the Archimedean point from which all else can be determined.[2] Yet despite a

---

1. Most famously in the Socratic injunction to examine one's life or care for one's soul (or the Delphic Oracle "Know Thyself," which Socrates takes as directing his search for truth). Pierre Hadot has examined this understanding of philosophy as "a way of life" or even a "spiritual" pursuit in the ancient and medieval world in his famous works *Philosophy as a Way of Life* and *What is Ancient Philosophy?* These works had a strong impact on many contemporary French thinkers.

2. For a good summary of both the "strong" (Cartesian) subject and the (Nietzschean) dissolution of the self, see the introduction to Paul Ricoeur's *Oneself as Another*, where he posits the two as polar opposites between which he seeks to negotiate in his own work on the self. Michel Henry calls "the critique of the subject" the main theme of twentieth-century philosophy in a text with the same title, "La critique du sujet."

strong conviction that this notion of the immutable and powerful subject is inadequate, the self and (since Lévinas) the other—hence the human, though not in the sense of traditional modern versions of humanism—can be said to be the most important topic of contemporary philosophy, beginning with a close examination of consciousness in early Husserlian phenomenology, via the analysis of Dasein in Heidegger, to the many iterations of the bodily and communal self in subsequent thinkers.

Yet the concept of the human is under attack not only from the "death of the subject." It is threatened also by the contemporary culture of death that surrounds it and seeks to consume it. Already Heidegger warned of the dangers of unbridled technological progress as worse than a possible third world war or a nuclear holocaust: the danger is that calculative thinking might become the only kind of thinking and that meditative thinking, namely the kind of thinking that gets to the core of the human being and makes us who we are, might be erased altogether: "The approaching tide of technological revolution in the atomic age could so captivate, bewitch, dazzle, and beguile man that calculative thinking may someday come to be accepted and practiced *as the only* way of thinking." If that were to happen, "man would have denied and thrown away his own special nature—that he is a meditative being. Therefore, the issue is the saving of man's essential nature."[3] This realization is carried to a new height in the late French phenomenologist Michel Henry who shows the ways in which what he calls tele-techno-science has begun to erase Life itself: the personal life of each human being, but also the life of culture, of art, ethics, religion, and academia.[4]

The strongest indictment of this culture of death is found in his book *Barbarism*, where he argues that science, technology, and the media effectively kill life, erase all its expressions, and lead directly to "the destruction of the human being."[5] Henry indicts technology as "nature without the human, abstract nature reduced to itself," which becomes a self-actualization

---

3. Martin Heidegger, "Memorial Address," 56; emphasis his.

4. Much of French philosophy during this time period is fairly critical of technology. See also the writings of Jacques Ellul, Jean Baudrillard, Jacques Derrida, and many others. Although I focus in the rest of this essay on Henry, his insights could easily be supplemented by drawing on other Continental philosophers of religion, such as Jean-Luc Marion, Jean-Yves Lacoste, Jean-Louis Chrétien, Emmanuel Falque, and others.

5. Henry, *Barbarism*, 3. For a fuller summary of Henry's view of technology and its detrimental effects, see my "What About Non-Human Life? An 'Ecological' Reading of Michel Henry."

of nature exclusive of the human being.[6] In contemporary technology, "objectivity is given as the site of every conceivable truth, while life and the individual, which are consubstantial, are eliminated. Whether it knows it or not, whether it wants it or not, the slogan of this theoretical objectivism rejoins the slogan that was formulated more clearly on the political level: 'Long live death!'"[7] He employs strong language:

> Technology is alchemy; it is the self-accomplishment of nature in place and instead of the self-accomplishment of the life that we are. It is barbarism, the new barbarism of our time, in place and instead of culture. Inasmuch as it puts life and its prescriptions and regulations out of commission it is not only barbarism in the most extreme and inhuman form humans have ever known, but it is pure insanity.[8]

The knowledge Galilean science pretends to give us is pure illusion and rejects the real knowledge we have of the life of the senses, of birth, growth, life, and death.[9] Technology leads directly to nihilism.[10]

Yet, Henry is not simply a Luddite (in the derogatory sense of that term), rather he is pointing to the ways in which the ideology of progress and techno-science has become the mantra of our society, the ultimate "truth" that frames our reality and determines and excludes any other insight. Genuine Life, truly human life, is erased. The two are utterly opposed to each other: "The knowledge of life is radically opposed to the knowledge

---

6. Henry, *Barbarism*, 52.

7. Henry, *Material Phenomenology*, 121–22.

8. Henry, *Barbarism*, 52 [translation modified].

9. Ibid., xiii (from the preface to the second edition) and 6–7.

10. And indeed, contemporary technology separates us from life by erasing our affectivity and replacing it with a virtual reality, in which the pleasures and pains of the pain are simulated and manufactured artificially. Much more profoundly than Henry could have realized at the time he died, our lives are increasingly conducted via a virtual reality, relationships maintained via social media, pains and pleasures "shared" or "liked" electronically. Our speech and writing become fragmented, brief "buzzes" twittered or tweeted. There is no longer any deep and thoughtful engagement with the deepest sorrows and joys of human life, which in the past gave rise to great works of literature, poetry, and art. Life is lived for us on screen or increasingly on endlessly multiplied smaller screens, which becomes so addictive that we can hardly stop to engage each other in meaningful conversation. Sustained critical thinking has become a rarity because attention spans do not last longer than a few minutes and concentrated work is made impossible by the clamor and glimmer of our many gadgets. Technology is increasingly turning life into pure simulacrum, as Jean Baudrillard and Jacques Ellul also show in detail.

of consciousness and science, to what we generally call knowledge."[11] He carries this argument further in *Seeing the Invisible* where he shows the access to Life in the abstract art of Kandinsky.[12] Kandinsky is able to paint the invisible reality of Life to which science has no access: "Art in general (and painting in particular) brings about the revelation of the invisible life that constitutes the true reality of the human."[13] The very essence of art is this reality of the human:

> What is the essence of life? It is not only the experience of oneself but also, as its direct result, the growth of the self. To experience oneself, in the way of life, is to enter into oneself, to enter into possession of one's own being, to grow oneself and to be affected by something "more" which is "more of oneself." This something more is not the object of a regard or a quantitative measurement. As the growth of the self and the experience of its own being, it is a way of enjoying oneself; it is enjoyment. For this reason, life is a movement: it is the eternal movement of the passage from Suffering to Joy. Inasmuch as life's experience of itself is a primal Suffering, this feeling of oneself that brings life to itself is enjoyment and the exaltation of oneself.[14]

Henry maintains over and over again that the life of which science (biology and physiology) speaks is utterly different from genuinely human life. Biology reduces life to molecules, neurotransmitters, and amino acid

11. Henry, *Barbarism*, 14. Henry reiterates this over and over in most of his works. See also chapters 1–3 of *I am the Truth*.

12. Already in *Barbarism*, Henry had indicted technology for its erasure of art. For example, he describes the scientific mutilation of the effort at restoration in the monastery of Daphne and concludes: "What science did in Daphne, it does everywhere. It does not know life, its fundamental properties, its sensibility, its pathos, or its essence. That is, it does not know what life is for itself, what it experiences constantly, and from where it draws the hidden but invisible motivation for everything that it does. These are the only interests that there are in the world, but their origins can never be discovered in the world, in objectivity. Without knowing life and its own interests, science is placed in nearly inconceivable solitude. This solitude of science is technology" (*Barbarism*, 38). He goes on to analyze the ways in which science abstracts from life and "rejects and wholly misunderstands the theme of life" (ibid., 39). See also his essay "La métamorphose de Daphné."

13. Henry, *Seeing the Invisible*, 20. He summarizes Kandinsky's insight: "This truth is that the true reality is invisible, that our radical subjectivity is this reality, that this reality constitutes the sole content of art and that art seeks to express this abstract content" (ibid., 21).

14. Ibid., 122. The final line of the book calls art "the resurrection of eternal life" (ibid., 142).

chains. Yet authentic life is defined by suffering and joy, needs and desires, hopes and pleasures; it is pure affectivity: "Transcendental affectivity is the original mode of revelation in virtue of which life is revealed to itself and is thus possible as what it is, as life."[15] This life, for Henry, is utterly immediate and immanent, it is directly felt without any distance intervening between feeling (in the nominal sense) and feeling (in the verbal sense):

> That is the mystery of life: the living being is coextensive with all of the life within it; everything within it is its own life. The living being is not founded on itself; instead, it has a basis in life. This basis, however, is not different from itself; it is the auto-affection in which it auto-affects itself and thus with which it is identical.[16]

And this life is material and fleshly. Although Henry draws stark divisions between the false "life" of the world and the genuine Life we live and which has nothing to do with "the world" at all, his phenomenology is a *material* phenomenology (heavily influenced by Marxism), a phenomenology of the body and the flesh.[17] Life is material in the sense that it designates the pathos of our flesh. A flesh without pathos is a corpse. The senses make us alive, there is no life without sensation. In *Material Phenomenology*, in a close engagement with Husserlian texts, Henry develops the notion of life as material in its essence, inasmuch as it is pure bodily self-givenness in the affectivity of the touch of the flesh. The body is not a thing in the world, but rather our self-affective flesh constitutes our original and authentic corporeality.[18] At the same time this makes possible a community

---

15. Henry, *Barbarism*, 14.

16. Henry, *Material Phenomenology*, 132.

17. This is first proposed in his *The Essence of Manifestation* and then worked out most fully in his *Philosophy and Phenomenology of the Body*, in *Material Phenomenology*, and his penultimate work *Incarnation: Une philosophie de la chair*, which is not yet translated. In *Material Phenomenology* he clarifies his project as follows: "'Matter,' which material phenomenology understands in its clear opposition to the hyletic [Husserlian phenomenology], no longer indicates the other of phenomenality but its essence. To the extent that in pure givenness it thematizes and explains its own self-givenness, material phenomenology is phenomenology in a radical sense. . . . It is no longer governed by the laws of the world and thought, but by the laws of Life" (*Material Phenomenology*, 42). In some of his work on art, drawing on Kandinsky, Henry contrasts "a cosmos of spiritually affective beings" with the "world" of things and objects.

18. He develops this in great detail in his text *Incarnation*. See also his essay "L'incarnation dans une phénoménologie radicale." In this essay he stresses in particular Christ's flesh as revealing human identity as flesh. His flesh is identical to ours and yet that does not mean primarily that it consists of blood or veins, but refers rather to his

of shared pathos via participation of all the members of the community in life as its source. Life, however, is not something separate from them—like a spigot to which we connect different hoses—but it "is experience itself" and "fills the whole world"; it is "not some thing," but "absolute subjectivity," the "original givenness as self-givenness." We "enter into this community on the basis of the life within" us.[19]

In these earlier works Henry primarily diagnoses the situation and seems to offer few concrete suggestions for how we might combat the current "culture" of death.[20] In his final works, however, he argues that Christianity might provide an answer to this contemporary dilemma. Both *Barbarism* and the first explicitly Christian work, *I am the Truth*, end on a similar note, with an indictment of the culture of death we have cultivated that seeks life in a false, "virtual" reality and thereby covers over or even erases genuine pathos. *Barbarism* still puts this in terms of a question: "But, then, what happens to culture and to the humanity of the human being?" Artists alone cannot combat this: "They would like to transmit this cul-ture, to enable one to become what one is, and to escape the unbearable boredom of the techno-media world with its drugs, monstrous growth, and anonymous transcendence. But it has reduced them to silence once and for all. *Can the world still be saved by some of them?*"[21] *I am the Truth* now offers an answer: "It is not just any god today who is still able to save us, but—when the shadow of death is looming over the world—the Living One."[22]

---

passion, his suffering in the flesh (ibid., 149–50). He refers especially to Irenaeus whom he credits with profound insight on this issue. Christ's flesh is defined most fundamentally by his suffering. The flesh hence is already capable of receiving life (ibid., 150–51). Henry actually contends in this piece that Christ has "two flesh," his human flesh that suffers on the cross and the "arch-flesh"—the bread of life that becomes our salvation ("L'incarnation," 154). He ends this text with a reference to the "Word of Life." See also his critique of a Christology that "gets bogged down in the presupposition of a 'human nature.'" *I am the Truth*, 100.

19. Henry, *Material Phenomenology*, 120. He also admonishes: "The attempt to oppose the community and the individual—to establish a hierarchical relationship between them—is pure nonsense. It amounts to opposing the essence of life with something that is necessarily entailed by it" (ibid., 121).

20. This cannot really even be called a culture, because Henry argues that contemporary techno-science destroys culture. The term "culture" functions ambiguously in English (to some extent also in French).

21. Henry, *Barbarism*, 136; emphasis mine.

22. Henry, *I am the Truth*, 275. The reference to a "god" who might be able to "save" us is presumably an allusion to the famous line of Heidegger's final interview with the magazine *Der Spiegel*, where he claimed that "only a god can now save us."

The Living One is Christ, Son of God, Son of Life who communicates Life and Truth to us, if we are willing to see the false reality of the world for the death that it is and to enter into Life, to become sons of Life, sons of the God who is Life.

In this book Henry reiterates and even radicalizes the stark distinctions between the false truth of the world, which knows absolutely nothing of life, seeking to reduce it to particles and molecules, and the genuine Truth of Life, the very life we live and that makes us who we are: our deepest joys and sorrows, the pathos that is the Life flowing within us and which we cannot give to ourselves. This generation in Life hence is not a single event (at the "beginning" of life), but a continual process and reality, our very being as incarnate, as pathos. We are ultimately not creatures of blood and bones for Henry, but are generated directly out of the divine Life. That is our genuine identity and it is now our task to recover this identity, to live again in Life instead of choosing death. The closing paragraph of *I am the Truth* puts this contrast between genuine Life and its false simulacrum in our technological society the most starkly:

> People debased, humiliated, despised and despising themselves, trained in school to despise themselves, to count for nothing—just particles and molecules; admiring everything lesser than themselves and execrating everything that is greater than themselves. Everything worthy of love and adoration. People reduced to simulacra, to idols that feel nothing, to automatons. And replaced by them—by computers and robots. People chased out of their work and their homes, pushed into corners and gutters, huddled on subway benches, sleeping in cardboard boxes. People replaced by abstractions, by economic entities, by profits and money. People treated mathematically, digitally, statistically, counted like animals and counting for much less. People turned away from Life's Truth, caught in all the traps and marvels where this life is denied, ridiculed, mimicked, simulated—absent. People given over to the insensible, become themselves insensible, whose eyes are empty as a fish's. Dazed people, devoted to specters and spectacles that always expose their own invalidity and bankruptcy; devoted to false knowledge, reduced to empty shells, to empty heads—to "brains." People whose emotions and loves are just glandular secretions. People who have been liberated by making them think their sexuality is a natural process, the site and place of their infinite Desire. People whose responsibility and dignity have no definite

site anymore. People who in the general degradation will envy the animals. *People* will want to die—but not *Life*.[23]

Henry speaks of this recovery of Life as a new birth (in *I am the Truth*) or as listening to the words of Christ (in his final book with that title). In order not to remain dead, we have to drink from the source of life.[24] We have to receive salvation as the manifestation of true Life and Henry contends that this is first of all a fundamentally *phenomenological* insight.[25]

He posits this as a response to the strong Cartesian, Kantian, or even Husserlian "I can," where the subject is conceived primarily in terms of its powers of self-determination and capacities for control.[26] Here, then, the "death of the subject" might actually become productive, because it weans us from a definition of the human in terms of powers and capabilities. Realizing the "pathos" of life also means to recover its connotations of *passivity*: we receive life, we do not give it to ourselves. This means that genuine life is pure passivity, but not in the sense that it is not active, but in the sense that it is not its own source: it is wholly receptivity. As Christ can do nothing without the Father and yet the entire fullness of the Father is in him, so we must become nothing as Life becomes everything within us: "I myself am this singular Self engendered in the self-engendering of absolute Life, and only that. *Life self-engenders itself as me*. . . . The generation of this singular Self that I myself am—the living transcendental Me, in the self-generation of absolute Life: this is my transcendental birth, which makes me truly human, a transcendental Christian."[27] We must become in Christ as "sons

---

23. Henry, *I am the Truth*, 275 [translation modified].

24. Ibid., 162. Henry points out that the more fundamental issue actually is how we could lose our condition of sonship in the first place. We have life and must merely regain or recognize it: "To come back to Life, to be reborn, is given as a possibility always present to one who is born of Life. A rebirth is thus implied in any birth because the new life to be reached, the second life, is just the first one, the oldest Life, the one that lived at the Beginning, and that was given in its transcendental birth to all living people: because, outside it and without it, no living person nor any life would be possible" (ibid., 164). This issue of how we might lose life if that is our true reality and what "forgetting" and "conversion" or "new birth" might mean in this context is maybe the central problem in Henry's late work, to which I will return below.

25. Henry, *I am the Truth*, 80–81. Later in the same chapter he puts this in terms of reversal between light and darkness. Although Christ's light shines into the darkness of the world it cannot be seen there, but is irreducible to the light of the world (ibid., 86–87.)

26. See also his much more extensive critique of the "I can" in *Incarnation* (especially §§30–45).

27. Henry, *I am the Truth*, 104; emphasis his [translation modified]. "This passivity of

within the Son."[28] Henry distinguishes between "individuality" as an object in the world and ipseity as the self-phenomenalization of life in a particular human being.[29] Because we have forgotten this condition of being sons within the Son, we must be born anew. We think of ourselves as egos, as in possession of powers and capacities that we exercise independently, yet we only access these powers through Life and hence our ability to wield certain concrete powers is rooted in a deeper passivity and inability to give ourselves any such power; it is rooted in our condition as sons of Life.[30] We must therefore "rejoin the absolute Life of God."[31]

Henry talks about the second birth as a complete setting aside of everything "worldly," including Western "humanitas" as "thought itself, knowledge, science, Reason."[32] We must recover the condition of divine sonship by remembering the divine life within us, which means to live no longer for the world or ourselves, but to allow God's life to flow through us in concrete acts of mercy.[33] He calls this "forgetting of self," abolishment of egoism (Cartesian and otherwise), and full realization of the divine power of Life within that roots the self not in its own ipseity but in the divine Life working within it:

> It is only with the elimination of the worldly self shown in the world and of the worldly relation to self in which the Self sees itself, desires to be seen, is concerned with itself, works with a view

---

the singular Self within Life is what puts it into the accusative case and makes of it a 'me' and not an 'I,' this Self that is passive about itself only because it is passive to begin with about Life and its absolute self-affection" (ibid., 107).

28. "It is this dual identification, the eternal birth of the Son and the birth of sons within the Son, that constitutes the foundation of Christian salvation" (ibid., 114). He links this again to the very possibility of the self: "Thus, there is no Self, no relation to self, except in Life's first relation to self and in the Self of this first relation. No self is possible that does not have as its phenomenological substance, as its flesh, the phenomenological substance and flesh of the Arch-Son" (ibid., 116).

29. Ibid., 124.

30. Ibid., 137–40. Henry also disputes Heidegger's claim here that human being consists in some essential way in care. Care is "of the world" and introduces distance into the self's ipseity. Christianity is completely opposed to care. He even says that "in care, man's forgetting of his condition of Son takes drastic form[;] . . . forgetting follows directly from the system of egoism, which follows from the transcendental illusion of the ego" (ibid., 147).

31. Henry, *I am the Truth*, 151.

32. Ibid., 153.

33. Ibid., 166–68.

to itself, that the advent comes of the true Self, which experiences itself within the Ipseity of absolute Life and is nothing other than that. . . . Here then is how each work of mercy leads to salvation. Each time, it produces a decisive substitution, by virtue of which the worldly acting of the ego concerned with things, others, and itself, with a view to itself, gives way to the original action of Life that gave this ego to itself. Because action is wholly phenomenological, the process of this substitution is phenomenological, too, and one who practices mercy has felt the eruption in himself of Life.[34]

Thus, the central question *I am the Truth* seeks to answer is how life can be communicated to us and recovered by us. *Words of Christ* carries this further by focusing on Christ's words as life-giving and attempting to solve the dilemma of how genuinely human words could be identified as also at the same time fully divine words that can communicate life to us. Christ comes to us as God, but looking like a human, speaking human words that we can understand, yet ultimately realize are not the words of a merely human being, but are the very words of (divine) Life, and communicate that Life to us directly. Again, Henry emphasizes the complete immediacy and immanence of the divine Life: Christ's words are powerful, precisely because they do not follow the conventions of human speech, which always distinguishes between the word and that to which it refers. Human words lead astray; they are lying, distant, and duplicitous. The words of Life instead are completely immanent, what they say is one with what they effect. They are their own reality.[35] Within the course of this larger argument

34. Ibid., 169, 170.

35. Although this final work puts this insight entirely in terms of an analysis of Christ, Henry already makes the same point in his earlier phenomenological work in strictly phenomenological terms: "Every Word (*Parole*) is the speech (*parole*) of life. What is shown in this Word, what is made manifest, is life itself. Saying is the pathetic self-revelation of absolute subjectivity. It says itself. It is the pathetic determination whose self-revelation is in every form of life. What it speaks about is itself, about the determination it is. It does not say what it says on the basis of something else about which it speaks; it says this on its own basis. That is what it means for the Word of Life to let something be seen by showing what it says in what it is speaking about. 'Letting be seen' is to reveal in the pathetic self-revelation of life, in the way in which all things arrive in us, prior to every conceivable seeing and outside of every possible world. 'That in which it speaks' is its pathetic flesh, while 'that about which it speaks' is this flesh. So the suffering of pain is 'clear' inasmuch as it is 'obscure,' which is to say that it is revealed to itself in and through affectivity as painful. *Language is the language of real life*" (*Material Phenomenology*, 97; emphasis his). Henry's insistence on the utter immediacy of Christ's words leads for him to a complete dismissal of hermeneutics, because interpretation implies at least some distance between

Henry is emphatic about the ways in which this word of life challenges the apparent (and false) truths of our world, frequently employing the terms "décomposition" and "bouleversement" (which roughly mean "undoing" and "turning upside down," but have a much stronger force in French). In two early chapters (which include those terms in the respective titles) Henry attacks the false humanism of contemporary society, which he judges incapable of grounding any sort of ethics. Christ in his message does not merely try to "better" things a bit, but rather pulls them completely apart. This is a radical transformation, a kind of transubstantiation and radical re-generation. It includes a complete rupture of standard human relationships, turns hierarchies upside down, and results in a cataclysmic upheaval of our assumptions and expectations about the human condition. Henry especially attacks the reciprocal nature of human relationships that rely on a kind of "tit-for-tat" version of social and economic relationships. He contends that Christ's message completely overturns these conceptions and instead shows an interior relation to the divine life.[36] Christ's words can become life in us, as we hear the divine life in our sufferings and joys. The issue is not "believing" in this word, but rather experiencing its life as we feel and experience ourselves.[37] The gift of life, offered by Christ, delivers us from evil and gives us access to true life.[38] This true life comes by hearing the Word and surrendering to the will of God in merciful action toward others.[39]

---

the text and its "truth." I examine and criticize his position on hermeneutics in my "Can We Hear the Voice of God? Michel Henry and the *Words of Christ*."

36. Henry, *Paroles du Christ*, 43. This new conception of human relationships within the divine life is his earlier philosophy of community (cf. the final chapter of *Material Phenomenology*) now translated into Christian terminology. The English translation of *Words of Christ* has a significant number of mistakes that, although corrected in the copy-edited version, were not amended before printing; I therefore refer to the French version.

37. Henry, *Paroles du Christ*, 149.

38. Ibid., 154.

39. Religious experience "comes to humans each time that, hearing the Word and surrendering themselves to it, they do the will of God. For example, forgetting themselves in the world of mercy and giving themselves entirely to the fulfillment of this commitment, they are no longer distinguishable from it. When their action has thus become the will of the Father, whoever accomplishes it experiences the extraordinary release of a heart delivered from all finitude and the burden of human egoism" (*Paroles du Christ*, 154). The book ends with a brief reference to the Eucharist as the Word of Life, the word of salvation.

Henry, then, gives us a phenomenology to combat a culture of death, a technological society that has reduced life to a simulacrum, a merely virtual reality. Genuine life instead is lived in the material flesh in which I intimately experience my suffering and pleasure, which can in no way be separated from me. We recover such genuine life by recognizing our essential receptivity, by allowing the words of Christ to work within us, drawing us into the divine life, which alone is our own authentic life, the divine life in which all humans together become truly alive and genuinely human. There are, to be sure, some problems with Henry's account: its lack of attention to hermeneutics and the need for interpretation coupled with the insistence that Christ's words are entirely self-verifying; its absolute distinctions between natural science and Christianity that seem to re-institute traditional science and religion debates that by now should have been laid to rest; its almost complete identification of divine and human life that creates difficulties of distinguishing between divine and human, Christ and other humans, and completely removes humans from any affinity or connection with animals or other living beings; its idiosyncratic use of scriptural texts to cement phenomenological claims.[40] One of the most significant problems in Henry's work, however, is the question of how access to Life can be recovered once it has been forgotten, how rebirth can become possible after succumbing to the world, or, if Life is never really lost, why a turning or conversion is necessary at all, why it might not just happen automatically. The question, then, is precisely that of the symposium and this collection: "What is the role of life in death?" or even more profoundly "What is the role of death in life?"[41] I will explore in closing how this particular question

40. Henry has been criticized on all these counts. See, for example, Antonio Calcagno's "The Incarnation, Michel Henry, and the Possibility of an Husserlian-Inspired Transcendental Life," for a critique of Henry's notion of incarnation; Emmanuel Falque's "Y a-t-il une chair sans corps?" for Henry's dualism between flesh and body; and Jean-Louis Souletie's "Incarnation et théologie" for a critique of Henry's close identification of human and divine. For other valuable articles on Henry's work, see Jeffrey Hanson and Michael R. Kelly, eds., *Michel Henry: The Affects of Thought*. I criticize Henry's lack of attention to other living beings in my "What about Non-Human Life? An 'Ecological' Reading of Michel Henry's Critique of Technology." The central problem I explore in the final part of the paper is raised most strongly by François-David Sebbah in his *Testing the Limit: Derrida, Henry, Levinas, and the Phenomenological Tradition*.

41. Although the topic of the symposium was framed as "The Role of Life in Death," phrasing it as how Christ's death shows us what it means to live and "to participate in the life of God" or the genesis of the human via death seems to suggest that the question also is about the role of death in life or even as a means to life. See John Behr's contribution on martyrdom.

of the *relation* between life and death might be posed in Henry's work in the hope that this might also provide greater insight for a more explicitly theological confrontation with that question.

Precisely because Henry draws such stark distinctions between the barbarism of contemporary society and genuine culture, between the false truth of the world and the Truth of Christianity, between the pseudo-life of Galilean science and the genuine Life of God, between the lying words of our world and Christ's words of life, he often struggles to explicate how this authentic Life or Truth is lost in the first place and what exactly it might mean to regain it. He tries to work this out most fully in two chapters of *I am the Truth*, the final part of *Incarnation*, and to some extent in *Words of Christ*. The chapter on "forgetting the condition of son" opens with a consideration of what it means to speak of ourselves in the first person as "I" or "me" and the contention that philosophy has not reflected on this reality sufficiently.[42] Henry claims that only Christianity has insight into the human condition because it alone communicates this truth from Life itself. Only Christianity enables us to give an account of ipseity:

> The possibility of saying "me," "I"—more radically the possibility that there exists something like a "me" and an "I," a living "me" and "I" who are always a particular one, mine or yours—this possibility is only intelligible within absolute phenomenological Life, in the Ipseity of which is engendered any conceivable Self and me. This is Christianity's thesis about man: that he is a man only insofar as he is a Son, a Son of Life, that is, of God.[43]

Henry contends that our loss of this insight is due to a deeper reason that is internal to the very process of self-generation within Life. Hence, "the occultation of the condition of Son coincides apparently paradoxically with the very genesis of this condition. . . . The birth of the me contains the hidden reason why this me unceasingly forgets this birth, or precisely his condition of Son."[44] This self-affection of the me as it is generated by Life according to Henry enables the "me" to "possess" itself and to make use of its "powers" (such as movement, touch, thinking, desiring). Henry refers to this as a "transcendental genesis." These powers are intimately linked with "non-powers," inasmuch as I have actually no control over whether I

---

42. In fact, Henry puts it even more strongly: "In truth, philosophy knows nothing about what concerns the me and the problems linked to it" (*I am the Truth*, 133).

43. Henry, *I am the Truth*, 134.

44. Ibid., 135.

have such powers and cannot "will" to be. Our "powers" and our freedom in exercising them, then, derive only from our generation in the divine Life via the Arch-Son, Christ.[45]

It is this freedom that leads, according to Henry, to the illusion that I am the source of my own power, which causes me to separate myself from the source of Life: "Exercising its power and taking itself as its source, as the ground of its Being, the ego believes it perceives its true condition and so suffers under the similar illusions of forgetting and of falsifying that condition."[46] Henry stresses the radical implications of this: Any pretense of power, even that of lifting an object, as self-initiated or having its source in the self's capacity is a lie, a "transcendental illusion of the ego." All of life is gift and should not be appropriated as possession.[47] In light of Henry's previous work, the "barbarism" of technology then emerges most profoundly as hubris. At its core it derives from the Frankensteinian assumption that we are the source of life and have the power to generate it and its various manifestations. Such illusion leads directly to a profound loss of self and a preoccupation with the illusory objects and gadgets of the world.[48] This obsession with things of the world, which is ultimately an obsession with the self, leads directly to the forgetting of Life: "The more the ego is concerned with itself, the more its true essence escapes it. The more it thinks of itself, the more it forgets its condition of Son."[49] Throughout this section Henry constantly contrasts the false sense of self with Christianity's true conception. The true conception is "forgotten" in the focus on the

45. He explores this issue and his critique of the capabilities of the self more fully in *Incarnation*, especially Part III.

46. Henry, *I am the Truth*, 140.

47. At the same time, this gift really is given and does enable the self to live and exercise powers. It is assuming oneself as the source of these powers that leads to the sinful forgetting Henry highlights (ibid., 141). One should also stress that this "forgetting" of one's condition and the "second birth" are not temporal, but phenomenological, events. It is not a Platonic drinking of the river of forgetting as the soul is reborn into a new body or a rebirth in death as the soul is released from the prison of the body. That sort of dualism makes no sense for Henry's account of the flesh. See also his analysis of Christianity's "entirely new and unusual conception of temporality" (ibid., 159).

48. This seems to me a trenchant insight into the way in which the technological gadgets of information technology and social media function in contemporary society. Henry is right, too, that it is not ultimately these objects themselves that interest us, but the value they seem to confer upon the self (ibid., 142). In this context Henry also analyzes and criticizes Heidegger's conception of Dasein as projecting itself in the world via care (ibid., 143–48).

49. Ibid., 144.

self characterized by care. This does not, however, really provide a good reason for how one would lose and regain life, but merely perpetuates the absolute distinctions he has drawn throughout the book and in his other work. Henry insists that this forgetting is in some sense internal to Life and thus "definitive and insurmountable"; it is not simply a memory that can be pushed to the back of the mind and then recovered.[50] If that is the case, however, then how can he simultaneously also maintain that each one of us has the self-affective reality of Life within us and that all that is necessary is to realize this? Henry argues that the forgetting of one's condition as son is not only necessary and inevitable, but also actually the proof of this very condition.[51] This makes his position essentially circular and self-verifying.

Part of the problem is that for Henry Christianity is entirely and exclusively identified with life and that this life is both the solution to the ills of the world and simultaneously our very condition. He posits salvation in terms of rejoining the divine life:

> Christianity asserts the possibility that someone may surmount this radical Forgetting and rejoin the absolute Life of God—this Life that preceded the world and its time, eternal Life. Such a possibility signifies nothing other than salvation. To rejoin this absolute Life, which has neither beginning nor end, would be to unite with it, identify with it, live anew this Life that is not born and does not die—to live like it does, in the way it lives, and not to die.[52]

This Life, however, was never genuinely lost. The second birth is really only a realization of one's true condition. Henry insists that this means that such a person "will not know death" but will "live henceforth from this Life that does not die."[53] Henry argues that this does not consists in a recovery of knowledge, thought, or consciousness. Rather, it is self-affectivity itself, an openness to the Life flowing within us. It is only as the Self forgets itself and remembers its reliance on the divine source that it can be regenerated in the divine Life (in which, however, it always already finds itself). "*If life escapes any memory even though it has never left us, it is because a memory without*

50. Ibid., 147. He reiterates these claims in *Incarnation*, where he explicitly identifies this forgetting as "sin," but does not really resolve the issue of how the forgetting occurs and how we move from one realm to the other.

51. Henry, *I am the Truth*, 150.

52. Ibid., 151. In *Incarnation*, he even speaks of the "originary impossibility" of "separating oneself from life" (252).

53. Henry, *I am the Truth*, 152.

memory has always already and for eternity united us to it. It has always already accomplished its work, it has always and already put us into our condition as living ones. This immemorial memory of life that can alone join us to Life, this is life itself in its pathos: it is our flesh."[54] Salvation is precisely the condition of being a Son of God.[55] Yet, how can that save us if it is our condition anyway?

Henry recognizes the crucial question: "How is it possible to live in any fashion if one is really dead? . . . Inversely, if one is really dead, how can one rediscover and drink anew the water of the source of life . . . ?"[56] Yet his answer to this question leaves something to be desired, because it erases the reality of death in favor of an exclusive focus on life. Henry consistently insists on the priority of Life within us. It can only be recovered because it is our very condition. We can only be reborn because we are always already born into Life. *Words of Christ* grapples with precisely the same problem, now put in terms of our ability to hear a word that seems essentially foreign to us. If we are fully human, how can we hear divine words and how can they transform our lives? Although Henry works out the role of Christ as both divine and human much more fully in this text, ultimately his answer comes down to a similar tautology as in *I am the Truth*: The words of Christ are self-verifying. We can hear them when we sense their truth within our self-affective life. Their powerful acting validates them as words of life. Henry employs the parable of the sower to point to the ways in which the word can be heard as evidenced by its ability to bear fruit. He reiterates our essential powerlessness and the absolute givenness of the divine Life. Being deaf to the word of life means to be closed in on oneself, relying entirely on one's own powers. Hearing the word of life means to be open entirely to the gift of Life, to its self-revelation that cannot be judged or justified but comes entirely from itself. Yet such listening and openness is only possible because this Life always already speaks within us.

Henry again wonders in this text how evil is possible and how one might turn away from evil and toward Life. As in *I am the Truth*, the answer lies in the realization that we are already within Life and that the Word always already speaks to us, we have merely to hear it. It is already present within our heart and speaks in an immediate self-revelation.[57] Henry

54. Henry, *Incarnation*, 267; emphasis his.
55. Henry, *I am the Truth*, 161.
56. Ibid., 162.
57. See the final two chapters of *Words of Christ*.

stresses repeatedly that this new birth occurs only because we are *already* born within life and merely need to recognize this; we can hear the word within our hearts because it *always already* speaks there and we merely have to listen to it. This does not seem sufficient for the radical distinctions he draws between the world and Life, between the words of the world and the words of Life. If the world were purely an illusion in the extreme sense Henry occasionally suggests, it could not have the power of barbarity and evil he also claims for it. There would be no need to fight it as intensely as he does, no such radical distinctions would need to be made. His phenomenology of life, if it is to be the radical insight he takes it to be, requires a more radical account of death, a dying to the "world" and not merely a forgetting of it. The "Christian problematic of salvation is" *not* "unfolded exclusively in the field of life" as Henry claims, it does not "escape death" but requires it.[58] Death is necessary for life and for becoming a self. Only if we really are actually separated from the source of Life can we turn toward it. Only if we genuinely die to the false truth of the illusory "world," can we be reborn to life. In order to become genuinely human—or, for that matter, genuinely "divine" in Henry's sense—death is a necessary step. If the two realms are really as fundamentally distinct as Henry claims, then nothing short of death in one enables entry into life in the other.

In light of this it is telling that Henry basically never speaks of the crucifixion.[59] Although he makes extensive use of all four of the Gospels, focusing on John in *I am the Truth* and analyzing the Synoptic Gospels more fully in *Words of Christ*, Christ's death and resurrection are hardly ever mentioned. Henry repeatedly quotes passages from the Gospels that speak of the overcoming of death or the fact that whoever believes in Christ "will never see death" and he makes quite a bit of Christ's declaration to Pilate that he is the truth, but he rarely addresses Christ's death directly. Apparently it is irrelevant for our recovery of life. When he explores our becoming sons "within" the "Arch-Son" in *I am the Truth*, he speaks of Christ consistently as the originary source of absolute Life, but never comments on Christ's death as somehow important for communicating this Life to us. Life is always already generated eternally and we are always already connected to it. No death is necessary. In *Incarnation*, he does actually

58. Henry, *I am the Truth*, 165.

59. It is very occasionally mentioned in his analyses of Christ's suffering and passion, but even there his argument always revolves around an affirmation of the flesh and its passions in terms of the self-affectivity of absolute life. Christ's death per se is not a concern.

once mention Christ's death in the context of his analysis of Irenaeus and Augustine (where that topic is hard to ignore): "In becoming incarnate, the Word has hence taken on himself our sin and the death inscribed in our finite flesh and has destroyed them by himself dying on the Cross." But he immediately goes on to put this entirely in terms of life: "What is hence restored is the original human condition, his transcendental birth in the divine life outside of which no life can reach life."[60] He speaks of this as the "Christian structure of salvation," but puts its "genius" entirely in terms of its recognition of the life we already have instead of the new birth made possible through death.

It is interesting in this respect that *Words of Christ* ends with a brief reflection on the Eucharist, which of course refers to Christ's broken body and shed blood, to his death. Henry does not comment on death but interprets the Eucharist as an assimilation of our flesh to Christ's flesh.[61] It is the bread of life that enables our life. That is obviously true, but such identification is only possible because of Christ's death, because his flesh was broken and his blood shed. The radical reversal Henry continually explores in *Words of Christ* requires the death of Christ and requires our death, if it really is the complete "turning-upside-down" of our world that Henry wants it to be. He stresses earlier in *Words of Christ* that "not only improvement but complete transformation is required. A transformation so radical that it properly signifies a change of nature, a sort of transubstantiation. The new nature that must be substituted for it can only result from a new generation."[62] And yet he goes on to identify this "new birth" again merely with a recovery of the life already flowing within us. The denial of self Henry counsels cannot consist in a mere forgetting of the self but must imply a genuine death of the self, a complete offering of the life of the self and its full entry into the death of Christ. Only taking death seriously can get Henry out of the circle he repeatedly recognizes and make possible a new birth that enables the radical transformation he desires.[63]

60. Henry, *Incarnation*, 334.

61. Henry, *Paroles du Christ*, 152–55. See also the final section of *Incarnation* where he talks about the "mystical body" though not in an explicitly Eucharistic sense (*Incarnation*, 350–59).

62. Henry, *Paroles du Christ*, 31.

63. What this means concretely for Henry's phenomenology must obviously be worked out much more fully. While it addresses the circular and quasi-tautological nature of some of Henry's claims, it would need be shown much more fully how taking death seriously makes his phenomenology of life overall more successful or coherent.

It is, then, only by genuinely dying to the world that we can enter into life, only by a radical turning that is not merely a recovery of a prior situation. If Henry really does want to maintain the absolute difference between the two realms, the false and the true phenomenological reality, then a real death must occur and not merely a realization of already being alive. This does not take evil or even the difficulty of hearing the word sufficiently seriously. We are not already automatically generated into the divine life, but become generated into it via our death to the world. We become a self only via a dying to the ego and a new birth through this death. Henry hints at this when he speaks of a "forgetting" of self in *I am the Truth* (not to be confused with the "forgetting" of our condition as sons of life). In aligning ourselves with the will of the Father via concrete acts of mercy, we are able to forget ourselves and to be reborn into the divine life. Forgetting the divine Life means to be absorbed in the Self and concerned only with the Self, while salvation is possible via a different forgetting of self and a realization that all action is actually generated by and within absolute Life. The only true humanity consists in this complete self-emptying that is simultaneously a being filled with divine Life. While *I am the Truth* puts this primarily in terms of acts of mercy, *Words of Christ* speaks of it more in terms of love. One might say (although Henry does not) that by claiming Life as our own we die and that only by dying to ourselves we recover the source of Life. There is, then, some recognition on Henry's part that a kind of death of self is required,[64] but the terminology of "forgetting" he uses instead creates more difficulties than it solves. The acts of mercy or love Henry counsels here just feel a little too cosmetic in response to the complete disintegration of culture he diagnoses. It is because we do *not* already have access to the divine life that we grasp at the false realities of our tele-techno-scientific consumerist simulacrum of genuine life. And it is only by dying entirely to the "world" that we can be born into life. Such dying must mean a real death to the false truth of the world and its false self and a rebirth into the genuine life that is not a prior possession, but is entered only via a radical conversion or turning (the kind of death traditionally symbolized by baptism).

Henry's phenomenology has profound implications for Christian theology: for the task of Christian theology in, and critique of, the contemporary world, for the ways in which Christianity often makes common

---

64. It is really the death of the self as an "individual" that is at stake here in favor of a life of the self as "son." See especially *I am the Truth*, 112–32.

cause with technology and the media,[65] for the role of the body, the flesh, and especially the passions in the Christian life, for how we explicate the incarnation and the ways in which it gives us access to the divine life, for how we speak of Christ's relation as Son to God as the very source of Life, and for how salvation might be utterly immanent (even "material") and yet not be "of the world." Even more profoundly, however, struggling with the hitherto unresolved question of the relation between life and death in Henry's work can help us work out theologically what it means that there is no life without death, that death is the opening of birth onto life.[66]

65. For a trenchant analysis of this, see Derrida's essay on "Faith and Knowledge: The Two Sources of 'Religion' at the Limits of Reason Alone" and the detailed exposition of Derrida's analysis in Michael Naas, *Miracle and Machine: Jacques Derrida and the Two Sources of Religion, Science, and the Media.*

66. I should acknowledge that it was the very question of the symposium and the invitation to reflect on the intimate link between life and death that led me to explore the need for a larger role for death in Henry's phenomenology of life. My reading of Henry here is throughout deeply informed by John Behr's *Becoming Human.*

IV

PERSPECTIVES FROM THEOLOGY

6

Life and Death in the Age of Martyrdom

John Behr

For the topic on the role of life in death and death in life, the age of martyrdom, here understood to be the first two or three centuries following Christ, offers much material for reflection. It presents us with a dramatic reversal of how we usually understand life and death, and does so in the immediacy of the event of Christ's own passion, understanding this defining event through the apocalyptic opening of the Scriptures (the "Old Testament") by the slain Lamb (cf. Rev 5) and interpreting current events in this light, rather than through the framework of a systematic theology elaborated after the Christian church adjusted to a more comfortable (though still tense and uneasy) relationship with the world. Having given a few examples from the martyrdom literature, this essay will draw out three key themes, pertaining to life/death, creation, and the human being, and offer a few concluding reflections.

The Martyrs

Ignatius of Antioch at the turn of the second century, that is, in a period still with a living memory of Christ and the apostles, while being taken under guard to Rome to be martyred for his faith, wrote to the Christians in that city, imploring them not to interfere with his coming trials. While journeying slowly but surely towards a gruesome martyrdom, he nevertheless embraces his fate with joy, exclaiming:

> It is better for me to die in Christ Jesus than to be king over the
> ends of the earth. I seek him who died for our sake. I desire him
> who rose for us. Birth-pangs are upon me. Suffer me, my brethren;
> hinder me not from living, do not wish me to die. . . . Suffer me to
> receive the pure light; when I shall have arrived there, I shall be-
> come a human being [ἄνθρωπος]. Suffer me to follow the example
> of the passion of my God. (Ign. *Rom.* 6.)

Life and death are reversed for Ignatius, compared to our usual patterns of speech. "Hinder me not from living," by seeking to stop my martyrdom; "do not wish me to die" by trying to keep me "alive"! He is in the
process of being born, in a birth through which he will become a "human
being"—a human being in the stature of Christ, the "perfect human being"
(Ign. *Smyrn.* 4) or the "new human being" (Ign. *Eph.* 20), as the martyr
refers to "the faithful Martyr, the Firstborn of the dead" (Rev 1:5), "the Pio-
neer of our salvation" (Heb 2:10).

Death, here, is a defining moment: not the end, but the beginning; not
disappearance, but revelation. As Ignatius also pointed out to the Romans:
"Now that Christ is with the Father, he is more visible than he was before"
(Ign. *Rom.* 3). That is, when Christ walked amongst us in the flesh his disciples never really understood who he was; now that he has passed through
his passion, the "exodus" that he accomplishes in Jerusalem (Luke 9:31),
and is with the Father in the kingdom, now they can finally "see" who he is.

A second example comes from later in the second century. Reporting
on a violent pogrom that had taken place in Lyons around 177 AD, the
author of a letter, probably Irenaeus of Lyons, addressed to the Christians in
Asia Minor and Phrygia, focuses upon the figure of Blandina.[1] As a young
slave girl—the epitome of weakness in the ancient world—she personifies
Christ's words to Paul: "My strength is made perfect in weakness" (2 Cor
12:9). She was so "weak in body" that the others were fearful lest she not
be able to make a good confession. Yet, she "was filled with such power
that even those who were taking turns to torture her in every way, from
dawn until dusk, were weary and beaten. They, themselves, admitted that
they were beaten . . . astonished at her endurance, as her entire body was
mangled and broken" (*Hist. eccl.* 5.1.18)

Not only is she, in her weakness, filled with divine power by her
confession, but she becomes fully identified with the one whose body was
broken on Golgotha:

---

1. Eusebius, *Hist. eccl.* 5.1–3.

Blandina, hung on a stake (ἐπὶ ξύλου), was offered as food for the wild beasts that were let in. She, by being seen hanging in the form of a cross, by her vigorous prayer, caused great zeal in the contestants, as, in their struggle, they beheld with their outward eyes, through the sister, him who was crucified for them, that he might persuade those who believe in him that everyone who suffers for the glory of Christ has for ever communion with the living God. . . . [T]he small and weak and despised woman had put on the great and invincible athlete, Christ, routing the adversary in many bouts, and, through the struggle, being crowned with the crown of incorruptibility. (*Hist. eccl.* 5.1.41–42)

Through her suffering, Blandina becomes identified with Christ: she no longer lives, but Christ lives in her (cf. Gal 2:20). This is, of course, only seen by those who are undergoing their own ordeal with her in the area, those who have also truly taken up the cross. Those looking down from the seats in the amphitheater would have looked upon the spectacle quite differently, though perhaps some were moved to reflect further on what kind of witness she was providing. Blandina's passage ("exodus") out of this world is Christ's entry into this world—and this is again described as a birth, both hers and that of Christ.[2] After describing her suffering, and that of another Christian called Attalus, the letter continues:

Through their continued life the dead were made alive, and the martyrs showed favor to those who had failed to witness. And there was great joy for the Virgin Mother in receiving back alive those who she had miscarried as dead. For through them the majority of those who had denied were again brought to birth and again conceived and again brought to life and learned to confess; and now living and strengthened, they went to the judgment seat. (*H.e.* 5.1.45–46)

The Christians who turn away from making their confession are simply dead: their lack of preparation has meant that they are stillborn children of the Virgin Mother, the church. But now, strengthened by the witness of others, they also are able to go to their death—and so the Virgin Mother receives them back alive, finally giving birth to living children of God. The death of the martyr is their "new birth," and the death of the martyr is celebrated as their true birthday (*Hist. eccl.* 5.1.63).

---

2. Cf. Ign. *Trall.* 11: "Through the cross, by his suffering, he calls you who are the parts of his body. Thus the head cannot be born without the other parts, because God promises unity, which he himself is."

Finally, Irenaeus of Lyons, the first Christian theologian to use all the standard features of later theology—using the writings of the apostles and evangelists as Scripture, appealing to a "canon of truth," tradition, succession—in the first comprehensive theological vision, encompassing creation and salvation together, also focuses on the martyr. In one of his most-quoted lines, he asserts: "The glory of God is a living human being," and continues, "and the life of the human being is to see God" (*Haer.* 4.20.7). As "a human being cannot see God and live" (Exod 33:20), it is not surprising that he too is speaking of the martyr as the living human being, the glory of God. For Irenaeus they exemplify the words of Christ that the Spirit is ready, while the flesh is weak, and so demonstrate what happens to the "pledge" of the Spirit given in baptism when it fully bears life in the witness of one dying in Christ:

> For it is testified by the Lord that as "the flesh is weak," so "the Spirit is ready" [Matt 26:41], that is, is able to accomplish what it wills. If, therefore, anyone mixes the readiness of the Spirit as a stimulus to the weakness of the flesh, it necessarily follows that what is strong will prevail over what is weak, so that the weakness of the flesh will be absorbed by the strength of the Spirit, and such a one will no longer be carnal but spiritual because of the communion of the Spirit. In this way, therefore, the martyrs bear witness and despise death: not after the weakness of the flesh, but by the readiness of the Spirit. For when the weakness of the flesh is absorbed, it manifests the Spirit as powerful; and again, when the Spirit absorbs the weakness, it inherits the flesh for itself, and from both of these is made a living human being: living, indeed, because of the participation of the Spirit; and human, because of the substance of the flesh. (*Haer.* 5.9.2.)

It is not that the martyrs think death to be of no account, or simply embrace it nihilistically, but rather do so as martyrs following Christ. It is, moreover, in their witness, their *martyria*, that God's creative work comes to fulfillment, for in their death the martyrs image Christ, who is himself the image of God, so that in this way the handiwork of God is perfected as a truly living human being, bearing witness to the paradoxical words of Christ that his strength is made perfect in weakness (2 Cor 12:9). The Spirit inherits the flesh, possesses it in such a manner that the flesh itself adopts the quality of the life-giving Spirit, and so is rendered like the Word of God (cf. *Haer.* 5.9.3). The paradigm of the living human being—flesh vivified by the Spirit—is the martyr.

These three examples, which could easily be multiplied, present us with very dramatic words and descriptions, inverting our usual understanding of life and death: one only becomes human, or rather one is born into life as a human being, through following the trail blazed by Christ. There are three key ideas at work here, which I will explore below, before offering some conclusions.

1: It is Finished

The first point relates to Ignatius' words that only through martyrdom will he finally become a human being. Ignatius, as also Irenaeus, comes out of Asia Minor with a theology shaped primarily by the evangelist John. It is well known that John presents his gospel in a manner that deliberately parallels Genesis: they both begin "In the beginning . . . ." But to understand the particularity of this gospel, and a further allusion to Genesis, we need to consider briefly its relationship to the Synoptics, that is, to Matthew, Mark, and Luke. In these gospels, it is only through the Passion of Christ that the disciples came to know who Christ truly is. This is often referred to as the "messianic secret": the Lordship of Christ is hidden from his followers (though not to the reader) until after the events of the passion. The only exception—Peter on the road to Caesarea Philippi (Matt 16)—is the exception that proves the rule: after making his confession ("You are the Christ the Son of the Living God") Peter is told that he did not know this "by flesh and blood" (by seeing Jesus), but by a revelation from the Father. When Christ then tells this supposed "rock" ("Peter" in Greek means "rock"), upon whom he will build his church, that he must go to Jerusalem to suffer and be killed, Peter bursts out "That will never happen to you," only to be called "Satan" by Christ, precisely for trying to separate Christ from the passion. When it comes to the crucifixion in the Synoptics, the disciples abandon Christ; Peter even denies him. When they find the tomb empty, they don't understand; nor do they immediately recognize the risen Christ when they meet him. It is only once he opens the Scriptures (the "Old Testament") to show how "Moses and all the prophets" spoke about how "the Christ should suffer these things and enter into his glory" (Luke 24:26–27), that their hearts start to burn, so that they recognize him in the breaking of the bread. At this point, however, he disappears from sight, so that the disciples are left to await his coming, looking backwards at the Scripture seen in the light of the passion to seek the coming Lord. And so it is in terms drawn from the Scriptures that they present Christ in their gospels.

The Gospel of John, however, begins where the other gospels conclude: that which the disciples only know at the end of the Synoptics—the opening of the Scriptures by the slain Lamb—is where John begins. After the opening verses (known as the "Prologue"), the narrative begins with the Baptist crying out when he sees Jesus: "Behold the Lamb of God" (John 1:29). Then, when Philip says to Nathaniel, "we have found the one of whom Moses in the law and the prophets wrote," that is, what the disciples are taught by the risen Christ in the Synoptics, Christ promises that "you will see greater things than these" (John 1:44–51)! The Gospel of John, known from the earliest times as the "spiritual gospel" written by "the theologian," thus reflects a movement from a human, historical perspective, recounting what had happened as it happened, to a divine, eternal perspective, telling all things, with the Scriptures already opened. And so, in his gospel, John depicts Christ as the exalted Lord from the beginning: Christ repeatedly tells his disciples that he is from above—from the heavens, born of the Father—while they are from below, from the earth, born of Adam. As such, if Christ goes to the cross, he does so voluntarily, and therefore his elevation on the cross is his exaltation in glory. Identified as the Lamb of God from the beginning of John's Gospel, Christ is crucified, naturally, at the time of the slaying of the lamb in the temple, rather than on the following day as in the other gospels. His crucifixion is also depicted differently: he is not abandoned and his words are not a cry of abandonment. Rather, after addressing his mother and beloved disciple, Christ says with stately majesty: "It is finished" (John 19:30).

What is it, though, that is "finished"? Here, perhaps, we can turn back to Genesis to catch a deeper allusion than simply the opening words of the book of Moses and that of John, "In the beginning." In the opening chapter of Genesis, there is a striking difference in the way that God's activity is described. Scripture begins with God issuing commands: Let there be light. . . . Let there be a firmament. . . . Let the waters under the heavens be gathered. . . . Let the earth put forth vegetation. . . . Let there be light in the firmament. . . . Let water bring forth swarms of living creatures. . . . Let the earth bring forth living creatures. . . . . God speaks everything into existence by his "fiat"—"Let it Be." This "fiat" is sufficient for the existence of the universe: "and it was so . . . and it was good."

But, having declared all these things into existence by a word alone, God then announces his own project—not with an injunction, but in the subjunctive: "Let us make the human being [ἄνθρωπος] in our image, after our likeness" (Gen 1:26). This is the only thing that God is described as specifically deliberating about; this is his divine purpose and resolve. That this is indeed the work of God is shown, for Irenaeus, by the manner in which Christ heals the blind man, recounted only in the Gospel of John. The blind man healed by Christ was born blind not because of his fault or that of his parents, but, as Christ says, "in order that the works of God might be made manifest" (John 9:3). As the way that Christ heals the blind man, mixing spit and earth, parallels our initial fashioning, mixing the power of God and the dust of the earth, Irenaeus concludes: "The work of God is the fashioning of the human being" (*Haer.* 5.15.2, *opera autem Dei plasmatio est hominis*).

However, returning to Genesis, this divine deliberation and resolve is the only thing in the creation account that is *not* followed by the words "and it was so." This project of God, God's own work, is not completed by his word alone. Only with the culmination of theology in the Gospel of John do we hear that the work of God is complete. Shortly before Christ declares that it is "finished," we hear confirmation of the completion of God's project in the words uttered unwittingly by Pilate: "Behold the human being" (John 19:5). That Christ is the first true human being in history is a position maintained right through the first millennium and more. Nicholas Cabasilas, writing in the fourteenth century, put it this way:

> It was for the new human being [ἄνθρωπος] that human nature was created at the beginning, and for him mind and desire were prepared. . . . It was not the old Adam who was the model for the new, but the new Adam for the old. . . . For those who have known him first, the old Adam is the archetype because of our fallen nature. But for him who sees all things before they exist, the first Adam is the imitation of the second. To sum it up: the Savior first and alone showed to us the true human being (ἄνθρωπος), who is perfect on account of both character and life and in all other respects.[3]

Although within the scope of our history, as we collectively and individually experience it, Christ comes later, nevertheless the biblical Adam is already made *in* image of Christ (Gen 1:27), who *is* the image of God (cf. Col 1:15). From a divine perspective (meaning, reading the books of

---

3. Cabasilas, *Life in Christ*, 6.91–94 (6.12 Eng)

Scripture in the light of the passion) Christ preexists Adam; Christ is "in the beginning" (John 1:1). As such, Adam is only ever, as Paul puts it, "a type of the one to come" (Rom 5:14), a preliminary sketch of the fullness of humanity that is Christ.

Finally, if this is the culmination of creation, then the Sabbath on which God rests from his work is none other than the day on which Christ rests in the tomb. As an ancient Eastern Christian hymn for Pascha puts it:

> Moses the great mystically prefigured this present day, saying: "And God blessed the seventh day." For this is the blessed Sabbath, this is the day of rest, on which the only-begotten Son of God rested from all his works, through the economy of death he kept the Sabbath in the flesh, and returning again through the resurrection he has granted us eternal life, for he alone is good and loves humankind [φιλ-ἄνθρωπος literally: loves-the human being].[4]

The project, the work of God announced at the beginning, is completed at the end by one who is God. As Maximus put it: Christ, as human, completes what he himself, as God, has predetermined to take place.[5] And, as such, for us to become human requires, as Ignatius affirms so resoundingly, our own *martyria*.

2: From Genesis ("coming-to-be") to Gennesis ("birth")

One further point to be drawn, from our consideration above, about how it was that the disciples finally came to know who Christ is, is that the revelation of Christ as God coincides with his death as human. It is in *the way* in which he died as a human being that Christ shows us what it is to be God. It is not by being "almighty," as we tend to think of this, but rather, in the Pauline inversion of the cross—strength in weakness, wisdom in folly—by his *all-too-human* act of dying, in the particular manner that he does, offering his life for others, that he shows us the life of God and the love that God is (1 John 4:8). It is not that Christ died because he was human, and that because he is God he was able to conquer death. That would "split" Christ apart, and be of no help to anyone else! Rather, as the disciples concluded—not simply by seeing the risen Christ but by going back to Scripture (in particular Isaiah 53, the suffering servant)—it was his death that conquers

---

4. Doxastikon, Holy Saturday Vespers.
5. Maximus the Confessor, *Ambig.* 41.

death, and so it is his death that is the means of life for others, because it was the death of an innocent victim, one over whom death had no claim, and so whose death for the sake of others was completely voluntary and freely given.

This is the heart of the theology defended by the councils of the first millennium. That which we see in the crucified and risen Christ—as proclaimed by the apostles through the words drawn from the Scriptures, the prophecies and narratives, the poetry and the prayers—is what it is to be God. This is the meaning of the affirmation that Christ is "consubstantial with the Father," asserted by the Council of Nicaea (325 AD): Christ is *what* it is to be God, and yet *other* than the Father, something only known in and through the Holy Spirit, by whom alone one can confess Christ as Lord (1 Cor 12:3) and through whom one adopted as sons of God, and so is also confessed to be what it is to be God, one of the Holy Trinity. The heart of the affirmation of Chalcedon (451 AD) regarding the person of Christ is that what it is to be human and what it is to be God—death and life—are seen together in one concrete being (*hypostasis*), with one "face" (*prosōpon*): that is, we do not look at one being to see God and another to see the human; both are revealed together in one, "without confusion, change, division, separation." What it is to be God and what it is to be human remain the same, but the miracle is that each is now revealed together in one and, therefore, also through each other: mortality is not a property of God, creating life is not a property of humans, but Christ has brought both together, conquering death by his death and in this very act conferring life, a life which can no longer be touched by death.

To take this reflection further, we should consider again the words of Ignatius, that, through his death in conformity with Christ, he is about *to be born* as a living human being. A contrast is implied here, which becomes fully explicit with Maximus the Confessor several centuries later, between *genesis* ("coming into existence") and *gennesis* ("birth").[6] Through *genesis* we have all come into existence, without any choice on our part (as Kirilov put it in Dostoyevsky's *The Demons*: "No one asked me if I wanted to be born!"). We are, to use Heideggerian language, thrown into an existence in which, whatever we do, we will die. Mortality, in fact, is the only thing that is common to life on earth; and the ability to contemplate and to use our

---

6. The two words, γένεσις and γέννησις, distinguished only in graphical not aural form, derive from two different verbs, γίγνομαι, "to come into being," and γεννάω "to beget."

mortality is that which is distinctively human. Despite our knowledge of our mortality, however, or rather because of it, we are tempted to hold on to this "life" as we know it, to do whatever we can to secure it, to live it as mine for as long as I can perpetuate it. It is the "fear of death," as the Letter to the Hebrews put it, that has held us "in life-long bondage" (Heb 2:15).

However, the Christian gospel turns this upside down: "whoever would save his life will lose it, and whoever would lose it for my sake will gain it" (Matt 16:25). Following the language of Hebrews, it is not from death itself that Christ has delivered us (we all still die, after all), but from "the fear of death". Through his death, as Maximus the Confessor puts it, Christ has changed the "use" of death for all men and women throughout time:

> When willingly submitting to the condemnation imposed on our passibility [that is, our passive subjection to suffering], he turned that very passibility into an instrument for eradicating sin and the death which is its consequence.[7]

Christ has provided, as Maximus explains: "another beginning and a second birth for human nature, which through the vehicle of suffering, ends in the pleasure of the life to come." In this way, Maximus continues, Christ has "converted the use of death," so that "the baptized acquires the use of death to condemn sin, which in turn mystically leads that person to divine and unending life."[8] Rather than being passive and frustrated victims of death and of the givenness of our mortality, in Christ we can freely and actively "use death," in Maximus' striking phrase, not as an act of desperation, bringing about the end, or as passive submission to victimization, resigning oneself to one's fate, but rather as the beginning of new life.

Losing life for the sake of Christ is the path taken by Ignatius and Blandina in the most dramatic terms possible, through their martyrdom, which is nothing other than their birth into life.[9] It is also, somewhat less dramatically, the step taken by those who would be baptized in Christ: "Do

7. Maximus the Confessor, *Ad Thal.* 61

8. *Ad. Thal.* 61.

9. The resonance of this with Michel Henry's Phenomenology of Life is striking and deserves further study. Cf. Henry, *I am the Truth*, 59–60: "To be born is not to come into the world. To be born is to come into life. . . . To come into life here means that it is in life and from out of it alone that this coming is capable of being produced. To come into life means to come from life, starting from it, in such a way that it is not birth's point of arrival, as it were, but its point of departure." See also the contribution of Crina Gschwandtner to this volume.

you not know that all of us who have been baptized into Christ Jesus were baptized into his death? We were buried therefore with him by baptism into death, so that as Christ was raised from the dead by the glory of the Father, we too might walk in newness of life. For if we have been united with him in a death like his, we shall certainly be united with him in a resurrection like his" (Rom 6:3–5). By freely "dying" to oneself (to "the old man," to "Adam," to our involuntary created existence) and beginning to live ecstatically, beyond ourselves, for others and for God, the life that is begun is, even now, a life that has been entered into through death and, therefore, a life that can no longer be touched by death. In so doing, we transcend the limitations of the life into which, through *genesis,* we have involuntarily come into existence. In and through Christ, we now have the possibility of freely using the givenness of our creaturely mortality to enter, freely and willingly, through birth, *gennesis,* into existence as a human being with a life without end, "born from above . . . from the water and the Spirit" (John 3:3, 5). In this way, freedom, rather than necessity, becomes the basis for a truly human existence in Christ. This is a new existence, beginning with an act of freedom—that of Christ voluntarily going to his passion, "converting the use of death" for all—and in this way, enabling us also to start over—*freely*—by following him.

To live in this divine manner, however, requires growth and maturity. At several points in his magnum opus, Irenaeus addresses the question of why God did not simply create human beings as such at the outset, and offered various reasons. He suggested, for instance, that Adam and Eve, whom he depicts as infants (having but recently come into existence) in paradise, needed to grow in order to achieve perfection, the fullness of being human to which they were called by God. He gives the example of a mother, who could give a newborn child meat rather than milk, though this would not benefit the infant at all, for the infant needs to grow before being able to receive such food. So also, he suggests, God could have given us a full share in his life and existence from the beginning, but we would not have been able to receive such a magnificent gift, without being prepared by learning through experience (*Haer.* 4.38.1). This doesn't necessarily imply any imperfection in that which comes into existence, but qualifies the notion of perfection: in the same way that a newborn infant may have "perfect" limbs, but needs to exercise (and to fall) before being able to walk and to run; so, too, a creature needs to be exercised in virtue before they can share in the uncreated life of God (cf. *Haer.* 4.38.4).

He further explains that this growth is bound up with different kinds of "knowledge" (*Haer.* 4.39.1). There is knowledge that is acquired by hearing and there is knowledge that is only gained by experience, such as, what it is for something, such as honey, to be sweet. Moreover, someone who has lost their sight, but then regains it will value sight much more than those who do not know what it is like to be blind. Likewise, he suggests it is only by our mortality, by the experience of death in our separation—apostasy—from God, that we come to value life, knowing that in ourselves we do not have life, but depend for it upon God. Our experience of death drives home this point in a way that we will never otherwise fully know. We need to know experientially what it is to be weak, if we are to know the strength of God, for as Christ both exemplified and affirms: "my strength is made perfect in weakness" (2 Cor 12:9).

Irenaeus points to the case of Jonah as an analogy for understanding the wisdom of God in these matters (*Haer* 3.20.1–2). As God appointed a whale to swallow up Jonah, not to kill him but to provide an occasion for Jonah to learn—so that having been in the belly of the whale for three days and nights and then unexpectedly cast out, Jonah would acknowledge himself to be a servant of the Lord, dependent upon him for his life—so, likewise, Irenaeus suggests that in preparing beforehand the plan of salvation worked by the Lord through the sign of Jonah, God allowed the human race to be swallowed up by the great whale from the beginning, not to destroy the human race, but so that once they unexpectedly received salvation, they would then know that they do not have life from or in themselves, and so be willing to receive it from God. In this overarching arc of the economy of God, which leads from Adam to Christ, the human race comes to learn of its own weakness, but also and simultaneously comes to know the greatness of God manifest in their own weakness, transforming the mortal to immortality and the corruptible to incorruption. In this way, intriguingly, Jonah is a sign of the perishing human race and, at the same time, a sign of the savior, for it is precisely by his death that Christ has conquered death.

Finally, Irenaeus adds that only in this way can there be created beings who can freely respond to God in love, who can adhere to him in love, and so, in love, come to share in his existence. Any other approach would have resulted merely in "automatons." He then concludes, rather shockingly, that if we ignore all this, and especially the need for experiential knowledge of our own weakness: "we kill the human being in us" (*Haer.* 4.39.1). From what we have seen, we might also say that in order to be a true human being in the image of God—who is Christ the true human being, "the firstborn of all creation" (Col 1:15)—we must be born into a new existence in Christ by a birth effected through our voluntary use of our mortality, as an act of sacrifice through baptism, thereby freely choosing to exist as a human being and grounding that being and existence in an act of freedom, and so living the same life of love that God himself is. Only in this way can a created being come to share in the uncreated life of God, a life that Christ has shown to be one of self-sacrificial love: one cannot come into existence (*genesis*) already "in" that state; it requires growth and maturity.

In this way, then, the desired intention of God expressed in Genesis, to make a human being, is realized, when the creature brought into existence gives his or her own "fiat"—"Let it be!" For every other aspect of creation, all that was needed was a simple divine "fiat"—"Let it be!" But for the human being to come into existence, required a creature able to give their own "fiat!"

This is accomplished sacramentally in baptism, and the life of the baptized thereafter is one of "learning to die," learning, that is, specifically to take up the cross of Christ. However, until I actually die and lie in the grave, I'm caught in the first-person singular. *I* can only say: "Didn't *I* die well to myself today?" It is still *I* who am working, while I learn how to let go of all that pertains to my self. Until I actually die, it is still *I* who am doing this, dying to myself. When, on the other hand, *I* am finally returned to the dust, then *I* stop working. Then, and only then, do *I* finally experience my complete and utter frailty and weakness. Then, and only then, do *I* become clay (for *I* never was this), clay fashioned by the Hands of God into living flesh. And so, it is also only then that the God whose strength is made perfect in weakness can finally be the Creator: taking dust from the earth which I now am and mixing in his power, he now, finally, fashions a true, living, human being—"the glory of God."

3: From Breath to Spirit

Another way of putting all this is in terms of the contrast between breath and Spirit, as Paul explains it with reference to Genesis. While the first Adam was animated by "a breath of life" to become "a living being" (εἰς ψυχὴν ζῶσαν cf. Gen 2:7), the "last [or final] Adam became a life-creating spirit" (εἰς πνεῦμα ζῳοποιοῦν 1 Cor 15:45). In context, Paul is discussing the resurrection of the dead and what kind of body the raised shall have.

The difference is not between a "physical" body (as the RSV translates ψυχικόν) and a "spiritual" body; the continuity is precisely the body itself, and the difference lies in the manner in which it lives, either as animated by a breath of life or vivified by the life-creating spirit. And the transition is effected through the death of the body: "What you sow does not come to life unless it dies" (1 Cor 15:35). Animated by a breath of life, Adam could have used this gift of life in a divine manner. But to do so, as Christ shows us, requires living not for oneself, but rather being willing to die to oneself and live for others. Christ himself shows us what divine life looks like by his own sacrifice. But, not having yet seen this, Adam took his life to be his own possession to do with as he pleased, and trying to secure his own immortality he ends up dying. Yet, through the work of Christ, our very mortality itself now becomes the very means by which we learn to live the life of God—through our experience of weakness and all the other things we considered. Through this mortality, when we now embrace it actively, by taking up the cross following Christ and living for others, we come to live, even now, the life given by the life-creating Spirit, a life that, as entered into through death (dying to ourselves, living for others), can therefore no longer be touched by death, but is eternal, everlasting.

This distinction could also be rendered in terms of a contrast between βίος (*bios*) and ζωή (*zoe*), both terms meaning "life," with the difference that, in Christian theology, the first is used of all that which is animated by a "soul" whereas the latter is that which comes about through Christ: "I have come that they might have life and have it in abundance" (John 10:10). Gregory of Nyssa, following the Stoic philosopher Posidonius, differentiated three different kinds of soul manifest in things that "live": the power of growth and nutrition found in plants; the power of sensation and movement found in animals; and the power of rational thought found in human beings. Each level of "soul" or animation includes the previous level and raises it up to a higher level, an order that he found in the opening chapter of Genesis, such that he was able to say that "nature makes an ascent as it were by steps—I mean the various properties of life—from the lower to the perfect form."[10] In contrast to such animation, life as *zoe* is what comes about in Christ: "what came to be in him is life."[11] Life, as *zoe*, lives when

10. Gregory of Nyssa, *De hom. op.* 8.7.

11. Cf. John 1:3–4: "All things came to be by him and without him nothing came to be. What came to be in him was life [ὃ γέγονεν ἐν αὐτῷ ζωὴ ἦν], and the life was the light of human beings." This is the way that many of the early writers, including Irenaeus, cite the verse, as well as a number of early manuscripts.

life, as *bios*, no longer lives for itself, but rather lays itself down for others, in the manner initiated by Christ and exemplified in the martyrs.

The pledge of such life, given in the Spirit through baptism, will be completed when we finally die and are raised in Christ. Breathing our last breath—expiring—we are no longer animated as by the breath of life, but rather, the pledge, which had been kindling the spark of new life, will be set ablaze in the fullness of the life-creating power of the Spirit through our actual death and resurrection in Christ: "What is sown in an animated body is raised in a spiritual body" (1 Cor 15:44). This movement, from breath to Spirit, is affirmed in the Psalm of creation, which may well antedate Genesis itself (and which is said at the beginning of every vespers in the Byzantine tradition, the beginning of each new day):

> When you take away their breath they die and return to their dust; when you send forth your Spirit, they are created and you renew the face of the ground. May the glory of the Lord endure forever and may the Lord rejoice in his works. (Ps 104 (103): 29–31)

From breath, through the earth, to the Spirit—and so, finally, created. It is, in fact, only with our actual death, completing that which begins in baptism, that we become earth: this is our end-point, rather than our beginning, but it is an end-point that becomes our beginning, as creatures of God, creatures not simply in the sense of having come into existence by creation, but creatures reflecting or embodying the will of the Creator through their own fiat and birth into life through death, thus completing at the end the stated intention of God at the beginning.

Conclusion

The witness of the martyrs, and the theology of those who reflected on their witness, provides a stark challenge to us today, on a number of levels: it consistently, and coherently, reverses our usual understanding of life and death, creation and what it is to be (truly) human, the beginning and the end. It is theologically challenging, for we have come to think of perfection much more in terms of protology, as the way things were in the beginning before "the fall," and of Christ's work as being a remedy for our deviation. That is, we tend to think of creation and salvation as being two distinct moments or operations, a Plan A followed, after human error, by Plan B. For these early theologians, however, Christ is not Plan B, but rather the realization of God's intention, stated at the beginning, and brought to completion by the arc that leads from Adam to Christ. The work of Christ in the passion is not simply a remedy, but the expression of the life, love, and being of God, which encompasses and transforms human deviation and death itself: our deviation becomes a pedagogic instrument (cf. Jer 2:19 "your own apostasy shall teach you," cited by Irenaeus in *Haer.* 4.37.7), and death becomes the means of life, not a resuscitated breath continuing our *bios*, but rather the life, *zoe*, created by the Spirit through the act of losing our life for the sake of Christ and others. Life comes through the cross, and only the one who lives in this way is truly a human being.

The challenge of this vision is accentuated greatly by the fact that in most Western countries we no longer "see" death today. People still die, of course, whether peacefully at home or tragically in accidents, and we hear of many more deaths than ever before, whether through warfare, or terrorism, or natural calamities such as famines and diseases. But in a very real sense, we no longer "see" death. Until a century or so ago, it was normal to have at least one sibling die in childhood and for one parent to die before one reached adulthood. Their bodies would be looked after at home, laid out in the bedroom or the dining room, tendered and cared for, with friends and neighbors keeping wake, until they were taken to church to be commended to God and interred in the earth. Today, however, the bodies are removed as quickly as possible, to the morticians, who prepare the body to be placed under pink lights in the funeral home, so that they appear to be living and that comments might be made such as "I've never seen him/her looking so good." The bodies are increasingly disposed of in crematoriums, with only a few people present, and a "memorial service" is held, without the person being there (for after all they have "left" the body behind) in which their "life" is celebrated. This discarding of the traditional funeral liturgy (in all the senses mentioned above), such that we no longer "see" death, is perhaps the biggest change in human existence in history. If it is true, as I have argued above, that, at least from a Christian perspective, Christ shows us what it is to be God in the way that he dies as a human being, the removal of the "face" of death from society and our experience, is simultaneously the removal of the "face" of God. It results in a very imminent perspective on human life—human life is what we now live, as we "live life to the full"— and a very odd relationship to our bodies: while we are "living," our life is all about our body and its plasticity, ready to be fashioned and refashioned as we desire, as traced out so well by Hervé Juvin, but when we die the body is discarded as nothing but our earthly shell.

In such a culture, the idea that life comes through death, and that death therefore has a role to play in life, giving birth to a life beyond the reaches of death, cannot but strike us as bizarre. Yet, as Irenaeus underscores, death nevertheless will have its final say, though, as he would add, the final say is that of God who uses our mortality to educate us of our finitude, our embodiedness, and our earthiness, and so enables us, finally, to receive that which we don't have in or from ourselves, that is, life. Or, as Juvin concludes his fascinating study: "Alone the body remembers that it is finite; alone, it roots us in its limits, our last frontier (for how long?); and even if—especially if—it forgets, the body alone still prevents us from being God to ourselves and others."[12]

12. Juvin, *The Coming of the Body*, 177.

7

New Life as Life out of Death: Sharing in the "Exchange of Natures" in the Person of Christ

Henry L. Novello

THE HYPOTHESIS OF THIS collection of essays is based on the grand reversal at the heart of the Christian gospel, from which arises the proposed idea that Christ offers us an alternative "use" of death as a way of participating in the life of God, and, in fact, becoming human. Talk of participation in the life of God is nothing new, of course, for it recalls the key principle of the "admirable exchange" of natures in the person of Jesus Christ, which was used by the early church fathers to convey the essence of the Christian faith; namely, the divinization or deification (*theosis*) of humanity. The latter does not mean that human nature ceases to be what it is and becomes a divine nature (as feared by Reformed thinkers). Rather, it is intended to stress that the difference between the two natures is not division, for the human becomes truly human only if it is united with the living God. The divinization of the human being, therefore, as John Zizioulas has asserted, attains its true meaning from the perspective of personhood.[1] The focus of this essay will be the systematic presentation of a particular conception of the admirable exchange of natures in the person of Jesus Christ and its specific implications for the hypothesis of the symposium. But before coming to the core section of the essay it will be necessary to first create a contextual framework for the argument. To this end, the first section

1. Zizioulas, "Human Capacity and Incapacity," 440.

will identify shortcomings in the manner that past theological traditions have approached the mystery of our death in relation to the unique death of Jesus Christ, while the second section will highlight what I regard as the most noteworthy and important developments in contemporary theological reflections on the role of death in life.

I: Past Theological Traditions—Dying to Sin

In the past, death was portrayed as having a wholly negative character, inasmuch as it was regarded as the wages of sin[2] and the end and limit of life.[3] The traditional teaching that the sin of Adam introduced death into the world is very difficult to defend nowadays, given what is now known about the origins of the universe and the emergence of life on planet Earth. A number of the essays in this volume highlight the import of scientific knowledge for a theological revisiting of traditional doctrines such as original sin. Alex Filippenko has articulated the current understanding of the origin of the chemical elements necessary for life, and what is clear from his essay is that without the continual birth and death of stars we humans would simply not exist: "We are made of star-stuff." In the processes of thermonuclear reactions taking place in stars, which produce heavy elements from lighter ones, we find a fascinating and powerful illustration of the role of life in death, and, conversely, the role of death in the formation of new stars, planets, and ultimately life. From a biochemical perspective, Luc Jaeger has sought to demonstrate that the process of natural adaptive selection is based upon the elimination (death) and conservation (life) of a certain kind of information. Without death as a means to eliminate some kind of information, top-down causation (TDC) by information control and adaptive selection would not be able to operate at the level of cellular life and cellular evolution would not be possible. From the standpoint of contemporary astrophysics and the biological sciences, then, there appears

2. Athanasius in the East and Augustine in the West gave this doctrine its classical expression.

3. In the Old Testament, to descend into the underworld (*Sheol*) is to be forsaken by God, thus the dead are called the *rephaim* (the powerless, the helpless). The final word of the Psalmist is a word of hope against hope—God's salvation will extend even beyond death so that God shall again be praised (cf. Pss 42:5, 11; 43:5). Karl Barth, reflecting on such psalms, comments that what lies beyond is "the absolute miracle of salvation out of the midst of death" (Barth, *Church Dogmatics*, Vol. 3.2, 593). At the heart of the Christian gospel lies this miracle of salvation.

to be a "structural" logic in the birth and death of stars and in organisms dying to make way for new, more complex forms of life. Death is primarily a natural happening that is intrinsic to the emergence of new forms of life in our universe.[4] The question for the human being therefore becomes: what possible significance could human death have in respect of the emergence of new forms of life in the world? The concrete event of Jesus Christ provides a definitive answer to this fundamental question.

Returning to the traditional theological treatment of death as the wages of sin, only what precedes death (the pilgrim state) and what follows death (the interim state) was deemed to be of theological interest, while the event of death itself was accorded no significance in respect of the person's final salvation. The emphasis was placed on *dying to sin* by progressively imitating Christ and growing in the life of virtue. At best, the topic of death received consideration in moral and ascetical theology where the concern was to prepare the person for a holy death (*artes morendi*).[5] In the West, where forensic-juridical categories tended to govern theological reflection on the Christian faith, the focus was well and truly on the pilgrim life and the need to die in a state of grace to avoid the punishments of hell and enter into the interim state of either heaven or purgatory. In the East, the notion of divine punishments for sin was also very real, although, by adopting a more ontological framework in which the Platonic idea of "perpetual progress"[6] towards God featured strongly, punishments were not seen as

4. The classical doctrine that physical death is the result of sin came under attack from modern Protestant theology, which contended that physical death is a natural occurrence related to creaturely existence. Recourse was made to Paul who talks of an earthly body that must die in order that it be raised a spiritual body (1 Cor 15:35–38). Karl Barth, for example, has followed in the train of modern Protestant theology when he asserts that death is a natural happening, yet at the same time he holds that from the perspective of believers death is the "sign" of God's judgment on sinners (Barth, *Church Dogmatics*, Vol. 3.2, 596). Once we acknowledge that there never was a "golden age" lost by Adam's sin, that the human is an emergent being on the cosmic stage, then the doctrine of original sin is in need of rethinking and reformulation. See, for example, Henry Novello, "Lack of Personal, Social and Cosmic Integration."

5. See, for example, Gregory of Nyssa, "On What it Means to Call Oneself a Christian" and "On Perfection," and Thomas à Kempis, *The Imitation of Christ*.

6. The Alexandrian and Cappadocian fathers, for example, taught the emanation of all things from God and the return of all things to God, who is unlimited goodness. This gave rise to a doctrine of *apokatastasis*, which was not uncommon in the East in the fourth and fifth centuries. After the condemnation of "Origenism" at the Council of Constantinople in 543, however, universalism was discredited in the theological tradition of the East. In the West, Augustine's strong refutation of universalism ensured that

forensic and retributive, but essentially pedagogical and purgatorial—their purpose was the formation of the human being who is created *imago Dei* and destined to union with God as its ultimate end.

But what all the theological traditions, both in the West and in the East, failed to do was to assign any saving significance to the actual event of our death as a dying into Christ who has conquered death by his unique death. If, as Irenaeus famously asserted, the life of the human being consists in "beholding God," then surely our death as a dying into Christ—who shows us by his dying on the cross what it is to be truly God as well as what it is to be authentically human—should be treated as a "privileged" moment for the beholding of God and the transformation of our being.[7] A further notable inadequacy, which is intimately intertwined with the failure to conceive of our death in essentially salvific terms, is that while the guiding principle of the admirable exchange of natures in the person of Christ was used to convey the essence of Christianity as a "partaking of the divine nature" (2 Pet 1:4), the communication of properties (*communicatio idiomatum*) tended to be thought of one-sidedly, so that a genuine reciprocity of communication in the hypostatic union was not really envisaged. The basis for this christological tendency can be traced to Greek philosophical thought, which attributes only negative characteristics to the temporal sphere. The eternal God who is immutable and impassible is defined as the opposite of creaturely existence and cannot be in union with perishability and temporality.[8] There can be, therefore, no penetration of the divine by the human; the emphasis is placed on the communication of divine properties to the human, which brings about the deification of the latter.[9]

---

his doctrine of hell prevailed for many centuries.

7. To emphasize the privileged nature of death, one of my published essays is titled, "Death as Privilege."

8. Eberhard Jüngel, in *God as the Mystery of the World*, by contrast, argues that God's identification with the crucified Jesus means God's union with perishability and temporality, hence the process of change and decay into nothingness is invested with "possibility." He affirms an "analogy of advent," rather than an analogy of being, to stress that God is more like us than unlike us, while still remaining God. The work of Jüngel will be discussed in Part II below.

9. The penetration of Christ's human nature by the divine received classical expression in the idea of "perichoresis" as formulated by John of Damascus (*De fide* 3.7). An analogy is glowing iron: the power of illumination and combustion, which is the property of fire, is transferred to the iron without any transformation of the properties of either the fire or the iron.

As Sergius Bulgakov has argued in his impressive work of Christology, the problem with patristic thought, which is summed up in the work of John of Damascus, is "the absence of an expressly established and consistently developed idea of *kenosis*."[10] Bulgakov is rightly critical of the fact that the incarnate Word's "state of humiliation" remains undeveloped in patristic thought, which has given rise to the constant deviations in the direction of monophysitism. This shortcoming must be addressed, for at the heart of the christological mystery is a movement of condescension of the divine being (*kenosis*-incarnation) which aims at the elevation of the human being to permanent participation in the divine life (*theosis*-glorification). Since the deification of the human being is effected by the humanization of the divine being, the christological mystery must be elaborated and articulated in a fashion that acknowledges genuine mutuality and dynamic interaction between the natures in the person of the incarnate Word. By so doing, the result will be an enhanced appreciation of the role of life in death, and, conversely, the role of death in the formation of new life. The main section, Part III below, will take up this fundamental issue of how best to conceive of the interaction between the two natures in Christ, as well as the implications of the argument for a contemporary theology of death that acknowledges the cosmological, social, personal, and eschatological dimensions of final salvation in his person.

But at this point it is worth noting that Bulgakov's assertion regarding the need to articulate an adequate notion of *kenosis*, which does justice to the authentic humanity of Christ the Son, is bolstered in this volume not only by the present essay, but also by two other contributors. First, Emmanuel Falque, guided by French phenomenological thought, argues for the need to acknowledge that nothing human, especially finitude and anxiety before death, escapes Christ, who suffers the weight of death in order that the human condition be radically transformed (i.e., resurrection of the body). Second, Daniel Hinshaw, writing from a medical perspective, proposes in his essay that the process of dying involves an invitation to healing inasmuch as the humble embrace of suffering and death is an inevitable form of *kenosis* that is a participation in the *kenosis* of the crucified one. Both Hinshaw and Falque are saying, in their respective ways, that only by acknowledging the reality of Christ's authentic state of humiliation is it possible to fathom the mystery of human suffering and death in essentially salvific terms. Once it is fully appreciated that the incarnate Word of God

---

10. Bulgakov, *The Lamb of God*, 248, n. 23; emphasis added.

knows all dimensions of finitude, suffering, and pain "from within" the human condition, then we can come to the view that life is always a suffering through to something higher, to a qualitatively new level of being in union and communion with the living God.

II: Positive Developments in Current Theology—Death as Salvific Event

(i) Some eminent contemporary theologians have attempted to address the inadequacies and shortcomings of past theological traditions by proposing that the death of Christ has given the death of all sinners a changed value.[11] Such a proposal is congruous, note, with the symposium hypothesis. Karl Rahner, who gave much impetus to a rethinking of a theology of death, writes that what distinguishes Christ's death from other deaths is that death as the consequence of sin, as the darkness of God-forsakenness, became in him a revelation of divine grace. Death "in itself" was accepted by Christ when he surrendered his whole person to the incomprehensibility of God and thereby transformed the emptiness of death into the plenitude of life.[12] Rahner recognizes *actual dying*, not merely dying to sin, as a dying with Christ, which leads him to posit death itself as a salvific event.[13] This, to my mind, is certainly a step in the right direction. But what is less convincing is that Rahner, whose thought is governed by a transcendental philosophy of freedom, regards the event of death as salvific only for those who undergo death as the "highest act of believing, hoping, loving."[14] The problem with this proposition is that everything in the order of salvation is decided by the person *on this side* of death. Too much emphasis is given to "subjective redemption," to how we can actively "use" death (see the essay by John Behr) to bring ourselves to personal consummation vis-à-vis God.[15] On a more

11. For a much more comprehensive critique of contemporary theologians, see my monograph, *Death as Transformation*, chap. 3.

12. Rahner, *On the Theology of Death*, 70.

13. Rahner, "Christian Dying," 252.

14. Rahner, *On the Theology of Death*, 71.

15. Later in life, Rahner argued that since something of eternal significance is realized in death as a personal act, then resurrection as the definitive validity of one's personal existence before God must take place at death. But what happens to those who say "no" to God at death—are they annihilated? Does Rahner's thought amount to a conditional immortality? If so, how can Christ be proclaimed as the Savior of the world? How can we be assured that the historical process will have a positive outcome?

positive note, however, it must be borne in mind that Rahner views human freedom as the capacity for the eternal, which is to say that freedom is not regarded as a neutral capacity; rather, freedom only becomes definitive in our "yes" to God, so that the human "yes" and "no" to God are not to be placed on the same plane.

This fundamentally important point can be seen as emerging from the traditional doctrine regarding the human being as created in the image of God (*imago Dei*): because the human being has the capacity for personal relationship with God, and the meaning of creation is that God enters into personal relationship with creaturely beings, then it follows that human freedom is perfected only in union with the eternal God who is the final end of temporality. When I criticize Rahner for placing too much emphasis on the decision of the person on this side of death, it is certainly not my intention to dismiss the traditional importance attached to human freedom in the process of the pilgrim life of imitating Christ, in the power of the Spirit, and participating in the sacrificial life of God himself. The issue here is how one conceives of human freedom becoming definitive vis-à-vis God, and, intertwined with this, how one intelligibly articulates the process of creation and history as coming to final salvation in the risen Christ who is the "new creation" in person. In what will become clearer later on in this essay, I would want to place more stress on God, not the human, as having the last word in the matter of our final salvation. I argue, therefore, for the need to place more emphasis on "objective redemption," on what God, in Christ, through the Spirit, has done "for us" (*pro nobis*). Rather than give prominence to how we humans can actively use death to consummate personal freedom vis-à-vis God, theological reflection should always be guided by the concrete event of Jesus Christ, so that we always have before us the mystery of God as the one who "uses" death as a definitive metamorphosis of the present state of things. It will be fruitful to think of death, as a dying into the Dead One, as a sacramental situation par excellence; that is, as the privileged and transforming moment in which God shows us what it is to be God (giver of the gift of ineffable life, love, and freedom) as well as what it is to be human ("clay in God's hands," receivers of the divine gift, which gives rise to doxology).

(ii) Hans Urs von Balthasar's theology of Holy Saturday provides more scope for reflecting on the mystery of our death as a dying with Christ. Unlike Rahner, who regards Christ as accepting death *in itself* in its emptiness and darkness, Balthasar insists that Christ's "descent into hell" be treated as his vicarious bearing of the *second death* for our sake. The overcoming of the rupture of death introduced by sin lies at the heart of redemption, thus Christ descends to the depths of hell in order to redeem the human condition "from within."[16] The latter phrase is laden with soteriological significance. It is clearly designed to steer away from the traditional (Reformed) interpretation of Christ being "made sin" (2 Cor 5:21; cf. Gal 3:13) for our sake, where the atonement effected on Calvary is conceived of as a mere substitution on forensic plane.[17] Over against the satisfaction theories of atonement of the past, Balthasar seeks to promote the idea that Christ the Son undergoes a real *kenosis*, that is, a radical self-emptying to the point of being in complete solidarity with the human condition, including the reality of hardened sinners. Although the Son was without sin and went to his death obediently out of unfathomable love for the Father, Balthasar contends that the Son nonetheless experienced hell in a way impossible for any other person.[18] Because the Son and the Father are so intimately one, we cannot say that the Son feels "damned" by God and placed in "hell," where there is hatred of God, but "it is quite possible to speak of the Son of God suffering what the sinner deserved, i.e., separation from God, perhaps even complete and final separation."[19] Since the Son alone has descended into the bottomless abyss, since he alone has endured the second death thereby sparing us sinners such a death, hell is regarded by Balthasar as a strictly christological concept. This means that hell truly belongs to the good news of Christ inasmuch as "hell is a part of the universe accepted by Christ; with that, it becomes a mystery of salvation. Christ takes everything upon himself—and with that, everything becomes different."[20]

The perspective of Christ's complete solidarity with the human condition from within is certainly conducive to further reflection on the inherently salvific nature of our death as a dying into the Dead One, for death emerges as the privileged locus for the manifestation and actualization of

---

16. Balthasar, *Mysterium Paschale*, 13–14.

17. Balthasar, while still employing the notion of substitution, distances himself from the traditional penal substitution theory where God's wrath against sinners (the divine thirst for retributive justice) is depicted as the cause of the passion of Christ. Instead, Balthasar stresses that God's love is the cause of the passion of Christ, although he still uses the term "punishment" to convey the sense of Christ's suffering endured as the "second death" for our sake.

18. See, for example, Balthasar, *Heart of the World*, 175.

19. Balthasar, *Does Jesus Know Us? Do We Know Him?* 71.

20. Balthasar, *Dare We Hope "That All Men be Saved"?* 112.

God's saving power as "life out of death."[21] God is the one "who gives life to the dead" (Rom 4:17), or, to state this point another way, in God death is the beginning of new life. Unlike Rahner, the soteriological import of our death as a dying with Christ is not dependent upon our condition at death, for objective redemption, not subjective redemption, is given priority in Balthasar's theology of Holy Saturday.[22] What Balthasar has in view is a truly ontological transference (cf. Col 1:13) in virtue of the exchange of places (*commercium*) spoken of in 2 Cor 5:21, which leads him to be critical of any theology of death that restricts Christ's solidarity with sinners to the act of decision (*pace* Rahner). This, to my mind, is a further step in the right direction. God, in weakness, has ways of persuading sinners to convert and realize their true freedom in the person of the Son whose death has given the death of sinners a "changed value."[23] The sinner can still resist God's perfect "yes" to humanity and lock themselves up in self-sufficient solitude, but for freedom to become definitive the human subject must say "yes" to God—the "yes" and "no" to God are not on the same plane. Rahner, we have seen, also acknowledges this insofar as he asserts that freedom is the capacity for the eternal, but Balthasar goes further when he claims that *our freedom exists within the freedom of Christ* who is in complete solidarity with the human condition, sin excepted.

At the heart of Balthasar's reflections on the christological mystery lies a well-developed notion of divine *kenosis*, which serves to dispel any inclination towards monophysitism (recall Bulgakov's criticism of patristic theology). What is distinctive about Balthasar's formulation of this concept is that he places the process of *kenosis* within the life of the immanent Trinity: he speaks of the eternal event of *kenosis* that constitutes the inner life of the Trinity—the "Urkenosis" of the Father—and views the event of Jesus Christ as the transposition of this eternal event of kenotic self-giving on the human, historical plane. The Son's descent into hell on Holy Saturday is the culmination of the radical dynamic of self-emptying love between

21. Balthasar, *Life Out of Death*, 39.

22. As in Karl Barth's theology, the ontological determination of the human being has been sealed in Christ, thus God's rejection of the sinner is excluded as a possibility. For Barth, though, Christ suffers hell on the cross (Good Friday) whereas Balthasar asserts that Christ descends into hell on Holy Saturday. A question that I would put to Balthasar is: Since the Son's abasement (going to the dead) and exaltation (going to the Father) form "one single reality," does this imply that those who say "yes" to the Son already share in his going to the Father and thus already enjoy the glory of the risen life?

23. Balthasar, *Theo-Drama*, vol. 5, *The Last Act*, 327.

Father and Son, for our sake, and, moreover, such a radical movement of love towards the other serves to undergird and guarantee the authenticity of Christ's human condition; to claim otherwise would be to undermine and distort the true nature of the divine persons in their complete self-giving to one another. According to Balthasar's idea of the inner-Trinitarian event of love, this kenotic event already contains within itself all the modalities of love (suffering, abandonment, death, descent into hell), so that the Son's human properties such as suffering and death should not be attributed univocally to God, but in a qualified, analogical sense. While some might question the adequacy of this proposition (see Jüngel below), nonetheless we should not lose sight of its effectiveness in establishing that human properties are communicated to the divine nature, that a genuine mutuality and dynamic interaction between the natures takes place in the person of Christ. Only in this way can it be asserted that in God death is the beginning of new life, that we are the recipients of a marvelous ontological transference from a situation of death and darkness to the everlasting kingdom of God who is life, love, and freedom. The condescension of the Son aims at the glorification of humanity in a new creation.

(iii) Balthasar has sought to highlight the salvific import of Christ's going to the dead, but it would be fair to say that the Lutheran theologian Eberhard Jüngel is *the* theologian of the grave of Christ. In an arresting fashion he maintains that the "death of God" is the story to be told by Christians. Jüngel, following Heidegger, views human existence as characterized by an inescapable rupture between being and time. The present situation of ontological anxiety simply cannot be alleviated by ourselves: only God who comes to us in Christ can overcome the struggle between being and non-being. In light of the Christ-event, we must reject the notion of the immutable and impassible metaphysical deity who is defined as the opposite of human existence, and affirm instead that *God is more like us than unlike us*, while still remaining God.[24] Because God must be thought of as being in union with all that is perishable and mutable, temporal existence is freed from an exclusively negative qualification and the process of change and decay is invested with the positive element of *possibility*.[25] The essence of

24. Jüngel, *God as the Mystery of the World*, 285, 288. He proposes an "analogy of advent" in contradistinction from an "analogy of being," which is designed to convey the sense of a greater similarity between God and humanity, while at the same time revealing the "concrete difference" between humanity and God.

25. Ibid., 184–225. Balthasar lends his support to this view when he says that the temporal sphere lies not "outside" eternity, but unfolds within it (Balthasar, *Theo-Drama*,

God is to exist through the giving of God's own life, a life that takes death upon itself for the sake of life. "Talk about the death of God implies then, in its true theological meaning, that God is the one who involves himself in nothingness."[26] Death is therefore no longer alien to God's own being, and it is this assertion regarding the death of God that ensures that the humanity of God is taken with full seriousness and is not compromised in any way. When God identifies with the crucified Christ, he defines not only himself—as love—but also the nature of death: death is now to be regarded as a *locus of relationship to God*. The concrete event of Christ reveals the humanity of God—which is ontologically definitive for all humans—and it directs us toward thinking of God as "the union of death and life for the sake of life."[27] God discloses himself as God precisely as the victor over death, as the one who calls into existence things that do not exist (cf. Rom 4:17).

In the theology of Jüngel, at the place where all relations end, God has interposed the divine being in order to create *new relations* in the midst of death. This, I believe, is certainly a further step in the right direction. For it points to the need to acknowledge that it is not just the pilgrim life which is a locus of relationship to God, but also the abyss of death, since God has created new relations in the midst of death. From the standpoint of the concrete event of Jesus Christ, the struggle between being and non-being has been overcome by God in favor of life, hence we are compelled to think along the lines of something new happening in the context of the abyss of death. We are also compelled to think of God in terms of "God's being is in becoming"[28]—God freely addresses us in the person of Christ and opens up to humankind a future that we are not capable of attaining by ourselves, a future in which God will be "all in all" (1 Cor 15:28). To think in terms of God's being in his becoming has the added value of effectively conveying the sense of this world of ours as created for the sake of God's history with human beings. Each human life-time is invested with worth and is irreplaceable because it is ontologically defined by the humanity of God, so that salvation can only mean that it is the life we have lived that is saved, not that we are saved *out* of this life.[29] Salvation in Christ is addressed to this

---

vol. 5, 126).

26. Jüngel, *God as the Mystery*, 218.

27. Ibid., 299.

28. See Jüngel, *God's Being Is in Becoming*.

29. Jüngel, *Death: The Riddle and the Mystery*, 120. Jürgen Moltmann (*The Coming of*

temporal life of ours lived in flesh and blood, and its definitive transformation in overcoming the struggle between being and non-being. Balthasar, we saw earlier, maintains that the human properties of suffering and death should not be attributed univocally to God but in an analogical and qualified sense, yet Jüngel is certainly prepared to be less reserved in affirming the genuine penetration of the divine by the human nature of Christ, without which there can be no proclamation of salvation in Christ. There is not so much as a hint of monophysitism in Jüngel's reflections on the christological mystery—the need to overcome the human struggle between being and non-being ensures that the Son's *kenosis* is accorded its full ontological realism.[30]

III: Future Directions—Death as Sharing in the Exchange of Natures in Christ

The above insights in respect of the "use" of death, both from the human standpoint and God's vantage point, can be developed further, I propose, by reflecting on death as a sharing in the "admirable exchange" of natures in the person of Christ.[31] The exchange principle, as mentioned earlier, was used by many of the church fathers to articulate the essence of Christian faith as the deification of humanity in the person of Christ, the incarnate Word. If, as John Behr has suggested in this volume, Christ shows us what it is to be God in the way that he dies as a human being, then perhaps it

----

God, 70–71) is emphatic on this point. He regards the deceased as having time in the "fellowship of Christ," when this mortal life is reconciled, healed, and completed for entry into eternal life. He does not subscribe to the notion of an immortal soul, or resurrection at death, or death as annihilation, or death as a deep sleep; rather, he claims that every life remains "before God" in the Spirit and thus has an ongoing history after death. But this is problematic, for the continuity of the "I" before and after death requires that something of the "I" must be the vehicle of this continuity, even if one wants to hold that the Spirit is integral to continuing personal existence after death.

30. There is, to my mind, one major problem with Jüngel's theology, namely, death is conceived of as the annihilation of the person and each personal history will be "recapitulated" at the end of time. Nothing, then, is envisaged as happening between the moment of our death and the end of time. I believe it is more feasible to think of our death, as a dying into the death of Christ, as the privileged moment for entering into new relations with God and beholding God as the victor over death. In such a perspective, the reality of the new creation can be affirmed as being in process and as furthering the nature of this world.

31. For a detailed development of the argument, see my monograph *Death as Transformation*, chaps. 1, 2, and 4.

would be profitable to explore the mystery of our death, as assumed into the death of Christ, as the privileged moment for the beholding of God as life, love, and freedom. To substantiate this claim, the ensuing discussion will pursue a number of converging lines of thought in respect of the exchange principle.

(i) The first line of thought has to do with an appreciation for the view that the exchange of natures in the person of Christ is not completed at the moment of his conception in Mary's womb. Rather than a static notion of incarnation that fails to recognize any process of development in the incarnate Word—and which tends towards monophysitism—the genuine *kenosis* of the Word requires that we embrace the notion of a progressive incarnation, which reaches its zenith in Christ's death and resurrection. The latter assertion regarding a dynamic incarnation is supported by the complex picture of Jesus depicted in the gospel story which simultaneously affirms the *ontological* aspect of the man Jesus as the incarnate Son of God, the *historical* element of Jesus' individuality as unfolding in the Jewish context of his earthly life and the hostile reactions to his preaching of the kingdom of God, and the *pneumatological* dimension of Jesus as the Son of God in the Spirit. Sergius Bulkagov, for instance, is emphatic about how the "divine-humanity" is realized and matures during the course of Jesus' earthly life, and he argues that such a view is not attested merely by scattered scriptural texts (such as Luke 2:40, 52), but by the whole content of the Gospels, which depict Jesus' earthly life as being on the *way* to fullness and accomplishment: "I have a baptism to be baptized with; and how I am constrained until it is accomplished" (Luke 12:50). The following citation can be taken as a key statement of Bulgakov's thinking on this matter:

> Nowhere in the Gospel can one find the notion that there is such a separation and sundering of the divinity and the humanity in the one life of the God-Man that God, abiding in His divine absoluteness, would only *pretend* to be subject to human becoming and development . . . while in reality having nothing to do with it. . . . The mystery, glorious and astonishing, consists precisely in the fact that God Himself lives an authentic life in the God-Man, humbling himself to the level of this life and maturing through it to the consciousness of the God-Man. The Divine-Humanity is a particular form of the Divinity's consciousness of itself *through* the humanity and of the humanity's consciousness of itself *through* the Divinity. It is the fusion of the Creator and creation, a fusion that is simultaneously the *kenosis* of the Divinity and the *theosis* of the

humanity, and that concludes with the perfect glorification of the God-Man.[32]

The idea of a progressive incarnation, or continuous deification of Christ's humanity, is required to ensure that justice is done to the genuine humanity and concrete historical existence of the incarnate Word (i.e., a true *kenosis*). But it is worth noting that this idea is also congruous with the modern tendency to regard the uniqueness and identity of a person as established by the particular character and unity of a whole life-history that is made up of the length of one's life (person as agent), the breadth of one's relationships (person as relation), and the depth of one's self-consciousness (person as subject). It is only from the perspective of Jesus' entire earthly life, suffering on the cross, and glorious resurrection from the dead, that his divine identity is established and he is proclaimed as "Lord" and "Christ" (Acts 2:36). The history of Christ is the history of God's engagement with humanity, so that every human lifetime is assumed into Christ's whole life-history. The issue here is ultimately about the nature of salvation, for if the Word is truly our Savior he must unite himself with a human life that is complete in every respect. As Gregory of Nazianzus aptly puts the matter, "that which has not been assumed has not been healed." This fundamental principle should alert us to the need to elaborate a genuine *kenosis* in the wondrous event of the incarnate Word, so as to be able to proclaim the fullness of final salvation in the risen Lord Jesus Christ.

How, then, given a progressive incarnation, should we conceive of Jesus' divinity? In the gospel story, the divinity of Jesus appears as his modus of being-related to the Father in unfathomable love. The "I" of Jesus is a responsive identity which is constituted by the Father's address to him and his perfect response to the Father in the limitations of his historical existence, so that the man Jesus really lets God be *God*: he is true God from true God. The radicality of his response to God also constitutes his true humanity, though, given the understanding that the human being becomes truly human only if it is united with God in love. The advantage of this particular perspective, where the second consubstantiality (Jesus' utter solidarity with us) is placed firmly within the first consubstantiality (Jesus' total self-surrender to the Father in unfathomable love), is that it ensures that Nestorianism (where the two natures are presented as juxtaposed to one another) is given a wide berth.[33] To state the matter another way,

32. Bulgakov, *The Lamb of God*, 242.

33. The view expressed here is in line with Cyril's single-subject Christology, the

Christ's humanity mediates his divinity: that is, the divinity reveals itself in the sphere of his humanity and his humanity expresses itself in the sphere of his divinity, so that the two natures progressively actualize themselves as the one and the other as they encounter and address each other in his person. Each nature, then, as Bulgakov makes clear in the citation above, is to be understood as advancing through the other in the authentic historical life of the God-Man.[34]

The union of Jesus' humanity with the Father is not complete from the beginning of his life, because Jesus, as the incarnate Son, undergoes development as a human being and encounters the *temptation* of evil on the way to the attainment of his glory. The union of his humanity with the Father is perfected on Calvary where he "learned perfect obedience as the Son" (Heb 5:8–9), and, moreover, the power of the Spirit is actuated in a new way in his resurrection from the dead (cf. Rom 1:4) where his humanity is raised to the glory of the "imperishable" (1 Cor 15:42). What is revealed in the glorious resurrection of Christ, where the process of the exchange of natures in his person reaches its final completion in the power of the Spirit, is the union of death and life for the sake of life. God, in Christ, takes death upon himself so as to transform the darkness and emptiness of death into the glory and plenitude of eternal life. The participation of the divine in the human (*kenosis*) arrives at its zenith in Christ's death and burial, but the participation of the human in the divine (*theosis*) reaches its completion in Christ's resurrection from the dead. This means that the resurrection enters into the very substance of salvation understood as a gratuitous sharing in the exchange of natures in Christ's person and thus being divinized.[35]

(ii) The second line of thought concerns a particular conception of the *communicatio idiomatum* (communication of properties or attributes) that is informed by the perspective of a progressive incarnation. What is

---

implications of which were not fully explored until taken up in the seventh century by Maximus the Confessor.

34. Maximus the Confessor also expresses the view that each nature advances through the other. In the fifth *Difficulty*, for instance, Maximus writes: "For who knows how God assumes flesh and yet remains God, how, remaining true God, he is true man, showing himself truly both . . . and each through the other, and yet changing neither?" (Translation by Andrew Louth, *Maximus the Confessor*, 177). On this point, see also Elena Vishnevskaya, "Divinization as Perichoretic Embrace in Maximus the Confessor," in Christensen and Wittung (eds.), *Partakers of the Divine Nature*, 133.

35. The resurrection is more than just God's vindication of Jesus and the revelation of the meaning of the cross. It reveals that humanity and the cosmos are destined toward a deified "new creation."

required is a reading that affirms a genuine mutuality and reciprocity between the two natures, so as to foster a true sense of wonder and appreciation for the process of the humanization of God (*kenosis*) in the man Jesus, the purpose of which is the divinization of humanity (*theosis*) as the final end of creation. All of the contemporary thinkers mentioned above are to be commended for regarding the death of Christ as a statement about God: the meaning is that *this* is God, and God is like *this*. Therefore, a concept of the unity of the two natures that remains abstract—the natures are treated as irreconcilable opposites—and does not think in terms of a concrete event between divinity and humanity, simply fails to grasp the history of the man Jesus as the history of God himself. The actions of Christ should not be divided up into divine and human actions, as if he had a divine miracle button in one hand and an ordinary human behavior button in the other, so he could act in each case as deemed appropriate; rather, his actions are at once both divine and human. Cyril of Alexandria was able to convey this effectively with his single-subject Christology, which features the notion of the "one incarnate nature of the Word."[36] In virtue of the interpenetration of humanity and divinity in the incarnation, the acts of Christ cannot be assigned separately to his humanity (i.e., those which arise from ignorance or fear) or to his divinity (i.e., those which manifest divine power).

For all the merits of Cyrillian Christology, the question does arise whether his Christology borders on docetism and/or monophysitism? While Cyril does acknowledge that the soul of Christ informs his humanity, which is in constant interaction with the Word, the problem is that the latter, as the governing principle, is regarded as immediately mastering every emotion experienced by Christ. When speaking about the fear of death that attempts to agitate Christ, for example, Cyril writes that "the power of divinity at once masters the emotion that has been aroused and immediately transforms that which has been conquered by fear into an incomparable courage."[37] Gregory of Nyssa offers us a very similar picture of the

36. See, for instance, Cyril's *Second Letter to Succensus*, in *Cyril of Alexandria: Select Letters*, 87–89. Nestorius, in contrast, put forward the idea of prosopic union—two different "prosopa" or roles, the human and the divine, forming a union by conjunction. As Norman Russell (*The Doctrine of Deification*, 191) explains: "Cyril took over Athanasius' scheme of salvation, the descending and ascending movement between the poles of human createdness and divine uncreatedness that Athanasius had derived from Irenaeus. The Word became human that humanity might become divine."

37. *Comm. Jo.* 8. 703d. Cited in Russell, *The Doctrine of Deification*, 198. What Cyril asserts is the very thing that Emmanuel Falque is at pains to repudiate in this volume. Falque argues rightly for the need to do away with false death scenarios that forbid Christ

Irenaean-Athanasian exchange principle when he asserts that the mingling of the two natures in Christ does not imply a symmetrical interpenetration of two equal constituents; rather, the divine swallows up the human like a drop of vinegar absorbed by a boundless ocean. In this manner, the human characteristics of finiteness and mortality are transformed and endowed with the divine characteristics of eternity and incorruptibility.[38] Cyril's single-subject Christology "from above" also governs Maximus the Confessor's presentation of the two natures. This is especially apparent in his contention that Christ has no "gnomic" will.[39] Fallen humankind have lost the sense of God as their true good, hence they need to consider various intentions and inclinations in order to deliberate on different possibilities—this is what Maximus calls "gnomic" willing, which is not infallible. In Christ, there are two natural wills, a human will and a divine will, but there is no gnomic will, because as a divine person he is without sin and knows God instinctively as the true good. The natural human will of the incarnate Word, then, is regarded by Maximus as wholly moved and shaped by the divine will.[40] Bulgakov has criticized this idea as tantamount to denying the divine will in the God-Man as *one of two* wills, and as implying the "*infallibility* of the divine volition."[41]

The upshot of all this is the failure to conceive of the interpenetration of the two natures in terms of a genuine mutuality of communication of properties in the historical life of the God-Man. What is lacking is an adequately developed idea of *kenosis* that acknowledges the becoming of the "divine-humanity" through a process of interaction and mutual reception of the two natures. Even John of Damascus with his classical formulation of the notion of *perichoresis* falls short in this regard. While he does affirm as a postulate that each nature accomplishes what is proper to it with the participation of the other one, so that the communication of properties goes in both directions, nonetheless he does not develop his thought on the

---

from inhabiting our own darkness. Christ does not simply "pass" from death to life; rather, he truly "suffers" the weight of death, in order to offer it to the Father who alone is capable of transforming it.

38. Cf. *Antirrh.* 42; *Ad Theoph.*; *Adv. Apoll*; *Eunom.* 3.4. Cited by Russell, *The Doctrine of Deification*, 229.

39. John of Damascus follows Maximus the Confessor in denying a gnomic will in Christ.

40. Louth, *Maximus the Confessor*, 61.

41. Bulgakov, *The Lamb of God*, 245, n.19.

communication of properties from the human to the divine nature. This is apparent, for instance, when John of Damascus writes:

> But observe that although we hold that the two natures of the Lord permeate one another, yet we know that the permeation springs from the divine nature. For it is that that penetrates and permeates all things, as it wills, while nothing penetrates it: and it is it, too, that imparts to the flesh its own peculiar glories, while abiding itself impassible and without participation in the affections of the flesh. For if the sun imparts to us his energies and yet does not participate in ours, how much the rather must this be true of the Creator and Lord of the Sun.[42]

John acknowledges that the Word appropriated the sufferings of the body, but he does not say that the nature of the Word suffered, for the divinity of the Word cannot suffer. John excludes the Word's "impassible" nature from this appropriation.[43] We can say that God suffered in the flesh, but in no wise can we say that divinity suffered in the flesh. The sufferings of the incarnate Word are regarded as having no relation to the divine nature, which is impassible. But how can one separate the hypostasis from the nature in this manner? If the natures are united without separation, how can that which occurs with one of the natures have no effect on and no relation to the other nature?[44] The problem with John's thought is that human flesh is received into the hypostatic union for the sake of its redemption, but in itself it remains outside the life of the God-Man; the human nature does not exist for the divinity itself, but is presented as a passive instrument of redemption.[45] This position is inadequate, for both natures are disclosed in the one life of the incarnate Word following the principle of mutuality in respect of the communication of properties.

The Lutheran formula also reflects this tendency to deny a genuine reciprocity of communication of properties in the hypostatic union. On a positive note, the Formula of Concord refutes the contention that there can be no communion whatsoever between the two natures themselves,

---

42. *De fide* 3.7.

43. Cyril holds the same paradoxical view when he speaks of Christ "suffering impassibly." Cf. Norman Russell, *Cyril of Alexandria*, 41.

44. This question is rightly raised by Bulgakov, *The Lamb of God*, 259.

45. Ibid., 256. Not only John Damascene, but also "Cyril with his unintentional docetism, the school of Antioch with its radical separation of the two natures, and monophysitism with its de facto abolition of the human nature, considered to be absorbed by the divine nature," all deny that the flesh participates in the proper life of the God-Man.

on the grounds that this would effectively result in the separation of the two natures and the emergence of two persons—Christ is one person and the Word of God who dwells in him is another. To avoid this unorthodox scenario, the Lutheran formula regards the natures as united in such a way that they have *true communion* with each other, which entails a "real exchange" of properties, as opposed to a mere "verbal exchange" or mere figure of speech.[46] All this is well and good, but what is less convincing is that the exchange of properties is limited to the *genus majestaticum*—only the divine properties of majesty (i.e., omnipresence, omnipotence, omniscience) are communicated to Christ's humanity.[47] But is it intelligible to separate off some properties from others belonging to the divine nature in the event of humanity being addressed by divinity in the person of Christ? A further problem with the Formula of Concord is that the communication of properties is envisaged as unidirectional: the divine communicates its properties to the human, but the human does not communicate its properties to the divine. Martin Luther himself, however, in contrast, did claim a genuine reciprocity and mutuality in the sharing of properties, and he did so on soteriological grounds: that is, to redeem humanity from the powers of death, God has suffered and died in the person of the Word made flesh.[48] When divinity is regarded *in abstracto*, God does not suffer and cannot die, but since the Word has *in concreto* assumed human flesh in the person of Christ, then divinity does suffer and we can talk about God's death, so that the ontological chasm between Creator and creature has been overcome (compare with Jüngel, who says that God is more like us than unlike us, while still remaining God). For Luther, the unity of Word and flesh signifies a "communion of being"[49] of God and humanity, which is integral to the fundamental union that obtains between creation and redemption. From the standpoint of the Son's death, then, there is simply nothing "outside" God, including suffering and death, which are now to be seen as loci of relationship to God, the very means by which divine salvation comes to us and makes all things new.[50]

46. *The Book of Concord*, edited and translated by Tappert, 603.

47. This is closely tied to the Lutheran doctrine of "consubstantiation" in sacramental theology.

48. See Lienhard, *Luther: Witness to Jesus Christ*, 342–43; and Nagel, "Martinus: Heresy, Doctor Luther, Heresy!" 47.

49. See Tuomo Mannermaa's essay, "Why Is Luther So Fascinating?" 11.

50. For a discussion of suffering and salvation as coming through suffering, see my essay, "Jesus' Cry of Lament: Towards a True Apophaticism."

In articulating an understanding of the *communicatio idiomatum* that does justice to the notion of a progressive incarnation, it is necessary to not negate the genuine mutuality of exchange of properties in the one life of the two natures. The natures are in dynamic interaction and each nature is to be seen as advancing through the other. The human nature is not absorbed into the divine nature like a drop of vinegar is absorbed into a boundless ocean; rather, the "divine-humanity" signifies that God humbles himself to the level of this historical life and matures through it to the consciousness of the God-Man. In the person of the incarnate Word, the divinity is conscious of itself through the humanity and the humanity is consciousness of itself through the divinity, so that the divine nature has a *real* relation to the human nature. In the process of becoming portrayed by a progressive incarnation, the whole of the human condition is assumed into the divine nature, and in this way God freely offers the totality of salvation to humanity and the world. God takes what is ours to himself, so as to impart what is his to us: God takes finitude, the pathos of the flesh, the reality of sin, and the weight of death to himself in order to impart righteousness, holiness, joy, freedom, and the eternity of the risen life to humanity.[51]

(iii) Finally, the third area of thought concerns the complex notion of salvation that emerges from the arguments presented in the previous two sections. On the view that the progressive exchange of natures reaches its zenith in Christ's paschal mystery, our own death, as ontologically joined to Christ's death, assumes the character of a complex salvific-transformative event that involves physical, moral, and eschatological dimensions. These dimensions, furthermore, can be set in relation to the complex view of the life-history of the person as made up of the length of one's life (person as agent), the breadth of one's relationships (person as relation), and the depth of one's self-consciousness (person as subject).

---

51. The "material phenomenology" of Michel Henry, which is the subject-matter of Christina Gschwandtner's essay in this publication, can be useful, I believe, for rethinking the doctrine of the *communicatio idiomatum* and supporting the view that each nature advances through the other. Henry talks of "transcendental affectivity" as the original mode of revelation, in virtue of which life is revealed to itself. Life is material and fleshy, and the pathos of the flesh, of the life flowing within us, is a givenness which underscores the passivity and receptivity of genuine life. Applied to Christ, this means that genuine life is communicated through the pathos of Christ's flesh, and his humanity advances as he grows in his consciousness of the Father as the source of life in him, so that he allows his flesh to be progressively divinized by bringing it into communion with the Father who is the fullness of life in him.

The physical aspect of salvation (regeneration) relates to death as a natural happening, as a situation of helplessness that represents an impasse for the person as agent who raises the question of meaning and hope: what is the point of human action and striving if death is the horizon of life?[52] As a natural happening, physical death should be thought of as the final *limit* set by God the Creator, in order that creatures might come to acknowledge their creaturely status and utter dependence on God who is the Life-Giver and source of ultimate meaning and hope. Genuine life is pure passivity and receptivity, which is to say that the source of life is not within ourselves, and only in death is this brought home to us with full force: becoming nothing as Life becomes everything within us.[53]

Furthermore, the scientific essays presented in this volume have shown that death is intrinsic to the production of the chemical elements necessary for life on earth, as well as being intrinsic to earth's biology. Without death, the world would be a static world with no development, there would be no emergence of new forms of life. The question in regard to human death therefore becomes: What is the new form of life that death can possibly bring? What happens in death as a dying with Christ is that humanity undergoes a metamorphosis: it receives the gift of a newly embodied self that is fitted for the glory of the risen life with its enhanced meaning and value, and heightened activities of mind and volition.[54]

The moral aspect of salvation (justification) relates to the complex reality of sin in the world,[55] the consciousness of which arises in the breadth

52. Douglas Davies, in this publication, has argued that immortality is the ideological form of hope, which in turn is the cultural-emotional form of the biological drive to survive. The notion of immortality cannot be thought of apart from the question of hope. In the Christian perspective, the risen Christ is the absolute hope and future of the world.

53. Michel Henry's material phenomenology underscores the need to recover the sense of passivity, of the receptivity of genuine life. See Christina Gschwandtner's essay in this volume.

54. Belief in the resurrected body means that not only material and efficient causes (ordered to function) but also formal and final causes (ordered to purpose) must be included in our thinking on the human body. Jeffrey Bishop, in this volume, has shown how the medical view of the dead body has shaped the way we think about living bodies. Once the dead body, not the resurrected body, becomes the epistemologically normative body for medicine, then the body is regarded as ordered to function, not to purpose. The body has no end in itself and is only a means to achieve ends. Thus it is easy to regard a failing body as spare parts that should be used to replace the failing organs of the living. There are clear dangers with the functional view of the body embraced by medicine.

55. Sin is a complex reality that involves interrelated anthropological (individual sin), cosmological (universal powers of sin), and eschatological (eternal death) aspects. See

of human relationships with others. The question here becomes the question of good living and justice: where can humankind attain forgiveness of sins, which renews the heart and empowers the person to enter into good relations with others? For the believer, death is not only a natural happening, but also the wages of sin, the "sign" of God's judgment on sin, hence there can be no physical redemption without moral redemption. To die with Christ is to receive definitive forgiveness and to receive a new heart that knows the good life intimately from within.[56] The baptized Christian who grows in virtue is already on the way to imitating Christ, but the process of divinization is completed in death understood as a sharing in the death of Christ who has conquered moral death by his actual dying on the cross.

The eschatological aspect of salvation (sanctification) concerns the person as subject, that is, the depth of one's self-consciousness as created in the image and likeness of God. The question here is that of the self's abiding outlook on life: What is the fundamental attitude that persists beneath one's actions and relationships with others? Since personhood is the capacity for union with God, freedom is not a neutral capacity but becomes definitive only in our "yes" to God. In our dying with Christ and participating in his divine identity, the perfect freedom of Christ becomes our freedom, and we receive the gift of an "original" identity with which we were only dimly familiar in this pilgrim life of ours.[57] This eschatological "moment" is inextricably connected to both the physical and moral moments in the event of the formation of being through death, understood as a sharing in the exchange of natures in Christ.[58]

---

my essay, "The Nature of Evil in Jewish Apocalyptic: The Need for Integral Salvation."

56. The moral aspect of redemption is apparent from the following logical argument. (1) Forgiveness of sins is through the death of Christ; (2) we suffer death as the wages of sin; (3) thus in the event of our death as a dying into Christ's death, our sins are forgiven and our guilt removed (cf. Rev 7:14).

57. Two propositions can be brought together to demonstrate this point. (1) Christ's freedom is perfected in his being "made sin" for our sake. (2) Sin as the perversion of freedom prevents us from realizing true personhood. It follows that (3) in death as a dying with Christ, not only are our sins forgiven but also our freedom is established definitively. I agree with Moltmann when he asserts a qualitative difference between God's decision "for us" in Christ and our decisions for faith or disbelief (Moltmann, *The Coming of God*, 240–46).

58. I use the term "moment" in the Hegelian sense. The moments do not follow one another sequentially; rather, in each of the moments the other moments are present as part of its own inner make-up. Since personhood is the capacity for union with God,

Actual dying, to conclude, conceived as a sharing in the exchange of natures in the person of Christ, becomes a privileged situation for the beholding of God as the giver of life, and for the revelation of the human being as receptivity of life. The human is an emergent being who is referred to the incomprehensible God and has a determination *from* the divine, while the divine is the one who loves in freedom and dies as a human being for the sake of our elevation to union with God: that is to say, the divine has a determination *to* the human and cannot be thought of apart from the concrete reality of the "divine-humanity." The event of Jesus Christ, in the first instance, is the participation of the divine in the human (through the *kenosis* of the Son, God redeems humanity "from within"), which attains to its ultimate depth as a gratuitous participation of the human in the very life of God (*theosis* and the glory of the risen life). The identification of God with the crucified and buried Christ defines not only the being of God as love, but also the nature of death as locus of relationship to God, as the beholding of God as the victor over death, as the one who calls into being things that do not exist (Rom 4:17).[59] Just as God set the conditions of creaturely existence at creation, so God creates the final conditions in death for entering into *new relations* with the divine, with one another, and with the entire cosmos in a "new emergent whole."[60]

It is best to avoid putting too much emphasis on death as a personal act of *self*-fulfillment, for the struggle between being and non-being is overcome by God, not by us. Death is primarily a situation of passivity and receptivity, of becoming "clay in God's hands," of becoming nothing as Life becomes everything within us. John Behr is certainly right when he concludes in his essay that since Christ shows us what it is to be God in the way that he dies as a human being, the removal of the "face" of death in our society is simultaneously the removal of the "face" of God. The removal of the face of death in our technological society is giving rise to a "culture

the eschatological moment is the principal moment in the complex system of salvation in Christ.

59. I propose that all enter into "essential beatitude" at death, yet are more perfectible ("accidental beatitude") given the diversity of merits. See my essay, "Heaven in Evolutionary Perspective," 144–47.

60. I regard the risen Christ as the "new emergent whole" in evolving nature. See my essay, "Integral Salvation in the Risen Christ: The New Emergent Whole." As we move up levels of organization in nature, the properties of each larger whole are determined not merely by the units of which it is composed, but also by the new relations between the units. Evolution involves not just a rearrangement of the parts, but change within the parts and in the organism as a whole.

of death" that erases Life itself by replacing genuine human affectivity by a "virtual reality" where pleasures and pains are manufactured artificially. The acceptance of death is the acceptance of our humanity as referred to the incomprehensible God, who offers us eternal life out of the midst of death. Death is a defining moment of humanity as the recipient of God's eschatological salvation, which brings to completion the pronouncement made by God at creation: "Let us make the human being in our image, after our likeness" (Gen 1:26).

8

Is There Life before Death?

Conor Cunningham

In memoriam: my friends, dearly missed, E. J. Lowe, John Hughes, and Stratford Caldecott.

A GREAT MANY WESTERN humans say there is no soul, but all, or nearly all, act as if there is—serial killers aside, and even they do; why else would you bother killing someone, when you might as well just watch the weather—it is, after all, more random. On the other hand, religious believers say there is a soul, but act as if there is no body. Whilst for many, Thomas Aquinas for example, the soul is the form of the body—a substantial form, and yet also a subsistent one; indeed he argues that the body is there to ennoble the soul. How, then, given our modernist logics, do we resolve this dilemma: is there a soul or not? If there is not, is there a person? And if we cannot give an account of a person, how do we give an account of crime, science, beauty, truth, etc., except without emptying the terms of all content, and therefore rendering them epiphenomenal? Indeed, as Peter van Inwagen writes, "One of the tasks that confront the materialist is this: they have to find a home for the referents of the terms of ordinary speech within a world that is entirely material—or else deny the existence of those referents altogether."[1]

---

1. Van Inwagen, *Ontology, Identity, and Modality*, 160.

Or as G. K. Chesterton put it, "There is no such thing as a thing."[2] As one Nobel-winning biologist put it: "Biology no longer studies life."[3] And as a philosopher of science tells us: "if we ask the question when did human life begin? The answer is never."[4] In light of such logic, which has been with us since what we might call the beginning, Gregory of Nyssa points out: "By their arguments they would prove that our life is nothing but death."[5]

Here are four more philosophers. First of all Paul Churchland: "Could it turn out that no one has ever believed anything?"[6] And another philosopher of mind, Thomas Metzinger is even more to the point, "No such things as selves exist in the world: Nobody ever was or had a self."[7] And it is not just the self that is lost, for we are told, by Ruse and Wilson, "Ethics is an illusion fobbed off on us by our genes."[8] Following in the wake of the demise of ethics is that of formal thought; according to Ruse and Wilson again, "Biological fitness is a function of reproductive advantages rather than a philosophical insight. Thus if we benefit biologically by being deluded about the true nature of formal thought, then so be it. A tendency to objectify is the price of reproductive success."[9] Rather tellingly, Quine once compared the simple belief in objects to belief in the gods of Homer.[10] How, then, if matter is all there is, can we discern real difference between *matter thus* and *matter so,* even if, in our folk language, that change might be termed (parochially and indeed colloquially) as murder, cancer, life, or death, and so on. This is, therefore, it seems to me, the very liquidation of existence. Against this nihilism, amongst many, C. S. Pierce puts it thus, "The soul's deeper parts can only be reached through its surface. In this way the eternal forms, that mathematics and philosophy and the other sciences make us acquainted with, will by slow percolation gradually reveal the core of one's being, and will come to influence our lives; and this they will do,

2. Chesterton, *Orthodoxy*, 59.

3. Jacob, *The Logic of Life*, 299.

4. Ghiselin, *Metaphysics and the Origin of Species*, 1.

5. Gregory of Nyssa, *De anima* 1.

6. Quoted in Rudder Baker, "Cognitive Suicide," 1.

7. Metzinger, *Being No One*, 1.

8. Ruse and Wilson, "The Evolution of Ethics," 310.

9. Ruse, *Taking Darwin Seriously*, 188.

10. Quine, "Two Dogmas of Empiricism," 44.

not because they involve truths of merely vital importance, but because they [are] indeed ideal and eternal verities."[11]

Atheist philosophers, Bunge and Mahner point out, "Radical reductionists reject the qualitative distinction between living and nonliving only at the peril of denying their own lives. Furthermore, it is inconsistent to deny a distinction between living and nonliving and to call oneself a biologist." Wisely, they point out, "one can only speculate over the origin of something if one has an idea what that something is, which is only possible if this something is distinct from everything else."[12] Those such as Daniel Dennett and Richard Dawkins might dream of letting the living world slide into the same category as the inanimate (we are, after all, only material machines), but we doubt that they will forget to bury their mothers or fathers; and, at the same time, we are pretty sure that they will forget to bury their kettles or washing machines when they no longer work.

As the philosopher Michel Henry put it: "Men turned away from Life's Truth, caught in all the traps and marvels were. Men given over to the insensible, become themselves insensible, whose eyes are empty as a fish's. Dazed men, devoted to specters and spectacles that always expose their own invalidity and bankruptcy; devoted to false knowledge, reduced to empty shells—to 'brains.' Men whose emotions and loves are just glandular secretions. . . . Men who in their general degradation will envy animals. Men will want to die."[13] This is a form of Docetism—we only *seem* to be, we only seem to be human, we only seem to be alive—we only seem to die.[14] Indeed we only seem to kiss; as Henry says: "The kiss exchanged by lovers is only a collision of microphysical particles."[15] Henry is no doubt correct, but there is something there that worries me: does Henry fall into the very same mistake he so profoundly critiques? After all, we *are* material creatures; sure, with dimensions that rise above any sort of reductionism, but in so doing they enable the material: I love microphysical particles—indeed I would kiss them. This is the point: in the wake of the incarnation, who cares about such things; for again, these particles are created, too. My lover is a physical mammal with all the fragility that that entails—from bacteria to menstrual cycles—but how would we have it any other way; my wife

---

11. Peirce, *Reasoning and the Logic of Things*, 121–22.

12. Bunge and Mahner, *Foundations of Biophilosophy*, 145.

13. Henry, *I am the Truth*, 275.

14. Docetism comes from the Greek *dokein*—to seem.

15. Henry, *Barbarism*, xiv.

is a real creature, one that can kiss, make love, go hungry, get sick, pray, and indeed die—forget the particles, for they help me kiss her, they help her be with me, and I with her, no doubt with all my fragilities. Yes, how we read creation (read materiality) is indicative of our metaphysics or lack thereof—though any such lack is impossible. But, crucially, Henry makes the point that "the negation of God is identically the negation of man."[16] Thunberg puts it thus, "human beings honor the very cause of the destruction of their existence. The unity of the human being falls into a thousand pieces, and human beings, like beasts, devour their own nature."[17] Over a millennium and half earlier, Athanasius said much the same: "As soon as they stopped attending to what is one and true (that is, to God) and stopped longing for him, all that was left to them was to launch themselves upon variety and upon necessarily fragmentary desires of the body."[18] But of course, then, there is no body—we are nobody.

This inability to die arises, of course, from a reductionist, or mechanistic, worldview; but as Sergei Bulgakov points out, "The world is mechanism only insofar as it is the kingdom of death."[19] Yet the provisional nature of such a situation should be immediately apparent, for any such kingdom must import its meaning and its terms, for even death eludes its grasp. In other words, even death, even the purely mechanical, cannot be articulated, for it has only *borrowed sense*—because "the horror of death can appear only in the land of the living." In this way, science is beholden to other discourses. Or, as Aquinas would put it, science, as we understand it, remains subalternate to philosophy and, ultimately, to theology, for, to quote Bulgakov again, "Science cannot comprehend itself, cannot provide an explanation of its own nature, without passing beyond the boundary of determinism and of a mechanistic worldview and entering onto the territory of metaphysical problems."[20] Moreover, mechanism and materialism are based on a series of mistakes—indeed on a form of Gnosticism—in which matter is deemed bad. Moreover, the drama of disappointment, the spectacle of materialism's supposed revelations is only fuelled by a seemingly demonic contempt for

---

16. Henry, *I am the Truth*, 263.

17. Thunberg, *Man and the Cosmos*, 58.

18. Athanasius, *Against the Gentiles*, 3.1.

19. Bulgakov, *Philosophy of Economy*, 191.

20. Ibid., 192.

finitude. But of course, for the theologian (and we are sure many others), this all seems to be stuff and nonsense.[21]

Any such accusation of being "merely material" is the equivalent of saying a theoretical physicist is made from carbon, and so being done with their thought—there goes E=mc²! How, then, can there be science if there is no soul, and therefore the normative, the metaphysical, life and death, and so on? Even if we provide a Darwinian or scientific analysis of some phenomenon, we do so only, reductively speaking, because *we are failing to provide an account of any such analysis:* its *telos,* its form, the goodness, indeed beauty of its truth—quite literally scientists know not what they do, for they know not why (see below). And, at the same time, is the common religious understanding of the soul not heretical or, less dramatically, inadequate, being an example of what I term "anonymous atheism"?[22] How does one give an account of the soul in light of evolution? But, at the same time, can we believe in evolution in the absence of transcendence? After all, we need *something* to evolve; otherwise, we have the mere flux of phylogeny. If that is the case, all our analyses are merely descriptions of configurations of material behavior, even if some of these configurations appear to be more prevalent, in terms of predictability; but then the dinosaurs were predictable for a while, presumably. As Robert Spaemann tells us,

> Nature becomes exteriority without selfhood (*Selbstein*). Moreover, to know something as existing by nature means to objectify and thus alienate it, "to know what we can do with it when we have it."[23] To know no longer means (in accordance with the classical axiom *inteleggre in actu et intellectum in actu sunt idem:* understanding in act is identical to the thing understood in act) to become one with that which is known. In the Hebrew Bible, the same word is used for the cognitive act and sexual intercourse—"Adam knew his wife" (Gen 4:1). But this becomes completely untenable where the ideal of cognition is self-contained enlightenment.[24]

Every time we think, just as when we are, we enter into a relationship. As Aristotle says, "For the mind somehow is potentially what it thinks

---

21. See Cunningham, "Nihilism and Theology: Who Stands at the Door?"

22 To corrupt Karl Rahner's notion of "anonymous Christians." Cf. Rahner, "Anonymous Christians"; See Cunningham, *Darwin's Pious Idea*, 393.

23. Hobbes, *Leviathan*, 13.

24. Spaemann, *Essays in Anthropology*, 9–10.

(*ta noēta*)"[25]—there is not domination, but intercourse. Again, "Knowledge that is activated is thus the same as the thing."[26] Once more, "Thus in general, the mind that is active is the objects."[27] This is the soul and the world together, and for this reason, the soul "is somehow all things."[28] This intercourse between thought and thing, and though offered by someone, a thing or at least an animal is the dance of all that we do, see, and believe: we know that which we think. This relationship gives birth to all thought and in this way to all things also. For just as there is no matter without form, and all forms, including souls, come into being only with matter, thoughts and things arrive together; yet any such arrival is always *in via*, that is, it never ends. In this way the thought of the simplest thing is analogous to the beatific vision, for there we will know all of God's essence, because God is simple (despite misguided thoughts to the contrary, all of which, I would argue, are self-undermining), but we will never comprehend God's essence. [29] Here Gregory of Nyssa's notion of *epectasis* becomes the basis of all thought, of all things, for just as we must traverse eternity to know God, we must also traverse time to know the slightest thing—that's why Aquinas says that we don't even know the essence of a fly.[30] Therefore, we can indeed, think of all knowledge as a form of marriage—we do become one with that which we seek to know, and this why Aquinas calls all thought *verbum cordis*. As Chesterton says,

> The mind is not purely creative . . . . But the mind is active, and its activity consists in the following, so far as the will chooses to follow, the light outside that does really shine upon real landscapes. That is what gives the indefinably virile and even adventurous quality to this view of life. . . . [R]eality and the recognition of reality; and their meeting is a sort of marriage. Indeed it is very truly marriage, because it is fruitful; the only philosophy now in the world that really is fruitful.[31]

We will return to this marriage.

---

25. *De anima*, III, 4, 429B30–31.

26. *De anima*, III 7, 431B21.

27. *De anima*, III, 7, 431B17.

28. *De anima*, III 8, 431B21.

29. See Cunningham, *Genealogy of Nihilism*, chapter 9.

30. So "the essential ground of things are unknown to us" (*De anima* 1.1.1n.15); thus "we do not even know the essence of a fly" (*In Symb Apost prol.*).

31. Chesterton, *Orthodoxy*, 148.

Now, persons are certainly unique, but we must approach this uniqueness in the correct way, otherwise we are led astray. As Spaemann argues, "Persons are not something else the world contains, over and above inanimate objects, plants, animals, and human beings. But human beings are connected to everything else the world contains at a deeper level than other things to each other. This is what it means to say there are persons."[32] And it should be noted that, before the fashionable despisers of humans tell us that such a view is pompous and self-serving, what in fact is special about humanity's place in the world is precisely our relation with the rest of nature. As Gregory Nyssa says, "There is nothing remarkable in Man's being the image and likeness of the universe, for earth passes away, and the heavens change . . . .[I]n thinking we exalt human nature by this grandiose name (microcosm, synthesis of the universe) we forget that we are thus favoring it with the qualities of gnats and mice."[33] Indeed, as Maximus the Confessor tells us, "Man was introduced last among existent things, as the natural bond mediating between the extremes of the whole through his own parts, and bringing into unity in his own person those things which are by nature distant from each other."[34] In other words, persons naturalize nature, which is to say they actualize nature, doing so because of the *imago Dei*. They reveal nature to itself, in all its forms, colors, and structures, for without them all is dark. Thus they do not flee nature, as do the philosophical naturalists who destroy all that is natural. But let us keep in mind that any such ability does not afford us domination. Again, as Chesterton says, "The mind conquers a new province like an emperor; but only because the mind has answered the bell like a servant."[35] John Damsacene makes a pertinent point when he tells us, "I do not worship matter: I worship the creator of matter who became matter for my sake, who willed to take his abode in matter, who worked out my salvation through matter. . . . Because of this I salute all remaining matter with reverence."[36] Indeed, following the apostle Paul we can speak of the mind of the flesh (*to phronema sarkos* Gal

---

32. Spaemann, *Persons*, 4.

33. St. Gregory of Nyssa, quoted in Alexei V. Nesteruk, *Universe as Communion*, 174. Or as Gregory again puts it: "Man is equivalent to the whole work of creation—but why was man created only on the sixth day? To make it possible to reply to him, if ever he were to become too proud 'You have nothing to be proud about—midges came before you in the order of creation.'" As quoted in Schönburn, *Man, The Image of God*, 71.

34. Maximus the Confessor, *Ambig.* 41.

35. Chesterton, *Orthodoxy*, 148.

36. John Damascene, *Imag.* 1.16.

3:3). As Pedersen points out, "Flesh is only a weak form of the soul. Flesh and soul are not contrasts as two absolutely different forms of existence."[37] Aquinas argues that "The human soul is a kind of horizon, and a boundary, as it were, between the corporeal world and the incorporeal world." Likewise, the soul "exists on the horizon of eternity and time."[38] Accordingly, the human is for Aquinas a little world (*minor mundus*). And importantly, the human is not just a horizon, but also a frontier (*horizon et continuum*). But any such horizon cannot be grasped, for the nature of humanity desires the supernatural, but cannot claim it.[39]

We can ask and answer causal questions about how we came to have certain characteristics. But when we give a genuinely teleological explanation of a piece of behavior, we are simply not asking that sort of question and we are not looking for that sort of explanation; rather, we are seeking to know the state of affairs toward which the agent's behavior was directed. And any such explanation is inherently normative and so supersedes any evolutionary account—not that these should be competing with teleological explanations, as they are addressing wholly different phenomena. Evolutionary explanations are causal, whilst common sense psychology, for instance, is irreducibly teleological. (Now, it should be pointed out that not for a moment do I think that cognitive science, evolutionary accounts of our mental apparatus, dispositions, and so on, do not tell us a great deal—they do—but they themselves are examples of teleological activity, otherwise a regress of sorts sets in.) Indeed, how can consciousness ever be understood in terms of survival when all its functions can easily be accounted for in physiological terms, of course with no actual reference to consciousness?

John Searle famously offered an argument against computers as mindful. While the content and reason of the argument bear no relevance here, the principle at work does. The argument is usually referred to as Searle's Chinese room. Imagine someone locked in a room, and this person does not understand any Chinese. In the room there are boxes in which there are Chinese symbols. In addition, there is a rulebook that instructs him how to respond to certain sets of symbols. He follows the rules and gives correct responses: "If I [the person in the Chinese room] do not understand Chinese on the basis of implementing a computer program for understanding Chinese, then neither does any other digital computer solely on that

37. Pedersen, *Israel*, 176.
38. Aquinas, *In III Sent. Pro.*
39. See Cunningham, "Natura Pura: Invention of the Antichrist?" 243–54.

basis, because no digital computer has anything which I do not have."[40] The point is that the man in the room has only a grasp of syntax, and not of semantics, for the latter requires an understanding of meaning and not just the application of rules. Right on! We agree because we believe in the existence of mind, but that is irrelevant here. Transferring Searle's argument to the question of what relation truth has with fitness, we can see that a syntactical grasp of Chinese is sufficient to get the job done. Moreover, a merely syntactical argument can go all the way down. In other words, there is no such thing as a semantical understanding of Chinese, thank you very much. We don't need it. Or, rather, natural selection does not need it. This being the case, Chinese is not about truth. There is no truth of Chinese, but simply the occurrence of tasks, so to speak. Call this major task SEX, and in this case many positions will do, the success of which is contingent and therefore completely retrospective. Put differently, any road that leads to Rome does, by definition, get us there, even if we thought we were going to Belfast, and even if we in fact believe that Belfast is Rome (though that's pretty hard to do). After all, Columbus never thought that he had discovered America. He had, but that was beside the point. His belief was irrelevant. In this way, ontological naturalism is the most syncretic, inclusive, and pluralistic of religions. It is not the case that any belief will do the job, however, but that any belief can do the job. And this is the case because, again, the intrinsic content of belief is irrelevant. Only its extrinsic relation to the major task—SEX—matters, as it were. But in fact we should point out that all such sex is frigid, tantric at best, and we could characterize it thus: Sorry, no sex, we're materialists. (In fact, I would wager my faith that no materialist can prove that eliminative materialists Paul and Patricia Churchland ever consummated their marriage; well they did, but that was a matter of grace, as always despite ourselves, or lack thereof, in their learned view). This is a long way from the aforementioned classical axiom *inteleggre in actu et intellectum in actu sunt idem.*

Humans Do Not Live by Bread Alone, But Bread as Well

The point of this idea is that mind does not live on its own—there is a brain, but the brain also requires the mind, and by mind I mean the soul, because there is no doubt that the reduction of soul to mind accommodates the reduction of the mind to the brain. The consequence of which, I would argue,

40. Searle, *The Mystery of Consciousness*, 11.

is the loss of the brain, just as it is a loss of the person. As Spaemann argues: "Scientism claims that *res cogitans* is in fact complex *res extensa*: thus the human being becomes an anthropomorphism to himself."[41] To paraphrase the scientist Gerd Sommerhoff: *in this way,* the physico-chemical picture of the living organism is only "half" the truth. The missing "half" concerns the nature of the organizational relationships that make the behavior of obviously living systems uniquely different from that of obviously non-living systems. In many ways this is the more important half—and I don't agree with the word "half" here. For here lie the differences between life and death. For even if we knew down to the last molecular detail what goes on inside a living organism, we should still be up against the fact that a living system is an organized whole which by virtue of the distinctive nature of its organization shows unique forms of behavior that must be studied and understood at their own level.[42] Echoing this insight, Young argues that the essence of a living thing is that it consists of atoms caught up into a living system and made part of it for a while.[43] But the physicalist worldview argues that the special sciences are reducible to the general science of physics, and, strangely, that includes biology too. There is then, no chance of causal pluralism. We are beholden, it seems, to a pre-Socratic model of thinking wherein what we are is always the configuration of some substance or other, call it water or fire, atoms or DNA—the point being that if there is only configuration, really there is nothing new at all. The whole problem in which we find ourselves is one that stems from a latent Cartesianism, and a willful sense that it is tenure-wise best to ignore that which we presume in our everyday lives, namely ourselves, and all those whom we know, love or hate. The famous philosopher of mind Jaegwon Kim calls this "Descartes' revenge," because if we are keen to point to dualists and say, "ha, how do you explain the interaction between mind and matter, silly Billy?"; well, the materialist's clever solution is to forfeit mental causation altogether, but as

41. Spaemann, *Essays in Anthropology,* xxiv. In other words, mind was made for the sake of matter, rather than the other way around. Echoing this, John Haldane ("Common Sense, Metaphysics, and the Existence of God," 383) says, "Ironically, one might even say that it was Descartes's dualism that made scientism possible by yielding everything publicly observable to reductionist explanation, thereby leaving the residue (mind) liable to elimination on grounds of empirical-cum-explanatory redundancy." David Braine (*The Human Person,* 23) argues, "for materialism to get going at all in its main contemporary form it is an absolute condition that one should have established a dualistic pattern of analysis of what goes on in human life."

42. Somerhoff, "The Abstract Characteristics of Living Systems."

43. Young, *An Introduction to the Study of Man,* 86–87.

another renowned philosopher of mind (Jerry Fodor) admits, this amounts to the end of the world.[44]

We will have more to say about the person below, but it may be important to note at this stage that the person (composed of body and soul, and as we shall see spirit) is a primitive indexical fact, namely the "I," which refuses, except under violence of willful elimination, to be captured by any reductive, materialist logic. The person, for example, is only contingently related to this body (yet for Aquinas the body is still specific—see *ScG*, IV, 81), in terms of the flux of matter that constitutes it. As E. J. Lowe says, "The obvious explanation for the contingency of the association [between mind and body] is that while these experiences are necessarily mine, this body is only contingently mine."[45] Or as Geoffrey Maddell puts it, the self, the primitive indexical fact that is the person, is an entity "which purely as a matter of chance alights on a certain set of properties in history but might equally have alighted on another set. This presents a dilemma of awesome proportions."[46] In short, the person is ungrounded. Therefore, it is no surprise that all this talk of the brain founding the person, and indeed behavior, is inaccurate. The crucial sign of this is that the person manifests a profound sense of ownership. Materialism lands us in the position analogous to that of Mrs. Gradgrind from Charles Dickens' *Hard Times*. When asked if she is in pain, Mrs. Gradgrind replies, "I think there's a pain somewhere in the room, but I couldn't positively say that I have got it."[47] Against this we must realize that all mental states to be just those must be "mine": "mental states are necessarily states of persons—they are necessarily owned, they necessarily have a subject." The point being that we cannot even individuate any such states in the absence of a person, for we would then be like the Cheshire cat, and be left with a floating, homeless smile, and therefore no smile at all.[48]

The mental/physical divide is question-begging to say the least, and a fallacy to say a little bit more. After all, it's always the mental telling us about the physical, and on the other hand, surely the physical qua physical is polite enough to accommodate, if not invite, such ruminations, equations, and so on. It is for this reason, among others, that the most we can

44. Kim, *Mind in the Physical World*, 38; Fodor, "Making Mind Matter More," 77.

45. Lowe, *Subjects of Experience*, 7.

46. Maddell, *The Essence of the Self*, 10.

47. Dickens, *Hard Times*, 224.

48. Lowe, *Subjects of Experience*, 25.

hope to say is that there are empirical correlations between "mental activity and brain-function, at least in persons. But the capacity for perception and agency does not of its nature reside in any sort of cerebral condition. . . . Thought can no more be (or be constituted by) a brain-process than a chair can be (or be constituted by) a set of prime numbers."[49] In fact, the notion of a brain-sate is a mental construction, a useful one, no doubt, but very accommodating to awful philosophy (see below).

Joseph Pieper, paraphrasing the work of Eric Przywara, noted that we must recall "the dimension of mystery in all our knowing."[50] But we have left the idea of marriage, metaphorically speaking, and lapsed into pornography, at least in terms of epistemology. Étienne Gilson, somewhat echoing Jean-Louis Borges, points out that we have committed the error of substituting "the definition for the defined, the description for the described, the map for the country."[51] Here, to paraphrase Jacques Derrida, there is nothing outside the text, at least nothing but atomless gunk, to use David Lewis' phrase. But of course, the flux creeps inside the text, so to speak, devouring the map, leaving merely instrumental reason and artificial reality, a skeleton, now without certain bones.

For Aquinas the mind/body divide is wrongheaded, for it is but a logical abstraction, and at times a vicious one (see below). Moreover, his notion of the soul not only makes what the scientists do possible, but also how we live, and what we are. But Aquinas is following in long hallowed tradition. For example, Irenaeus of Lyons who, writing in the second century, argued that a person was neither body or soul, but the union or commingling of both. Gregory of Nyssa, Augustine, and Maximus in the following centuries all argued the same. As also did Aquinas who (echoing Tertullian) tells us that Christ is "written on our flesh." Indeed our "flesh is the hinge of salvation" (*adeo caro salutis est cardo*), as Tertullian rightly insists. Michel Henry radicalizes this insight: "In the depth of its Night, our flesh is God."[52] In addition, he argued that all of the most sublime intellectual operations take place "in the flesh, with the flesh and through the flesh." (In fact, Tertullian is following the Stoics to the point where they argued that the soul is corporeal, and in a sense Aquinas will follow him, at least in certain way.)[53]

49. Ibid., 44.

50. Pieper, *Living the Truth*, 36.

51. Gilson, *The Unity of Philosophical Experience*, 72.

52. Henry, "Phenomenology of Life," 259; Aquinas, *Sermon on the Apostles' Creed*, 3.2.

53. Tertullian, *Res.* 8.2.

The point, put simply, is that matter is a result of soul, not its antithesis: "Form is directly related to matter as the actuality of matter; once matter actually is, it is informed. Therefore, just as the body gets its being from the soul, as from its form, so too it makes a unity with this soul to which it is intimately related" (Aquinas, *De anima*, II.1. 380–84). No soul, no matter— the soul is the possibility of the material, for we must pick out something that is material. Why no soul, no matter? Well we must remember that for Aquinas, "Form is something divine and best, an object of appetite. It is divine, because every form is something of a participation by likeness of the divine act of being [*divini esse*], which [divine act of being] is pure act: for, each thing just to this extent is actually [*est in actu*], that is, inasmuch as it has form."[54] Crucially though, the soul is the "place of forms (*topos eidōn*)" (*De anima*, III.4.429a, 27), Aristotle tells us, and Aquinas follows him. Indeed, the soul is the "form of forms" (*De anima*, III.7.432a, 1–2). Consequently, we can understand that the soul "is the cause of being for living things, for through the soul they live; and living itself [*ipsum uiuere*] is their being [*esse*]. Therefore, the soul is the cause of living things in the role of form" (*De Anima*, 2.7, II,176–81). Below we will see that Christian anthropology is tripartite (soul, body, spirit), something reflected in how we are to understand not only the person, but also by extension Scripture, and indeed the relation between philosophy, science (understood in modernist terms), and theology. For the moment, this tripartite logic is evident between matter and form, but only as it appears in relation to *ipsum esse* (which we can think of as spirit). As Aquinas says, "*ipsum esse* is the actuality of all things, even of every form" (*ST* 1.4.1 ad 3); so matter is actualized by form (most essentially by the soul), yet matter and form, body and soul, are themselves actualized by *ipsum esse*. Here is the crux of creation, for *esse* is the advent and upholding of all creatures, indeed of both the animate and the inanimate, for *esse* is the very presence of God: "Being is that which is most intrinsic to anything whatsoever, and that which is most deeply within." (*ST*, 1.8.1).

Importantly for Aquinas, matter yearns for form, it seeks it out, so that it can be actualized, so that it can be real, be some thing—a frog, an atom, a giraffe. (*Physics* 9, 1045b, 17–19). Matter is pure potential, crucially this means it is non-individual, an idea that Wippel rightly describes as Aquinas' "finest metaphysical statement."[55] Pure matter is radically dependent, fully inherent, and it is only through the priority of *ipsum esse* that we under-

54. Aquinas, *Commentary on Aristotle's Physics*, 1.15.7.
55. Wippel, *The Metaphysical Thought of Thomas Aquinas*, 25.

stand the profound concert between matter and form, indeed portions of matter, so to speak, are mere "stuff," but as Hegel rightly said, who can find such stuff: no form, no matter.[56] This marriage between form and matter, which is consummated by *esse*, is so important for Aquinas that not even God can create matter without form, and for this view he was condemned in Paris 1277. People such as Suarez were later to understand matter and form as separate principles, a view that arguably led to the dissolution of the Thomistic view of existence. It is because of the intrinsic intercourse, or entwinement between form and matter, that Aristotle said, "there is no part of an animal that is purely material or purely immaterial."[57] The aforementioned pre-Socratic temptation was already diagnosed by Plato, for in the *Sophist* he tells us about war between giants who say the person is only a body, and friends of the forms who appeal only to the immaterial.[58] But the point is that the person is *both*. Fundamentally, it must be understood that I am not my soul (*anima mea non sum ego*): "It is plain that a human being naturally desires his own salvation. But the soul, since it is a part of the human body is not the whole human being, and my soul is not I. So even if the soul were to achieve salvation in another life, it would not be I or any other human being" (*Super I ad Cortinthios*, 15.2). Elsewhere Aquinas repeats this telling insight: "Abraham's soul is not, strictly speaking, Abraham, but a part of him" (*Sent.*, IV, 43.1.1.1 ad 2). We will return to this below. Before doing so, it is important to take note of another radical view held by Aquinas when he tells us that the soul contains the body—here again, the Stoics are being followed, to some degree. It is true that form is in matter, but it also contains matter; thus we read, "though corporeal things are said to be 'in' something as in what contains, nevertheless spiritual things contain those in which they are: as the soul contains the body" (*St*, 1.8.1 ad 2). Again, form (soul) is in matter (body), but matter is in form and both participate in *esse* (the spirit).

Now, this means that when we talk about personality change due to physical trauma, and then conclude that the soul is reducible to the mind, and the mind to the brain, we have quite simply grasped the wrong end of a very long stick indeed, for as already suggested, the brain is not a stand-alone-term—just think of the enervatic system: we have neurons in our digestive system. My personality pretty much changes when I'm killed, say,

56. For a positive reading of prime matter see Fabro, *Participation et causalité selon s. Thomas d'Aquin*, 413–16.

57. Aristotle, *Part. an.* 1.3643A, 24–26.

58. Plato, *Soph.* 245e–249d

by starvation, just as a lack of nutrition, bereavement, the loss of legs in war, and so on changes me, so does a pole in my head, and surely that's not surprising. The point being that the body needs the soul, so that it can be a body, but conversely the soul needs a body that is operational—just as the corpse leaves it bereft, so does trauma. As Gregory of Nyssa says, "The power of the soul appears in accordance with the condition of the body."[59] And, it should be remembered that for Christianity the soul too can perish.[60] In short, we must relearn how to think of the soul, for it is a different creature than the body, but a creature nonetheless. As we know, only a mind can speak of a brain or a body, just as all bodies speak of souls: plant, animal, human.

Aristotle, and once again Aquinas following him, argues that the soul is the first principle of life (*arche ton zoon*), in those things in our world which live. The soul allows living things to be, and from that to be known, but as already read all form is divine, so all things are made possible by soul. It must necessarily be allowed that the principle of intellectual operation, which we call the soul of man, is a principle both incorporeal and subsistent. For it is clear that by means of the intellect humans can know all corporeal things. "Now whatever knows certain things cannot have them in its own nature, because that which is in it naturally would impede the knowledge of anything else."[61] So the soul cannot be a body, because then it could not know bodies, and so on. For Aquinas the soul has a twofold nature: on the one hand, it is the substantial form of the body, and on the other, it is also a subsistent form—hence it is the possibility of a body, but it is not reducible to a body. But we tend to succumb to an intellectual temptation here. We start to think of the soul as superior; after all, it is a subsistent form, and therefore it can live apart from the body. And that is true, but one tends to think that is a good thing, whilst Aquinas does not. To repeat, my soul is not me (*anima mea non sum ego*), and that any separated soul is an inferior,

---

59. See John Cavarnos, *St. Gregory of Nyssa on the Human Soul*, 69.

60. Matt 10:28. As Origen (*Comm. John* 13.427–30) says, "For on the one hand, because the soul is capable of sin, and the soul that sins shall die, we also say that the soul is mortal. But if he supposes that death means the total dissolution and destruction of the soul, we will not agree, because we cannot conceive, so far as the concept goes, of a mortal essence changing into an immortal one, and a corruptible nature changing to incorruption." In more Thomistic terms, the soul is incorporeal and incorruptible, but the soul is not eternal as it too is a creature. Why? Because, quite simply, existence does not belong to its essence; in short it comes into being.

61. *ST* 1.75:2 c.

unnatural thing, as its nature is to be in union with a body. Indeed Aquinas says that any resurrected body will have the same kind of organs, muscles, and so on, that we have here—though no doubt transformed.[62]

The soul is to be thought of as a proper part, and a proper part cannot be predicated of the whole: *nulla pars integralis praedicatur de suo toto*. As a proper part, the soul can be thought of as an incomplete substance, with a mixed subsistence—it subsists, but away from the body does so unnaturally. Again, the person is body and soul, or as Lowe says, "The self is what it is, and not another thing."[63]

Humans, who are what G. K. Chesterton called a fabulous animal, and this animal, the person, requires a body, soul, and spirit—therefore, as we know, our anthropology is always tripartite.[64] A body without a soul is meaningless, and a soul without a body is unnatural—like the proverbial fish out of water. As mentioned already, the soul is to be thought of in one sense as being corporeal, at least insofar as it is a creature. The person is made in the image of God, certainly, but without likeness it threatens to suffer dissolution. Tatian, writing in the second century, makes clear the Christian position: "The soul is not in itself immortal, O Greeks, but mortal. Yet it is possible for it not to die."[65] Origen concurs, "the soul is immortal and the soul is not immortal."[66] Accordingly, Origen speaks of the mutability of the soul, and of its fragile movements.[67] Indeed, he speaks of the death of the soul.[68] Crucially, Tatian and Origen speak about two varieties of soul.[69] As Origen says, "The soul of the sinner is in the flesh, while that of the just is in the Spirit."[70] Irenaeus argues similarly: "If the Spirit is lacking in the soul, he who is such is indeed of an animal nature and being left carnal, shall be an imperfect being, possessing indeed the image of God in his formation, but not receiving the likeness through the Spirit—and so his being is imperfect."[71] To repeat, the body is lost without the order of the

---

62. See Updike, "Seven Stanzas at Easter," 72–73.

63. Lowe, *Subjects*, 51.

64. See de Lubac, *Theology and History*, 132.

65. Tatian, *Address to the Greeks*, 13.

66. Origen, *Dialogue with Heraclides*, 25.

67. Origen, *On First Principles* 1.8.4.

68. Origen, *Commentary on Romans* 6.12.4.

69. Tatian, *Address to the Greeks*, 12 and 15; Origen, *Commentary on Matthew*, 13.2.

70. Ibid.

71. Irenaeus, *Against Heresies* 5.6.1.

soul, but the soul without the Spirit becomes itself a type of body itself, as Origen makes clear.[72] In light of such logic, maybe unsurprisingly Ratzinger says, "Creator-creature (instead of soul-body) is at the root of the biblical doctrine of salvation."[73] In this way we should understand that body and soul are coprotagonists in the pursuit of salvation. What is being advocated here is the intimate conjunction of Platonism and Incarnation (at least the Platonism to be found in *Philebus*, which is much more in keeping with Aristotle). Crucially, as Origen warns, "They should learn that a divine being came into a human body, but also into a human soul."[74] It is for this reason that Christ's resurrection does not exist without ours, nor of course ours without Christ's, likewise Christ is incomprehensible without Christians, and Christians without Christ.[75] As Tertullian says, in Christological terms, "so intimate is the union [between the divine and the human natures] that it may be deemed to be uncertain whether the flesh bears the soul, or the soul the flesh; whether the flesh acts as servant to the soul, or the soul to the flesh."[76] We, as the church, are the very body of Christ.

According to Aquinas,

> Something is one simple thing only through one form through which it has being; since it is from the same principles that a thing is a being and is one thing. And so things that are described by diverse forms are not one simple thing. . . . If, therefore, a man were to live on account of one form (the vegetative soul), and to be an animal on account of another form (the sensitive soul), and to be a man on account of still another form (the rational soul), it would follow that he would not be one simple [substantial] thing.[77]

Or Gregory of Nyssa:

> For this rational animal man, is blended of every form of soul; he is nourished by the vegetative kind soul, and to the faculty of growth was added that of sense, which stands midway, if we regard its peculiar nature, between the intellectual and the more material essence, being as much coarser than the one as its more refined other; then takes places a certain alliance and commixture of the

72. Origen, *Against Celsus* 20.134.

73. Ratzinger, *Dogma and Preaching*, 269.

74. Origen, *Homilies on Luke* 19.1.

75. Vagaggini, *The Flesh*, 24.

76. Tertullian, *De Resurrectione* 7. In CC 2, 921–1012.

77. Thomas Aquinas, *ST*1,76.3, *respondeo*.

> intellectual essence with the subtle and enlightened element of the sensitive nature; so that man consists of these three . . . body and soul and spirit.[78]

Consequently, the intellect is not discontinuous with the sensitive and the vegetative, so that there is no such thing as mere animality. Interestingly, this would in effect necessitate defining *Homo sapiens sapiens* as an animal devoid of content, a pure abstraction, whilst the other approach speaks of man as "mere animal." For example, John McDowell refers to human infants as "mere animals, distinctive only in their potential." But for someone like Aquinas "mere animal" is an abstraction (just like mind and body). As John O'Callaghan says, it is a vicious abstraction "if it is then projected back on to reality." O'Callaghan continues: "McDowell's mere animal is unique in reality, a living animality that is a member of no species, who yet stands waiting to be granted admittance by the members of one particular kind of animal."[79] To repeat, the body to be a body requires the soul; just look at a corpse, and yet the soul to be itself requires a body—so as the body languishes in the ground, rotting, so too, the soul languishes in a different form of grave. The soul has a nature and a mode of being; the nature remains the same, but its mode of being changes. As is said, when the worms eat the body, it hurts the soul (or as the Middle Platonist, Celsus said, resurrection was merely the hope of worms).[80] According to the Jesuits (and quite rightly, we might add), we cannot know what Scripture means *ab initio* ("from the beginning"), nor the aforementioned primitive indexical fact of the "I," the person, and once again, neither theology, philosophy and science, when kept wholly separate. Interestingly, Origen's tripartite understanding of the person is reflected in how we are indeed supposed to approach Scripture. We have the narrative or letter, which is equivalent to the body; its moral or dogmatic content, its soul; and lastly, its mystical instruction, which is its spirit. Like the person, this multifaceted approach ontologically preserves or saves the phenomenon, forestalling all attempts at reduction.[81]

We cannot, therefore, approach science or the empirical as if we could do so outside tradition, outside selected values, criteria, etc. And this is not to advocate relativism. Indeed, to deem this a form of relativism would be to share the same default position as the creationists regarding what

78. Gregory of Nyssa, *De hom. op.* 8.5.

79. O'Callaghan, *Thomist Realism and the Linguistic Turn*, 296.

80. See Pedersen, *Israel*, 180.

81. Origen, *On First Principles* 4.2.4.

constitutes truth. It would bespeak a vulgar form of literalism, one that is, in the end, devoid of people. Rightly, to my mind, Edmund Husserl rails against the substructions of science which are approached as if they were reality itself. As Husserl puts it:

> Whatever may be the chances for realizing, or the capacity for realizing the idea of objective science in respect to the mental world (i.e., not only in respect to nature), this idea of objectivity dominates the whole *universitas* of the positive sciences in the modern period, and in the general usage it dominates the meaning of the word "science."[82] This already involves a naturalism insofar as this concept is taken from Galilean natural science, such that the scientifically "true," the objective world, is always thought of in advance as nature, in an expanded sense of the word. The contrast between the subjectivity of the life-world and the "objective," the "true" world, lies in the fact that the latter is a theoretical-logical substruction of something that is not in principle perceivable, in principle not experienceable in its own proper being, whereas the subjective, the life-world, is distinguished in all respects precisely by its being actually experienceable. The life-world is the realm of original self-evidences.[83]

It is for this reason that objective knowledge is bankrupt, for it is a lie, denying its own animality, its own life, indeed its own evolution, and, lastly, its very possibility. Now, of course, such bankruptcy is not inherent in science, but rather contingent. As Baas Van Fraassen rightly says, science is an objectifying discourse, one that has brought us untold riches. But, he asks, "what does it profit us to gain the whole world and lose our own soul? Riches come with a temptation, a tempting fallacy, namely, to have us view them as all there is to be had, when they are so much. This is true of all riches, and it is true of the riches of objective knowledge. Poor are the rich who succumb to this fallacy."[84] And scientism is just such poverty, as Bulgakov tells us, "Scientism is but a pose assumed by life, a moment in life. Therefore it cannot and should not legislate over life, for it is really its handmaiden. *Scientia est ancilla vitae.* Scientific creativity is immeasurably narrower than life, for the latter is living."[85] And all moments, if they are

82. Husserl, *The Crisis of European Sciences*, 127. For a comparison of van Fraassen and Husserl on this point, see Bitbol, "Materialism, Stances and Open-Mindedness," 234.

83. Husserl, *The Crisis of European Sciences*, 88.

84. Van Fraassen, *The Empirical Stance*, 195.

85. Bulgakov, *Philosophy of Economy*, 182.

to be true to themselves, must pass. Rather than the humanities being a proto-science, and therefore guilty of folk psychology (in a pejorative sense), science is a proto-art; for all science is thought by people, we happen to call them scientists, and therein lies science's beauty, its truth, and even its goodness. Why, after all, get out of bed and bother going to the laboratory? If, that is, the desire for truth was something that summoned one, if rationality (whatever that might mean) is better than irrationality—that's good, right, and maybe even beautiful? As said, science is subalternate to philosophy and theology; moreover, science is an act of inchoate theological thinking, at least at its best, and one of pomposity, and self-denial, at its worst; self-denial is all around, and, for what it's worth, for me, that is a deep shortcoming. But theology (read spirit) requires philosophy (read soul), and the body (read science), for theology does not stand alone. Again, Christ does not make sense in the absence of Christians, nor does Christ's resurrection, and as we pointed out, Christ assumes a human body and a human soul.

But in many a trendy Parisian café (as in many an austere Anglo-Saxon philosophical lecture hall) there is a rumor afoot, uttered in conspiratorial tones: *there is nothing but matter.* Like some scary bedtime story (Brothers Grimm, no doubt), we are supposed to both enjoy this story and be fearful of it. Enjoy it, because it is supposed to be radical, even emancipatory, because such materialism is thought to topple every church, make a mockery of all religions—for how can you have religion in the face of materialism? Where would you locate the soul, not to mention the mind? So we are told that all our cultural pretensions skate on very thin ice—love, poetry, literature, intercourse, etc.—for they are but a façade, behind which lies the truth of us all and of everything, the *réel* hiding behind every face, our closest yet most foreign neighbor. As Jacques Lacan says, "What we see in there, these turbinate bones covered by a whitish membrane, is a horrendous sight. . . . [T]here's a horrendous discovery there, that of the flesh one never sees, the foundation of things, the other side of the head, of the face . . . the flesh from which everything exudes, at the very heart of the mystery . . . formless. . . . Spectre of anxiety . . . the final revelation, you're this—You are this, which is so far from you, this which is ultimate formlessness."[86] Without any solid reference points (solid self, or definite soul), disorientated material man stumbles around the rooms of his own house—his own body and life—as

86. Lacan, *The Seminar of Jacques Lacan, II: The Ego in Freud's Theory and in the Technique of Psychoanalysis, 19541–955*, 1545–.

if it were someone else's home. What was once familiar seems strange, odd, even threatening. Sigmund Freud refers to this as the Uncanny. We do not, it seems, want to know what lies behind that thin veil of skin that we call the face, just as we are ashamed of our faeces, making sure that the toilet is the first thing cleaned before visitors arrive, indeed even making sure our lovers do not catch sight of what we release for fear that it might reveal our truth: that we are of the same as that which we excrete. Moreover, think of that beautiful person after whom you lust—distant, mysterious, unknown. But that is why you desire them, for if you knew them—if, that is, you were married to them, so that your eyes caught sight of their humanity, which is of course animality—then desire would hemorrhage away, leaving only a material thing. Maybe this is what Lacan's gnomic statement—"there is no such thing as a sexual relation"—means. In other words, we can only desire that which we do not know, for if we knew it, desire would evaporate. But that means that we cannot in truth desire anything or anyone. All desire is, therefore, a lie, relying on what Lacan calls misrecognition (*méconnaissance*)—roughly translated.[87]

So, according to those who peddle the rumor of materialism, the truth of our situation is like that of a Magritte painting (*La Reproduction Interdite* of 1937), in which the man looking in the mirror sees only what appears to be the back of his head, because the truth is that the face is merely material. In other words, the face as some sort of special, iconic site is a fiction generated, not by what is real, but only by the nominal play of language. For it is language that fools us into thinking we exist; it seduces us into being. Here we have a case of false positives, probably due to HADD—*hypersensitive agency detection device*. There you are lying on your back in summer looking up at the sky, seeing all those lovely clouds, saying that one looks like X—but we do the same with faces, with our lovers, children, enemies, and so on, which is to the say a face is a *false positive*—here we are back with both Docetism and importantly the Chinese room argument, for we have theoretical false positives, insofar as we think there is such a thing as theory. The ontology available to naturalism means that third person subpersonal analyses are all that is available to us—whoever *us* is.

This reminds us of that great nihilistic comic sketch by Dudley Moore and Peter Cook—or Derek and Clive:

Clive: "a man walks up to me in the street and says 'hello.'"

---

87. See Cunningham, "Lacan, Philosophy's Difference, and Creation from No-One," 445–79.

Derek: "that's a bit provocative."

This is our Kierkegaardian leap of faith, wherein we leap, not somewhere else, but into the air, landing eventually from where we rose, but now, after this moment (*Augenblick*) all is new, all is real—the person is real: *ecce homo*. Now what is revealed is an apparent nominalism in our pretence to order and classify, to parse the world in real terms, an eminent example being the abolition of species, which as Hans Jonas tells us, "completes the liquidation of immutable essences, and thus signifies the final victory of nominalism over realism, which had its last bulwark in the idea natural species."[88] Alas, forms, essences, and natural kinds all fade away. In their wake is the now-ubiquitous threat of dust, pure matter, merely arranged, maybe thus rather than so. This is what Henry names "murderous madness."[89]

As Alain Badiou says, "The void proper to life, as death shows, is matter." In other words, "Everything that is bound testifies that it is unbound in its being."[90] This truth of all beings—namely their unboundedness or their unruly nature—becomes obvious in Edgar Allen Poe's tale, "The Facts in the Case of M. Valdemar." For there the eponymous character sits up and announces, "I'm dead," and after uttering these words he immediately decomposes.

> "For God's sake!—quick!—quick!—put me to sleep—or, quick!—waken me!—quick!—I say to you that I am dead!" . . . For what really occurred, however, it is quite impossible that any human being could have been prepared . . . amid ejaculations of "dead! dead!" absolutely bursting from the tongue and not from the lips of the sufferer, his whole frame at once—within the space of a single minute, or even less, shrunk—crumbled—absolutely rotted away beneath my hands. Upon the bed, before that whole company, there lay a nearly liquid mass of loathsome—of detestable putridity.[91]

This is the suicide of suicide, of life before death, for now we have only the mere flux of phylogeny, and a rather boring descriptive manner of speaking about it—Manchester United 3, Liverpool 1—giraffe 1, tiger 2—mental disposition 1, vs., mental disposition 2.

88. Jonas, *The Phenomenon of Life*, 45.

89. Henry, *Barbarism*, xvii.

90. Badiou, "The Event as Trans-Being," 99.

91. See Cunningham, "The End of Death?"

Two behaviorists have sex, and afterwards, one turns to the other and says, "that was great for you, but how was it for me?" Indeed, Aristotle argued that a corpse was only homonymously a dead body; that must now be reversed—a body is only homonymously a body, it is more of a corpse.

As Stevie Turner puts it in the poem entitled, *The Conclusion:*

> *My love, she said*
> *That when all's considered*
> *We are only machines.*
> *I chained her to my bedroom wall*
> *For future use*
> *And she cried*[92]

As Henry already pointed out, the book of Revelation tells us: "During those days men will seek death, but will not find it; they will long to die, but death will elude them."[93] In line with this, Sigmund Freud warned us that "We may be astonished to find out how little agreement there is among biologists on the subject of natural death and in fact that the whole concept of death melts away under their hands." Lynn Rothschild makes much the same point: "It is impossible unambiguously to determine death in a reductionist way"; Wilford Spradlin and Patricia Porterfield: "With the dissolution of absolutes, we may speculate that old concepts like God and man died into each other or dissolved into each other to form a uniform continuum. From this point of view, the merger of God and man is a conquest of death, which moved from a definitive event or entity to a fluid process in which life and death are relative organizational patterns."[94] And they are not alone, for it seemed fashionable, at least for a time, to argue that life was dead, or at least did not exist. For example, the biologist Ernest Kahane published a book in 1963 entitled *Life Does Not Exist.*[95] And as we know, biologists no longer study life (what do they do, then, and why should they

---

92. Turner, *Up to Date Poems, 1968–1982*, 24. Or as William James put it: "I thought I would call an 'automatic sweetheart,' meaning a soulless which should be indistinguishable from a spiritually animated maiden, laughing, talking blushing, nursing us, and performing all feminine offices as tactfully and sweet as if her soul were in her. Would anyone regard her as a full equivalent? Certainly not." As quoted by Putnam, in *The Threefold Cord*, 73.

93. Rev 9:6. See Cunningham, "The End of Death?"

94. Freud, "Beyond the Pleasure Principle," 617. Rothschild, "The Role of Emergence in Biology," 159; Spradlin and Porterfield, *The Search for Certainty*, 236.

95. Kahane, *La vie n'existe pas!*

still be called biologists? we would be inclined to ask). More recently, Stanley Shostak joined the wake, publishing the *Death of Life*—whither the soul I ask?[96] Again, to invoke Henry, "The naturalization of the human being, in all its forms and various guises, is the latest avatar of the Galilean *a priori*. The human being is no different than a thing."[97] But more than that, as we read above, there is not even a thing.

We are, therefore, not as Samuel Beckett suggested, *born astride a grave,* but in a grave, it just happens to be above the ground—there just may be some twitching, not sure. Why? Because as should be apparent by now, death (not to mention, truth, goodness, beauty, rape, genocide, and so on) are not real phenomena in the world of ontological naturalism, reductionism, and materialism—how could they be, death especially? Their collective ontology, so to speak, is too weak, too one-dimensional to accommodate anything as exotic as death—it is a wine beyond their purse. To the point, materialism, physicalism, and ontological naturalism—which are three flavors of the same ice-cream, are the equivalent to an ontological stroke, on par with locked in syndrome, or better Cotard syndrome (those people who are biologically alive, but are convinced they are in truth actually dead—maybe they are the smart ones, and the rest of us are just whistling in the wind). Claude Benard rightly tells us, *"La vie, c'est la mort,"* but this only makes sense in light of Christ, otherwise, as said, there is no death, and most certainly no life.[98]

Now, as we know, for those such as Irenaeus, Gregory of Nyssa, and Maximus, to mention but three, death was a blessing and not a curse, for if humans were immortal, that means their sin would be forever. Moreover, the holocaust they inflict in pursuing sensible things would have no end. For them such gifts are jagged, but they cut us free. But death is a blessing in another sense; we must be alive to die. That being said, Joseph Ratzinger is correct when he says, "Death does not belong fundamentally and irrevocably to the structure of creation, to matter."[99] How then do we reconcile this with the idea of a good creation? Alexander Schmemann moves us towards understanding this profound and disturbing conundrum when he says that "Christianity is not reconciliation with death. It is the revelation of death, and it reveals death because it is the revelation of Life." And

---

96. Shostak, *Death of Life.*

97. Henry, *Barbarism*, xviii.

98. Cunningham, *Darwin's Pious Idea*, chapter 7.

99. Ratzinger, *The God of Jesus Christ*, 100.

this places Christianity in stark contrast to both secularism and religion: "Religion and secularism by explaining death give it a 'status,' a rationale, make it 'normal.' Only Christianity proclaims it to be abnormal, and, therefore, truly horrible. At the grave of Lazarus Christ wept." (Not to mention Gethsemane, and of course the crucifixion.) Schmemann mentions "religion" here because there is a temptation in religion to hand this world over to death and then to build the dream of another world, a world in which the mystery and horror of death will not exist. "To accept God's world as a cosmic cemetery which is to be abolished and replaced by 'another world' which looks like a cemetery ('eternal rest') and to call this religion, to live in a cosmic cemetery and to 'dispose' every day of thousands of corpses and to get excited about a 'just society' and to be happy!—this is the fall of man."[100]

Christianity is not, therefore, about reconciling us to death. On the contrary, Christianity reveals death to be what it is: abominable, or unnatural. Indeed, without this perspective, we can never speak of the horror of death, for it would be only a natural event, a moment in a process, and any resistance to it would be the result of an illusory sense of worth. Moreover, in being part of a natural process, the problem of actually picking it out, that is, noticing it when employing only natural terms, would be intractable. In short, death is horrific and abnormal, and such imitations of its unnaturalness point to it being overcome—not by positing some heaven in the sky, or through talk of a soul slipping away to some ephemeral realm, but rather by speaking of the hope of bodily resurrection, hope already present, however implicitly, in our noticing death and our sense of repulsion from it. Therefore, in terms of the prodigal son(s) and of the sins of Adam, we can understand death to be educative in at least one sense. As Behr points out, until we "lie with our bodies decomposing in the grave . . . our temptation will always be to think that we have life from ourselves."[101] Ratzinger echoes this understanding when he talks of the tribunal of death.[102] Baptism is the profound mark of this tribunal: "As sacramental dying with Christ, it is an anticipation of real death: all our dying, which marks and permeates our whole life as the constant *processus mortus in vitam* is now no longer merely our own dying but, rather, because of baptism and for the sake of baptism and act of divine grace: the birth of the new Adam, the

---

100. Schmemann, *The World as Sacrament*, 124. Also see Schmemann, *O Death Where is Thy Sting?* 11–12.

101. Behr, *The Mystery of Christ*, 100.

102. Ratzinger, *Dogma and Preaching*, 253.

onset of resurrection."[103] This is not to be thought of as a theodicy for death reminiscent of the work of John Hick, rather a complete engagement with the reality of death: that it is unnatural (as Aquinas insisted it is), but yet it is; something we do not realize outside Christ, at least not fully. Again to quote Ratzinger (here being influenced by Henri de Lubac, who is in turn influenced by, among others, Nicholas Cabasilas), "Only the humanity of the Second Adam is the true humanity, only the humanity endured on the Cross brings the true man to light."[104] Through Christ we now have the reality of death, in all its horror, but also our overcoming its evil—the poison does become cure, as Hölderlin might suggest.

And because we do not have life from ourselves, because our life is not our own, we are the sign of another, that is, we are the sign of God. Here the message of Christ is most obvious: "Whoever finds his life will lose it, and whoever loses his life for me will find it" (Matt 10:39). It is very interesting that Origen spoke of three types of death, not one:

> I will reply that the soul is both immortal and not immortal. First, let us carefully define the word "death" and all the meanings that come from the term "death" and all the meanings that come from the term death. . . . I know of three deaths. What are these three deaths? Someone may live to God and have died to sins, according to the Apostle (Rom 6:10). This death is a blessed one. . . . I also know another death by which one dies to God. About this death it is said, "The soul that sins shall die" (Ezek. 18:4). And I know a third death according to which we ordinarily consider those have left their body are dead.[105]

The biblical quote of "Let the dead bury their dead" (Luke 9:60) is most telling, offering us a much more expansive view of reality, of life and death, and likewise "do not be afraid of those who kill the body but cannot kill the soul" (Matt 10:28); no wonder that Homer spoke of those living dead as "headless heads," and mourned them so. Indeed, for Irenaeus the soul was a creature, and therefore was only ever contingently immortal, and here, what it means to be immortal returns us to Homer.

If, to paraphrase Gerard Manley Hopkins, we seek to hold fast to our prodigal portion and *snatch* at our own lives, then death will be our only

---

103. Ibid., 251.

104. Ibid., 159. See also Cunningham, *Darwin's Pious Idea*, chapter 7; and Riches, *Ecce Homo*.

105. *On First Principles*, 4. 4.9–10; as quoted in Blosser, *Become Like Angels*, 241.

possession, for in the violent exchange of any such market, or economy, the only wages paid will be those of death. But instead of ownership and possession we give thanks for that which we are, for what we have received, and in this way a new economy is possible, that of the resurrection. But as already suggested, there is another resurrection needed—*one before death*, let us call it that of Lazarus, one that will save nature, and indeed science: *Et expecto resurrectionem morturoum. Et vitam venturi saeculi.* And this resurrection is enacted by the rejection of materialism and ontological naturalism with all their myths and fundamentalist ideology. For, it should be pointed out, materialism fails on every count. It is vacuous and question begging, unscientific, and indeed self-hating. In other words, materialists hate matter. Moreover, they misrepresent matter, but in so doing they are, like some latter-day Macbeth, forever haunted by the ghost of the very thing they have sought to kill, namely, the material.

A major problem facing materialism stems from something referred to as Hempel's Dilemma. In general terms, naturalism is usually thought to assert that all that exists can be explained naturally, using the laws of nature and so on; but of course what "nature" is, what qualifies as "natural," seems to be rather open. The next move is to appeal to physics, arguing that philosophy should invoke whatever physics says is the basic and therefore true description of the natural or physical world. But the problem then becomes one of adequacy, for in terms of the mind, for example, there is no worked-out physical theory. So we must appeal to some future physics. But because we have no idea what that future, supposedly complete physics will say (what its terms, concepts, or content will be), the whole procedure appears to be wholly vacuous and question begging. Here is Smart's definition: "By materialism I mean the theory that there is nothing in the world over and above those entities which are postulated by physics (or, of course, those entities which will be postulated by future and more adequate physical theories)."[106] Imagine a creationist saying something similar, such as—okay, okay, the current fossil record may not wholly support my views, *but you wait and see*, future discoveries will.

As David Lewis said, "Materialism was so named when the best physics of the day was the physics of matter alone. Now our best physics acknowledges other bearers of fundamental properties. . . . But it would be pedantry to change the name on that account."[107] Goodness, on this occa-

---

106. See Smart, *Essays Metaphysical and Moral*, chapter 16.

107. Lewis, "Reduction in Mind," 413.

sion surely pedantry is to be welcomed, if that indeed is what it is. For you can, after all, only move the goal posts so far before you are no longer on the actual playing field. Because, after all, some future physics might discover ghosts. But that means any current doctrine of physicalism or materialism is beside the point. As Tim Crane and David Mellor point out, "The 'matter' of modern physics is not at all solid, or inert, or impenetrable, or conserved, and it interacts indeterministically and arguably sometimes at a distance. Faced with these discoveries, materialism's modern descendants have—un-derstandably—lost their metaphysical nerve."[108] By this Crane and Mellor mean that materialism has just rolled over, remaining now only as a slave to a theoretically complete physics, which now defines the empirical world. In other words, materialism is a misnomer. Moreover, it is so weak and paltry that it cannot even hold onto its one, primitive term, namely, matter.

For what at first glance appears to be all ruddy, full of the meat of the Earth, dealing only in the soil of the empirical, is rather more ephemeral, immaterial, if you will, at least insofar as it is an ideal, if anything at all. This is indeed, why we can speak of materialism's ghosts. As Bertrand Russell said, "Matter has become as ghostly as anything in a spiritualist séance."[109] In short, as Chomsky makes clear, "The notion of 'physical world' is open and evolving." So we must not beg the question, for "If the scientific under-taking has limits, why should we stick on them the label 'matter', with its old-fashioned connotations of 'extended impenetrable stuff.'"[110] Or as W. H. Auden put it, "love, like matter is much odder than we thought."[111]

Consequently, this once laudable philosophical tradition (well, I'm being kind) is now more like a prostitute who will go by any name science wishes it to be called, not that science pays it much notice, mind you. Crane and Mellor continue: "For those whom reduction to physics is the touch-stone of the physical does not propose to do it in practice. They simply insist that it can be done 'in principle.' But what is the principle? It cannot be physicalism. These sciences cannot be reducible in principle because they are physical, if reducibility in principle (RIP) is supposed to tell us which sciences could 'in principle' be reduced to physics."[112] It seems there is no principle involved; rather there is only the dogma of ideology, in this

108. Crane and Mellor, "There is No Question of Physicalism," 66.

109. Russell, *An Outline of Philosophy*, 78.

110. Chomsky, *Rules and Representations*, 5.

111. Auden, *Collected Poems*, 259.

112. Crane and Mellor, "There is No Question of Physicalism," 67.

case, "no theology." Indeed, as they point out, "Reducibility to physics or to microphysics is a hopeless test of the ontological authority of science: a test that not even a physicalist can apply consistently."[113] Indeed, the whole appeal to the physical is one purely of emotion and not argument. And there is something else rather strange going on in this hopeful appeal to the physical, for why should the "physical" permit reduction? In other words, why are sub-atomic particles, or whatever, so destructive that their very existence would suddenly rid us of the natural world, of the human mind, and so on? Surely, this is just Gnosticism in spades.

Baas van Fraassen refers to the "contrastive nature of explanations." In other words, explanations that say X=B do so in a manner that inform us of why this is the case—why, that is, X is not C. But materialism and physicalism appear to fail this test miserably. Rather, all they offer is the desperate sweat of the compulsion to destroy. It is the Freudian death drive made manifest, for they would rather deny the world, and have nothing, than have something there for which they just might have to give thanks, or at least for which they should be thankful. The elusive (nay, slippery) nature of naturalism is revealed when we realize just how hard it is to give it substantive definition; and this inability surely belies its ideological nature, as is the case with materialism. As Barry Stroud points out, naturalism is a bit like world peace: everyone advocates it, but no one has a clue what it means. As a result, Stroud recommends a much more open form of naturalism but points out that we might just as well call it open-mindedness and therefore drop the otiose, or maybe even distracting, tag of "naturalism," because in the end it is just dogma (again in the pejorative sense).[114]

To conclude, if death exists, God exists; Aquinas said as much about evil: "If evil exists, God exists."[115] Now, this may sound very strange indeed, and we must be careful not to misunderstand it, for Aquinas is not saying that if God exists then evil exists. Rather, it suggests that if evil exists—that is, if we really believe that certain acts, events, and so on, deserve to be called evil—then for this to be legitimate, God is required. Otherwise our pronouncements and judgments are arbitrary and thus cannot be thought of as anything other than possibly *useful fictions*. This is what I elsewhere have called the argument to evil.[116] Joseph Ratzinger makes the crucial

---

113. Ibid., 70.

114. See Stroud, "The Charm of Naturalism," 22.

115. Thomas Aquinas, *Summa contra Gentiles*, 3, pt.1, c. 71, n.10.

116. See Cunningham, *Darwin's Pious Idea*, 282–90.

point that "If the world and man do not come from a creative intelligence, which stores within itself their measure and plots the path of human existence, then all that is left are traffic rules for human behavior, which can all be discarded or maintained according to their usefulness."[117] Here we are, once again, back with Searle's purely syntactic Chinese, the functionalization of truth, which is the advent of physicalist nihilism. As one translator of Aristotle's *De anima* put it, "There are two major ways to go in thinking about everything there is. The way adopted for the most part in recent centuries, not in practice [of course not!] but in the most approved kind of theories, has been to posit a picture of the world that excludes souls, and to try and cope with the wreckage."[118] From traffic rules to a metaphysical and therefore ethical car crash, to the point, as Lynne Ruder Baker argues, we cannot even speak of a car crash anymore, for all we are left are meaningless configurations or aggregations of matter, which we might term carwise. The ultimate crash is that there cannot be a crash at all.[119]

Like some latter-day doubting Thomas, we are incredulous—we need to see the wounds (and we can't even see them), we need to see the soul, to see the person—but where are the wounds for any such test, for wounds are surely impossible, cancer is impossible, likewise murder, rape, and genocide. Take a wound or cancer, for example; one needs a rich enough ontology—in this case an ontology of oncology, if you will—to allow for such imperfections, such phenomena. Speaking purely through the lens afforded by materialism, with maybe an auxiliary logic such as Darwinian survival, well, on the first count there is no real organism, as we know; and on the second, the "radical democracy" of Darwinism offers cancer as much suffrage as the bearer of this condition—pick your team and perhaps cheer: chemo vs. cancer. And it would be anthropocentric of us to oppose cancer; after all, cancer is merely trying to stop cells committing suicide (apoptosis), least that's how one could moralise it. Augustine knew as much, but the metaphysics that imbued his theology allows us to seemingly understand that there is a wound, or disease; that being the case it exists and so in fact does have a certain value: The body "has a beauty of its own, and in this way its dignity is seen to fair advantage in the eyes of the soul. And neither

---

117. Ratzinger, *Introduction to Christianity*, 27.
118. Fuchs, *On the Soul and Memory and Recollection*, 7.
119. Baker, *The Metaphysics of Everyday Life*, 7, 27.

is the wound nor the disease without the honour of some ornament." There is, after all, an intelligibility to cancer, and that demands our attention.[120]

To end, according to the Gospel of John, "He who believes in me, though he dies, yet shall he live, and shall never die" (11:25). I would say also he who believes in God lives and therefore can die, and does so in the hope of resurrection, for in one particular sense (say, molecular turnover), the days when they breathed already intimated that very possibility—their materiality was always in flux, but they were still called by their baptismal name—"Adam, where are you?" Where are we? Indeed, *are* we? This is indeed death in life, but also life in death, which is not, as Celsus argued, the mere hope of worms.[121] As Lowe argues,

> A consequence of the ungroundedness of the self's identity over time is that there is, and can be, no definitive condition that necessarily determines the ceasing-to-be (or indeed the coming-to-be) of a self. . . . [W]hile many will believe that we have good scientific grounds for believing that the functioning of the brain is necessary for the continued existence of the self, nonetheless, in the nature of the case, such evidence as he possess for that is bound to be inconclusive (and not just for the reason that all empirical evidence is defeasible), since we lack any proper grasp of what would constitute the ceasing-to-be of a self. This is why the prospects for life after bodily death must inevitably remain imponderable and unamenable to empirical determination.[122]

Richard Jones says something similar; "We may be an evolved, complex form of animal life ceasing at death, or there may be more levels of reality working in us, some of which will survive death in some way—the scientific study of the body . . . or the correlation of physical and mental states will never prove either possibility."[123] Science, philosophy, and theology (body, soul, and spirit), and indeed the very lives we live, are replete with goodness, no matter how limited, they sing to the possibility of all such life; the sheer beautiful intelligibility of all, and I heard a rumor that apparently intelligibility is a good thing—well, as said, scientists, you are all proto-theologians, and we all must listen to what you teach us, but you must learn why you teach, for, as said, you know not why, and we must with all our ef-

---

120. Augustine, *De Musica* 4.7.

121. See Origen, *Contra Celsum* v.14.

122. Lowe, *Subjects of Experience*, 42–43.

123. Jones, Reductionism, 351.

CONOR CUNNINGHAM   IS THERE LIFE BEFORE DEATH?   151

fort be true to it, that is, to what you tell us, and why you tell it if we are to be truly enlightened. But after all is said and done, we are indeed here, science is here, life is here to which we are beholden.[124] This is the adventure, the very meat of reality, as Chesterton calls it.[125] No wonder then, that Christ tells us to eat (*eisthein*) his flesh, but then tells us to chew it (*trogein*) (John 6:53–56), for only then will we be true to that which lies before our very eyes, or lies under our very sharp blades.

124. Henry, *Barbarism*, xvii.
125. Chesterton, *Orthodoxy*, 148.

V

PERSPECTIVES FROM MEDICINE AND BIOETHICS

9

The Kenosis of the Dying:
An Invitation to Healing

Daniel B. Hinshaw, M.D.

"Blessed are you poor, for yours is the kingdom of God"
(Luke 6:20).

T HE TERSE ALMOST UNCOMPROMISING character of this quote from the
Gospel according to Luke presents an interesting contrast to the more
familiar statement from the Beatitudes by Christ in the Gospel according
to Matthew: "Blessed are the poor in spirit . . ." (Matt 5:3). The lack of the
qualifying statement, "in spirit," forces one to confront the relationship of
poverty to blessing in all its different aspects. The focus of this essay will be
to explore the blessings of poverty in perhaps its ultimate sense, the poverty
of the dying.

Profound demographic changes are affecting the human condition in
the twenty-first century. For the first time in the history of the planet it is
anticipated that by the year 2045 the number of older persons (sixty years
of age and greater) will exceed the number of children (fifteen years of age
and less) in the world.[1] This shift had already occurred by 1998 in the more
developed portions of the world (e.g., Western Europe and North America)
and has largely been attributed to a universal reduction in fertility and

---

1. United Nations, "World Aging Report 2009," viii.

greater longevity among the elderly.[2] The proportion of the world population made up by older persons in 1950 was 8 percent, in 2009 it was 11 percent, and in 2050 it is projected to be 22 percent. Within the population of the elderly, the fastest growing segment is the so-called oldest-old, i.e., persons who are eighty years of age and older.[3] Increasingly difficult economic, social, and medical challenges will confront the nations of the world as a result of this phenomenon.

A proportionate decline in younger persons will replenish the workforce to a lesser extent in coming years, while at the same time the proportion of unemployable dependent older persons will expand dramatically. Another way to appreciate this problem is to examine the potential number of support persons available per person sixty-five years of age and older. In 1950, there were twelve potential workers to support each elderly person, in 2009, there were nine and in 2050 there will be approximately four.[4] The ability of pension plans to address the needs of retirees in developed countries will be increasingly threatened, especially to the extent they depend on taxation of current workers to support current retirees.[5] As the world's population has aged, a major shift has also occurred in the types of illnesses that predominate as sources of human suffering and death. Until recent times, communicable or infectious diseases, especially in the forms of childhood illnesses or epidemics had represented the major sources of mortality in the world. With better public health measures and developments in medicine since the end of World War II, there has been a transition; non-communicable diseases (NCDs, such as cardiovascular disease, cancer, diabetes, and chronic respiratory disease) that are associated with aging have become the major sources of morbidity and mortality, especially in developed countries wherever increasing healthcare budgets struggle to address the challenge.[6] What has often not been so well appreciated is that while NCDs are the major cause of mortality and morbidity world-wide, they particularly cause very high levels of suffering in nations with limited resources where struggling health systems become rapidly overwhelmed by the scope and extent of the problem. "Of the 57 million global deaths in

2. Ibid.,

3. Ibid., ix

4. Ibid., x

5. Ibid.,

6. World Health Organization, "Global Status Report on Noncommunicable Diseases 2010," Executive Summary.

2008, 36 million, or 63%, were due to NCDs . . . as populations age, annual NCD deaths are projected to continue to rise worldwide, and the greatest increase is expected to be seen in low- and middle-income regions."[7]

Most recommendations to address this epidemic of NCDs have been directed at preventive health measures intended to reduce the incidence of potentially preventable NCDs (e.g., reduction of tobacco use and harmful consumption of alcohol), disease surveillance, and treatment to limit mortality, with only a brief reference to palliative care for relief of pain and other symptoms in advanced cancer.[8] In tension with this is the recognition by the World Health Organization of the enormous burden of unrelieved suffering that currently exists, much of it directly related to NCDs. "In September 2008, the World Health Organization (WHO) estimated that approximately 80 percent of the world population has either no or insufficient access to treatment for moderate to severe pain and that every year tens of millions of people around the world, including around four million cancer patients and 0.8 million HIV/AIDS patients at the end of their lives suffer from such pain without treatment."[9] Thus, the likely numbers of persons with cancer worldwide who will suffer physically will expand dramatically in coming decades, especially since the introduction of pain relief and palliative care remains largely a secondary priority. One might reasonably ask if this emphasis in the response of the WHO to the growing crisis in healthcare related to NCDs worldwide is a reflection of some form of institutionalized denial, the same denial that individually afflicts so many members of the human species when confronted with mortality.

The roots of this institutionalized form of denial may be traced to a significant degree to the dramatic changes and successes, which have transformed medicine since the middle of the nineteenth century. With the emergence of the disciplines of anatomic pathology and microbiology, the understanding of human illness underwent a revolution. The phenomenon of human illness became increasingly understood as being caused by specific identifiable derangements, either initiated by the effects of invading microbial organisms or by the breakdown or distortion of normal anatomy and physiology within tissues or organs, i.e., diseases. The disease model has been a powerful impetus for medical progress, whether it has been on the level of public health measures to prevent the communicable diseases of

---

7. Ibid., 1

8. Ibid., 5

9. Human Rights Watch, "Please, Do Not Make Us Suffer Any More . . . ," 2

childhood, the introduction of antimicrobial medications to combat infection, or surgical advances among numerous other innovations, which have saved many lives. Many former scourges of humanity have been tamed or even eliminated by this revolution in medicine. Although this has facilitated greater longevity, especially in developed portions of the world where medical advances have had their greatest effects, aging with its attendant diseases continues to proceed, apparently unaware of its relentless pursuit by medical progress.

The essential optimism, sometimes approaching hubris, of the medical profession about the inexorable nature of scientific progress has led to a view that all illness and human suffering are in essence products of diseases whose mechanisms can eventually be understood; with understanding, effective treatments will inevitably follow. However, among great challenges that remain are infectious diseases afflicting human beings in low resource countries that are not deemed of sufficient interest to funding agencies in developed nations, chronic mental illnesses, and the NCDs of aging identified above. This latter category has proven to be much more intractable to address than originally thought by medical scientists. No cure for aging and death appears even remotely imminent.

With the great focus on the curative, disease-focused model of health care, there has been a substantial shift away from concern about the suffering of individuals who are ill to an intense interest in discovering clues to the diagnosis of their underlying diseases. Unfortunately, in this model the person who is suffering can often be neglected in favor of the disease afflicting the person. "The curative approach views patients in terms of their component parts or as repositories of disease. Where the only goal is cure, facts become differentiated from feelings, and the body becomes dissociated from the mind."[10]

As the primary goal of most health policy makers appears to be the conquest of disease (and by implication aging and death), it seems quite likely that those individuals in the present and coming generations who are not so fortunate as to be prevented from developing NCDs will continue to expand in numbers as will their suffering and mortality. While we await further medical conquests, what is to be made of suffering and death?

10. E. Fox, "Predominance of the Curative Model of Medical Care."

The palliative care movement has been a response, in no small measure, to the denial of death both within the medical and scientific community as well as in the greater culture. The WHO definition of palliative care is:

> . . . an approach that improves the quality of life of patients and their families facing the problem associated with life-threatening illness, through the prevention and relief of suffering by means of early identification and impeccable assessment and treatment of pain and other problems, physical, psychosocial and spiritual. Palliative care:
>
> • provides relief from pain and other distressing symptoms;
>
> • affirms life and regards dying as a normal process;
>
> • intends neither to hasten or postpone death;
>
> • integrates the psychological and spiritual aspects of patient care;
>
> • offers a support system to help patients live as actively as possible until death;
>
> • offers a support system to help the family cope during the patient's illness and in their own bereavement;
>
> • uses a team approach to address the needs of patients and their families, including bereavement counseling, if indicated;
>
> • will enhance quality of life, and may also positively influence the course of illness;
>
> • is applicable early in the course of illness, in conjunction with other therapies that are intended to prolong life, such as chemotherapy or radiation therapy, and includes those investigations needed to better understand and manage distressing clinical complications.[11]

Eric Cassell has defined suffering as "the state of severe distress associated with events that threaten the intactness of the person. . . . Suffering is

---

11. World Health Organization, "National Cancer Control Programs."

experienced by persons" and "occurs when an impending destruction of the person is perceived; it continues until the threat of disintegration has passed or until the integrity of the person can be restored in some other manner." It "can occur in relation to any aspect of the person, whether it is in the realm of social roles, group identification, the relation with self, body, or family, or the relation with a transpersonal, transcendent source of meaning."[12] Dame Cicely Saunders, the founder of the modern hospice and palliative care movement, coined an expression—"total pain"—to embody the full experience of suffering she witnessed among her patients with terminal cancer. She recognized that there are multiple domains in which pain can be experienced: physical, psychological, social, and spiritual.[13] Thus, suffering is experienced by persons and is typically centered in relationships, since one becomes a person in relation to other persons. How does this relate to the Christian tradition and its understanding of suffering?

Sin, suffering, and death are inextricably linked to one another in traditional Christian anthropology. In the ancient Christian understanding, sin (in Greek, *hamartia*) is a break from the way things should be, as much in the natural world as the supernatural, affecting the entire cosmos, most particularly in its relationships. As a result of sin, bad things happen, are experienced by persons, and suffering (in Greek, *pathos*) occurs. Sin and suffering are ultimately connected and lead to death. But, suffering and dying have been transformed by Christ's victory over death into a passage through death to life.[14] "Have this mind among yourselves, which is yours in Christ Jesus, who, though he was in the form of God, did not count equality with God something to be grasped, but *emptied* (in Greek, *ekenōsen*[15]) himself, taking the form of a servant, being born in the likeness of men. And being found in human form he humbled himself and became obedient unto death, even death on a cross" (Phil 2:5–8). Also, "Was it not necessary that the Christ should suffer these things and enter into his glory?" (Luke 24:26).[16] Thus, for Christians, the apparent order has been

12. Cassell, "The Nature of Suffering and the Goals of Medicine."

13. Saunders and Sykes, *The Management of Terminal Malignant Disease*, 1–14.

14. Hinshaw, *Suffering and the Nature of Healing*, 58

15. *hē kenōsis*, meaning "emptying," "depletion". Cf. Liddell and Scott, *Greek-English Lexicon*, 939

16. The Greek grammatical forms used (accusative absolute for *pathein ton Christon* and *eiselthein eis tēn doxan autou*) that have been joined by the conjunction *kai* could be understood as happening in parallel or as one fully integrated experience rather than one

inverted. Ultimate glory comes not through achievements or acquisition of power and wealth, but in imitation of Christ through a humble embrace of suffering and death, the inevitable "facts of life." Suffering and death, which are universally experienced within the life of each person, are from the Christian perspective opportunities for each person to participate in the kenosis of the Crucified One.

Whereas the kenosis of Christ, his self-emptying, was completely voluntary, human persons who experience the process of dying undergo an involuntary form of kenosis, which begins at the biological or physical level. It is a stripping away of those elements, which support function and independence. Just as Cicely Saunders' concept of suffering as "total pain" embraces all aspects of the person, so also the involuntary kenosis of the dying spreads from the physical to the psychological, social, and ultimately spiritual aspects of the person. Interestingly, one aspect of this involuntary kenosis is operative throughout the life of each person, maintaining health at the cellular level. In many organs, healthy fully differentiated cells respond to a program for cell death (apoptosis[17]) and undergo a highly choreographed dying process so that their host, the larger organism, might live. Cancer, to some extent represents a failure to respond to the "kenotic" program for death, a cellular act of autonomous "rebellion" that seeks immortality, but in the process brings death to its host along with the tumor. When individual cells lose their ability to respond to the apoptotic program and eventually are transformed by unrestrained signals for growth they also lose their connectedness, their *koinonia,* with the larger community of cells in their tissue of origin. The behavior of cancer cells is a powerful metaphor for the isolation that affects the whole organism when it seeks purely its own interest and no longer responds to the other, to the non-self. Self-absorption, pride, and ultimately presumption of the divine prerogative—the worst of the passions are spiritual forms of the cancer state.

Traditional understandings of life and death have emphasized their transitional character, particularly in the context of community. The states of being alive or dead have both physical and social aspects in this understanding. Just as one can be socially dead in the midst of life, one can still

---

following the other. Thus it could be translated, "it was necessary for the Christ to suffer, entering into his glory."

17. Kerr, Wyllie, and Currie, "Apoptosis." *Apoptosis* (Greek) suggests a meaning of falling away, like leaves from a tree or petals from a flower and is descriptive of the morphological changes that accompany the breakup of cells undergoing programmed cell death.

be socially alive even while physically dead. Social death implies passage out of the collective memory of the community. By the same token those who are approaching their death sense its imminence in their experience of personal kenosis and begin to prepare socially and physically for its arrival. Modern so-called "developed" societies have tended to adopt a very different view of life and death driven from a medical perspective in which there is an abrupt transition from one state to the other. Such a view has also been consistent with an increasing denial of death at both an individual as well as cultural level.[18]

In the medical context, chronic advanced illnesses associated with the aging process are the physical manifestations of the involuntary kenosis that is offered to all persons, except perhaps those who die suddenly. Organ failure syndromes (e.g., advanced heart failure) and cancer are very common examples of illnesses that initiate this process of kenosis. An examination of the cachexia of cancer will help illustrate the process of involuntary kenosis in stark terms.[19]

With progressive cancer a metabolic syndrome known as cachexia quite frequently develops, initiated and sustained by a complex inflammatory response triggered by the cancer. The hallmark of cachexia is the progressive loss of skeletal muscle mass, which adds to the suffering caused by other common cancer symptoms, such as pain, breathlessness, nausea, vomiting, anxiety, and depression. As cachexia progresses, the suffering person experiences increasing weakness, fatigue, lethargy, and poor appetite, which produce a downward spiral limiting function. The constrained function creates social isolation, indifference, worsening mood, and often overt spiritual distress in the form of loss of meaning and purpose. A very common response to such dramatic physical changes, at least initially, is denial with the pursuit of rescue treatment strategies in the face of death's imminence. To the extent that denial is embraced as a coping mechanism, those who are dying deny themselves and loved ones the greatest opportunity of their lives. They are now offered at the eleventh hour to live out that great precept of the spiritual life: "In everything you do, remember your end, and you will never sin" (Sirach 7:36).

18. For excellent discussions of these concepts, see Counts and Counts, eds., *Coping with the Final Tragedy*, chaps. 3, 13, and 16.

19. For a recent review, see Fearon, Arends, and Baracos, "Understanding the Mechanisms and Treatment Options in Cancer Cachexia." It is important to note that the cachexia phenomenon so well described in the context of cancer may also occur in advanced forms of congestive heart failure and chronic obstructive pulmonary disease.

From a Christian perspective the role of palliative care is to limit the burden of distressing symptoms so that dying persons can fully engage in an active remembrance of their death. The process of kenosis beginning with the physical decline of aging and more dramatically manifested for some in the phenomenon of cachexia extends to all aspects of the person, stripping away any remaining illusions and pretense. This is the beginning of the blessed poverty mentioned in the Gospel according to Luke; not only are the dying invited to experience poverty of spirit but theirs is a poverty that if they can accept it,[20] is complete, encompassing their whole being. With this poverty as a solid foundation, the dying person can now fully engage and reconcile with the other, first with one's neighbor and then with the ultimate Other. Barriers erected by the self have been eliminated. What remains is a healing encounter with the Crucified One, which is fully consummated in death.

20. The Viennese psychiatrist and survivor of the Holocaust, Dr. Victor Frankl emphasized the vital importance of the human person's ability to choose one's response to unavoidable suffering in his classic book, *Man's Search for Meaning*. This is especially true for the dying.

10

On Medical Corpses
and Resurrected Bodies

Jeffrey P. Bishop

MR. JAMESON IS A fifty-two year-old man suffering from amyotropic lateral scelerosis (ALS), which is a motor neuron disease that is usually fatal within five years of diagnosis. He has suffered with it for about seven years, with gradual decline. Currently, Mr. Jameson is progressing toward the end of the disease and has increasingly had difficulty clearing his respiratory secretions, and has had several bouts of bronchitis and pneumonia. During one episode of pneumonia, the patient required intubation and mechanical ventilation. After the intubation episode, Mr. Jameson decided that he did not want to be intubated again. He is currently not ventilator dependent.

Over the past six months, Mr. Jameson has repeatedly said to his family and to his doctor that he would like to be an organ donor someday. Jameson is an intelligent and determined man. In fact, he has done some research on what it takes to become an organ donor, and he understands that, in the United States, only dead patients can donate their organs. He also knows that there are two ways that people are declared dead, and that it is only after a declaration of death has been made that the person becomes eligible as a donor. Each of the two methods of death determination has a different pathway to donation.

First, the typical path to donation begins with a person that has sustained a severe brain injury in which his whole brain is dead. These patients usually suffer catastrophic brain injury, either through massive head trauma, or through ischemic or hemorrhagic stroke. These patients will always be unconscious and intubated, as they will not have the brain stem breathing reflex. These patients are usually pronounced dead by whole brain death criteria. Even before the patient is pronounced dead, the patient is assessed as to which organs are healthy enough to be procured. Once that determination of death has been made, the patient can be taken to the operating room and the long process of removing and prepping his or her organs begins. At the end of the surgery, the patient is taken off the cardiovascular bypass machines and the remains are taken to the morgue.

The second pathway to donation has been developed relatively recently. It is referred to as Donation after Cardiac Death (DCD). While traditionally cardiac arrest (cardiac death) was the major means of defining death, organ donation after cardiac death arose as a way to increase the number of organs available. The procedures for procuring these organs are tightly controlled in order to maximize the viability of the organ transplantable organs. Patients are usually taken to the operating room as life support machines are removed and after the patient's heart has stopped for five minutes, the surgery begins with the purpose of procuring organs like kidneys and liver.

Mr. Jameson suggested to his primary care doctor that he would very much like to donate his organs and realized that he could not do so with a high likelihood of success because his heart would slowly dwindle, leading to hypoxia of his organs, rendering them unsuitable for transplantation. He became frustrated and brought the following plan to his primary care doctor. The patient suggested to his primary care physician that, the next time that he got sick and required intubation, he would like to be intubated. But the goal of being placed on the ventilator and the goal of treatment would not be to save his life, but to keep his organs in transplantable condition. After stabilization, but before he could be weaned from the ventilator, the patient asked to be removed from the ventilator and that the DCD protocols be put into place. The policies at his hospital required that if death occurred within 120 minutes of removal from the ventilator, Mr. Jameson's organs could be procured. If his cardiac death took longer than 120 minutes, his organs will have been hypoxic for too long. The patient's wife and children were supportive of his wishes to donate his organs, but they also wanted Mr. Jameson to die naturally at home and with a minimal of suffering. The goal of donating his organs was incompatible with the goal of dying at home.

Mr. Jameson's desire to be an organ donor presents many ethically challenging problems: 1) is it morally legitimate to start mechanical ventilation to carry out a patient's wish that is not directed at the patient's own good? 2) Is it legitimate for his insurer to pay for his care while in the ICU when that care is not directed at Mr. Jameson's benefit? There is also a practical problem: the intubation—place of the endotracheal tube to support breathing—and subsequent extubation present a technically difficult problem, namely that one is aiming at keeping the patient's organs perfused enough to be good candidates for procurement, but with a plan to withdraw the patient from the ventilator at a time when he is not likely to survive on his own and when he is likely to die in relatively short order.

However, these morally problematic issues melt away if we would but be willing to explore another approach, as recently suggested by Franklin G. Miller and Robert D. Truog.[1] In this work, Miller and Truog suggest that there is no distinction between killing a patient and allowing a patient to die, that brain death is not only extremely difficult to be absolutely diagnosed, both it is also an euphemism and a legal fiction. Given these points, Miller and Truog go on to suggest that we ought to remove the dead donor rule as a pre-condition for organ donation and organ procurement. If their suggestion that the dead donor rule be removed is widely accepted, then Mr. Jameson would be able to do what he wants to do, namely to give the gift of life through the donation of his organs. If the dead donor rule is removed, Mr. Jameson could agree to be admitted to the hospital while he is stable. He could then be intubated, taken to the operating room, and have all his organs removed, including his heart. At the end of the operation, he would then be pronounced dead and his mortal remains could be sent to the morgue.

In this essay, I will lay out the thesis of my first book, *The Anticipatory Corpse: Medicine, Power, and the Care of the Dying*, and I will briefly describe how it is that Miller and Truog's position comes into being. I will first describe the epistemological and the metaphysical thinking that animates modern medical thought such that Miller and Truog's position can come to cohere. The epistemologically normative body for modern medicine is the dead body. (Or as Conor Cunningham asks, is there life before death? Medicine essentially says no to this question.) Under this epistemologically normative dead body, medicine's metaphysical stance has become one in which material and efficient causes are elevated, while formal and final

---

1. Miller and Truog, *Death, Dying, and Organ Transplantation*.

causes are deflated; put differently, the meaning and purpose of the body is deflated and the mechanical function of the body is elevated. Put differently yet again, in modern medicine, the body is merely dead matter in motion; and if its healthy functioning organs are not donated when they are no longer useful to the patient, then that body is ordered to no good. Thus, the logic of medicine has become such that drawing a line that demarcates acceptable from unacceptable organ procurement is merely a choice, as Mr. Jameson would like it to be (along with Miller and Truog).

In the first part of this essay, I will lay out thesis of my book in conversation with Miller and Truog. I will then turn to the final sentence in my book, which is a question: "Might it not be that only theology can save medicine?"[2] In the second part, I will begin to sketch how it might be that the resurrected body of Christ could become normative for medicine.

On Medical Corpses

The Anticipatory Corpse is about death; it is about our dying. It is about how the dead body—the cadaver—came to shape the way we doctors think about the living body. This book asks the question: what would we have to believe about the body such that we in medicine can come to treat bodies in just the way that we do? Specifically to Mr. Jameson's case, why is it that it is so easy for us to think of a failing body—our own failing bodies—as spare parts? I argue that we in medicine think about bodies as dead matter in motion, ordered to function, but not to purpose, and this is the reason that we repeatedly find ourselves in a kind of health care that we find so inhumane, and why it is that so many of us come to see the body as mere means to achieve ends and not as end in itself. For instance, the thought of taking someone to the operating room and removing their organs in order to place them in another living human being would have been unthinkable at one point in our history; now it is not only thinkable, but it is something that has both intellectual support from philosophers and practical support from the powerful transplantation community.

How is it that we have come to this point? How can it be that we see such shifts in the way that we think about bodies? I am not intending to argue against organ donation and transplantation in this essay. Instead, I want to illustrate how it is that we have come to the point where the living body of a thinking being can be understood as only having value insofar

2. Bishop, *Anticipatory Corpse*, 313.

as it is donated to others. It is *not* only that our mores have shifted or are shifting; rather, it is that our thinking about bodies, about the ontology of the body, has also changed. That is to say, ultimately, our metaphysics has shifted. I have argued that the way we think about the living body is grounded in the way we think about the dead body. The medical corpse came to transform how we think about the dying body, but also about the living body.

This shift in our thinking began to occur a long time ago. In fact, it began when we began to open up a few corpses; it began with the rise of modern anatomy. The dead body—the medical corpse—became the epistemologically normative body. What does that mean? The dead body began to shape the way we think about living bodies. By 1780, the law had allowed for doctors and medical students to dissect bodies and the church had given its blessing to dissection for over three hundred years. So why was there a new interest in the corpse at the end of the 1700s? Michel Foucault argued that by the 1780s, the dead body became the fetish of medical students. At this time, medical students all over Europe would wander the streets of London and Edinburgh and Paris noticing who was sick among the poor, and after the sick died, the students would proceed to the cemetery to dig up the dead body. What animated this macabre behavior? They thought they were saving the truth of the body from being lost with the decaying flesh of the dead. Why? Why did this become such a fetish? Because they believed that the dead body contained a kind of truth that had to be seen before the body began to decay. Speaking the truth, the dead body spoke eloquently about anatomy and disease. The truth of the dead body lies in the fact that it is static and not in flux. Life is flux; life is change. It is hard to build an efficacious knowledge on things that are constantly in motion. The corpse is static (well sort of) and can be better known. . . . Put differently, the dead body became an ideal type, the ideal type against which life would be measured. The dead body began to be mapped onto the bodies of the living.

While my thesis may sound strange at the moment, let me push further into the history of medical theory. Surely, you may say, physiology is the science of life, the science of the living body. I argued that the corpse in the anatomy lab moved into the physiology laboratories of Xavier Bichat and Claude Bernard. In the early part of the nineteenth century, physiologist Bichat noted that, "Life consists in the sum of the functions by which death is resisted."[3] Life wells up out of the processes found in dead matter; dead material is foundational. Claude Bernard, the great physiologist of the nineteenth century was eulogized as the Isaac Newton of physiology; he defended the practice of vivisection. "[T]o learn how man and animals live, we cannot avoid seeing great numbers of them die, because the mechanisms of life can be unveiled and proved only by knowledge of the mechanism of death."[4]

Bernard would go on to conclude that the terms "life and death have no objective reality in medicine and physiology."[5] The living body is nothing more than dead matter in motion. On Bernard's understanding, one could not seek the first causes of life in physiology, because to do so one would have to accept vitalism and commit to believing to something akin to the soul as the cause of life of a body. The body, at least since Francis Bacon, has had no first cause and no ultimate purpose. For the physiologist, there is only function and no purpose, only motion but no first or formal cause of motion.

So, what is *life*? Life is when the blood goes round and round. On Bernard's construal, life has no fundamental ontology, at worst, and at best the fundamental ontology is nothing more than dead matter and the forces that make matter what matter is. The observable body is mere efficient cause. Life is a series of causes, within which forces lead to effects, like when a cog turns a wheel, which turns another cog, turning another wheel, and so forth and so on for no particular purpose. Thus medical thinkers began to see the body as the aggregate of forces and causes that force the blood to go round and round. And medicine became a discipline bent on the control of those cogs and wheels. Medicine became about how the failing cogs and wheels can be manipulated to keep the dead body in motion.

Take as an example the way that brain dead people were referred to prior to the birth of the concept of brain death: "living cadavers" or "heart lung preparations." It is clear that the term "living cadaver" comes from the anatomy lab. Yet, the origin of the term "heart-lung preparation" is not as clear. A "heart-lung preparation" was a term that referred to a lab animal that had been prepped for experimentation. The heart would have been

3. Bichat, *Physiological Researches on Life and Death*, 9–10; Bishop, *Anticipatory Corpse*, 67.

4. Bernard, *An Introduction to the Study of Experimental Medicine*, 99; Bishop, *Anticipatory Corpse*, 73.

5. Bernard, *An Introduction to the Study of Experimental Medicine*, 67; Bishop, *Anticipatory Corpse*, 76.

cannulated, an arterial line would have been placed, the animal would have been put to sleep and ventilated (in most, but not in all instances), and a central line placed. The medical students or experimental scientists would then give the animal drugs or cut off its oxygen supply to see what happened to things like blood pressure and heart rate. In other words, the animal would have had its heart and lung prepared or prepped for experimentation. The animal was thus called a "heart-lung preparation." Thus in 1966, people who were unconscious and ventilator-dependent were referred to as "heart-lung preparations." The names and values of the anatomy or physiology lab moved directly into the clinical language of the ICU. The concept of brain death would be a further development out of the anatomy lab and the physiology lab.

So, these ideas grounded in the dead body moved into our debates about brain death, and our understanding of transplantation, where the living organs of the dead are taken and placed into the dead bodies of the living. Once we have climbed into medicine's epistemology of the dead body, we find medicine's metaphysics to be one of efficient causation, the efficiency of the machine of the body. In other words, we are stuck in the normative and normalizing epistemology of medical science, rooted in a metaphysics of efficient causation bent on control. The ontology of the dead body governs what we do to the living body.

In *The Anticipatory Corpse*, I trace this out in several other domains beside brain death, including the practices of the ICU, the euthanasia debates, the spectacle of Terri Schiavo, the rise of biopsychosocial medicine, and even palliative care. I even describe how it is that autonomy reigns supreme in health care ethics. The point is this: what medicine believes about the body, shapes its practices toward the body, leaving us all rather cold. In addition, I trace the way these attitudes toward the efficient control of the dying shapes palliative care and how it also shapes the drive to remove the dead donor rule. I even show how these attitudes toward the body move into the political arena.

So, I would like to briefly describe how this happens, and to do so, I need to give a little background on the relationship of modern science to modern politics. I think medicine is, and always has been a Baconian project—that is to say, we are all indebted to Francis Bacon. It is no accident that the greatest thinkers of the early modern period were not only scientific thinkers, but also political thinkers. Bacon, a political operative his entire life, is the father of the new empiricism. Hobbes, the geometrician, served as Bacon's secretary and models the polis according to geometric science, under the influence of Descartes. Locke, who we think of as a political philosopher, was a physician, who thought of himself as first and foremost a natural philosopher (i.e., a scientist). Thus, knowledge and politics, science and politics, knowledge and power have been caught up together.

Bacon states that of Aristotle's four causes—formal, material, efficient, and final—the quest for knowledge of final causes leads only to confusion. The final cause is of course the telos, the purpose, that for the sake of which something is done, and Bacon thinks that when thinking about the final cause or purpose of nature, we are deceived. The final cause, according to Bacon, obscures our knowing. He notes that formal causes are essentially the laws of nature, and these laws cannot easily be known. What matters most for science is material and efficient causes; that is to say that the only thing that science can know—or at least science in its modernist modes—is matter and mechanism. In other words, in the metaphysics of the modern natural sciences, we must set aside the meaning and purpose of the world in order to know the material and mechanisms of the world, or for our purposes, the material and mechanisms of the body.

How do we know when we know that something is true about the world? When we can manipulate the matter and mechanism of the world. What justifies the new knowledge? What justifies the activity of science? Bacon says that the purpose of knowledge (*scientia*) is to relieve the human estate. What does Bacon mean by this? First, Bacon is interested in how we can be justified in saying something is true; he is interested in epistemological justification. On Bacon's rendering, we are justified in saying something is true if we can manipulate the world with our knowledge; it is knowledge we can do something with. If we can bring effects into existence with information, it must be true knowledge. In fact, that is the very definition in both European and American law for patentable knowledge. If you can manipulate the world with the information, it can be patented knowledge. Second, Bacon holds that we are morally justified in the knowledge we pursue if we can intervene in the world of humankind to relieve the human estate of its frailties. On Bacon's reading, that we can do something in the world with that information, that we can relieve the human estate of its frailties, that we can manipulate the machine of the body, shows us we have the truth about humanity and that it is ordered to the good.

Bacon makes no bones about it though: nature—the bodies and objects of nature—must be coerced in order to get at the truth of the world.

The rock must be shattered, the atom must be split, the living organism must be killed in order for its truth to be revealed in order that the power of that truth can be harnessed for the political purposes of relieving the human estate of its frailties. Put differently, the meaning and purpose of the world are shattered in order to gain mastery over it. Put differently again, the formal and final causes are set aside in order for humankind to become the master of its own fate, the center of its own universe, the god of its own world. That is the move made by early modern philosophy and early modern science: it evacuated the world of its meaning and its purpose, in order to gain control over it. Or, as E. A. Burtt said in 1925, with the rise of the modern natural sciences, humankind with all of her "purposes, feelings, and secondary qualities was shoved apart as an unimportant spectator and semi-real effect" of the great mechanistic drama that is the world, that is the body.[6] Put differently, in Baconian medicine, the line between nature and artifice is blurred.

If medical epistemology and medical metaphysics is grounded in a Baconian project that always already blurs the lines between nature and artifice, then the machines of the ICU can replace the "living machines," as Bernard consistently called the organs of the body. Of course, "life" has no objective reality, but the machine of the body does. The metaphysics of medicine is geared toward efficient and material causes, and meaning and purposes are post-hoc additions to the meaningless mechanism of the world and of the body. The body is meaningless except insofar as it is order to relieving the human estate. And when Mr. Jameson can no longer participate in the good life, we think it is praiseworthy for him to give up his organs, so that they can be used by others who can contribute further to the relief of the human estate. We moderns increasingly are coming to think that the only purpose to which his body can be put is to promote social goods, such as organ transplantation. There is nothing special about Mr. Jameson's body, it is just so many interchangeable parts, which he is not using to the greatest social effect. In other words, Jameson's body becomes a good only insofar as it is utilized for other social goods.

Modern reductive science has consistently claimed that it has no metaphysics. It assumes that it is dealing solely with physics. Mr. Jameson's body is not useful to him, but he sees subtle pressure beginning to mount, arguing that it is praiseworthy for him to allow it to be used by others in society for the good of society. If he no longer finds his life meaningful, then

6. Burtt, *The Metaphysical Foundations of Modern Physical Science*.

he comes to believe that his life can only have meaning and purpose insofar as it can be put to use by others for the good of society. We do not have to think of the body as having an integrity, a meaning, a purpose in Mr. Jameson's dying, precisely because we think of the body as little more than dead matter in motion, ordered to the good of society, having no purpose except that to which it can be put to work for the social and political order.

There is another subtle point, which I did not bring into stark relief in my book, but that I want to highlight here. I did not say that medical science cuts out formal or final causes, believing that reductive science is truly reductive to mere efficient and material causes. I said that in the metaphysics of material and efficient causation there is already a different understanding of final causation, not the absence of a final causation. I did not claim that there is no final cause in modern medicine. The final cause of the body is the purpose to which it can be put by either the individual or the polis. That means that modern medical science is not just a mere reductive science. Modern medical science imports a *robust* metaphysics. It sneaks its much thicker metaphysics into these equations in the service of the politics that grounds modern medicine's formal structures and toward its telos of relieving the human estate of its frailties, of using the spare living parts of the dead to replace the dead parts of the living. For modern medical science the human body has a fundamentally different ontology than that of most people who live in and through their bodies.

For patients like Mr. Jameson, they come to think of themselves in this way. They come to see their lives as burdens to society and to themselves. They come to believe that human meaning and purpose is only possible in donating one's organs. There is little hope in facing death and transcending it in any other way than to participate in the great mechanical drama. Put differently, Mr. Jameson comes to see his own body with functioning heart, lungs, kidneys, and liver that support bare life, but do not allow him to have a good life as he (or society) understands it. There is then in this metaphysics of efficient causation—where the dead and static body is epistemologically normative—a kind of subtle logic bent toward moving us to demeaning the body as mere matter that can have no meaning in itself, but only meaning insofar as it is productive for society. And when the body is perceived to be meaningless to oneself, and one is unable to produce for society, the only way to find meaning in one's death is to offer the body as spare parts. In Mr. Jameson's case, it means his organs can be spare parts for those who might find better functioning in and for society.

A new formal cause is in place, namely the decision of Jameson to give his organs to others; a new telos is in place, namely the telos of relieving the human estate as defined by the polis. And Jameson whose body has all along been really dead matter in motion, might become spare parts for the failing bodies, the failing machines of the body, the failing organs. The living organs of the dead come to replace the dead organs of the living.

On Resurrected Bodies

At the conclusion of *The Anticipatory Corpse* I asked a question. "Might it not be that only theology can save medicine?"[7] When I wrote the last question—or rather, made that last statement, for it is more than a question—of my book, I suspected that there might be many different theologies of medicine. I expected theological responses to my book to be highly particular theological accounts that are dependent upon robust metaphysical and moral commitments. In theology, meaning and mechanism are inseparable from one another. I had hoped for non-generic responses of the one-size-fits-all variety that we usually see in medicine. Typically that will mean something about spirituality and medicine where spirituality can mean virtually anything. I wanted to see highly particular Christian responses that do not shy away from the scandal of Christianity. I also hope to see robustly Jewish or Islamic theological responses as well. However, I am only in a position to assess Christian theological responses, as I am a Christian. In this section, I shall begin a reflection on what I think the resurrected body of Christ might have to say about medicine. I expect that for a truly Christian medicine it will be the resurrected body that is epistemologically normative and not the corpse of medicine.

I want to make two points, the first of which is a brief description of where it is that we find a medicine built around the resurrected body already in action. The second point describes where it is that we should draw out the meaning of the resurrected body of Christ for medicine.

When I said, "might it not be that only theology can save medicine?" I had just two or three sentences earlier said another thing, namely, that perhaps we can learn from those whose practices have been marginalized by modern secular medicine, those who are theologians in the more ancient sense of the word. Perhaps it is they who can direct us. Here I convict myself more than anyone else. I love being a scholar. I love the history of thought.

7. Bishop, *Anticipatory Corpse*, 313.

And even though the theologians think of me as a philosopher, and the philosophers think of me as a theologian, by "theologians" or by "theology," I do not mean those engaged as scholars. I mean those who know God and who enact the love of Christ in the world, not us scholars. Moreover, while I love ideas, I like to see where and how ideas are instantiated in practices.

Our modern hospice care takes its name from ancient theological practices; it is what was offered in the *hospitum* of monasteries. All over Europe, Benedictine Monasteries were set up. St. Benedict believed that his order was called to live out Matthew 25. The poor, the prisoner, the hungry, the thirsty, the widow, the orphan, and the sick were to receive free hospitality in the monastery. Hospitality, the word from which we get the words hospital and hospice, was the chief virtue of the Benedictines. The monasteries had infirmaries where the monks would convalesce, replete with kitchens and chapels for prayer. In addition, the *hospitum* and the *hospitale pauperum*, were for anyone who needed care, whether they were orphans, the poor, wayfarers, prisoners, or the sick. We get the words "hotel" and "hostel" from the Benedictine spirituals. You went to the *hospitum* if you needed food, or shelter, or if you had a cough. So in this setting, disease was seen as just a part of the great list of human afflictions for which the Christian community was called to offer care.

Suffice it to say that, in the monasteries from the earliest time all the way up through the medieval period, the *cura animae*, the care of the soul through Christian worship and learning, went hand in hand with the *cura corporis*, the care of the body. It is also true that Dame Cicely Saunders—the founder of the modern hospice movement—drew her inspiration from the Irish Sisters of Charity in London, who offered care not only to the sick, but the poor of inner-city London. Their hospice was like those of medieval monasteries. Saunders took the idea of their hospice and turned it into the modern concept of hospice, taking it out of the monastic traditions and practices of its origins. But now I want to draw your attention to the margins of hospice care where we can find the resurrected body of Christ enacted.

Harold Braswell, in his dissertation written at Emory University in Atlanta, identifies himself as a secular Jew. His research project for his dissertation was to compare the different forms of care at the end of life. As part of his project he did research on various hospices and their practices of care. An example of the latter of these is a hospice called Our Lady of Perpetual Help Home in Atlanta, Georgia. This hospice is run by a group of Dominican sisters called the Hawthorne Dominicans. Their peculiar name comes from their founder Rose Hawthorne Lathrop. Lathrop was the youngest daughter of Nathaniel Hawthorne, and in 1900 she converted to Roman Catholicism from Unitarianism, and she started offering care to cancer patients, who at the time were marginalized. At the time, germ theory was just getting off the ground and it was believed that cancer might be caused by contagious pathogens. Lathrop offered free care to people with cancer. Lathrop was joined by numerous women in this work, and over the next few years they petitioned to become an order of Dominican sisters. To this day, they are referred to as the Hawthorne Dominicans and they have hospice houses around the world, and they continue to offer free care to dying patients.

Our Lady of Perpetual Help does not accept payment, and does not accept Medicare or Medicaid, because they would be forced to accept Medicare rules. In fact, the Home is technically a nursing home as they cannot call themselves a hospice because they do not meet Medicare definition of a hospice. Oddly enough, the Hawthorne Dominicans hearken back to the traditions of medieval monastic communities, where hospitality was offered to the sick and the dying, extending hospitality, but they cannot take on the word "hospice." So despite adhering to the hospitality of the monastic houses, the Our Lady of Perpetual Help cannot call itself a hospice.

Braswell also notes that Our Lady of Perpetual Help is not primarily a medical establishment. It is primarily a religious institution. The sisters at Our Lady of Perpetual Help understand the medical care that they offer to be primarily a vehicle for the resurrection, which the sisters bring to every patient. Braswell notes that he does not see Our Lady of Perpetual Help as a medical establishment, nor as a nursing home, which is its official designation. He states that Our Lady of Perpetual Help is "rather a hospice, within the Christian hospice tradition."[8]

Braswell describes the care offered in Our Lady of Perpetual Help. The sisters are trained religiously, then they are trained in nursing. They are taught to see the resurrected Christ in the face of their patients. The daily routine of care that the nuns offer to their patients includes praying the hours and daily Eucharist. They move seamlessly between prayer and liturgy to care of the dying. Braswell quotes Fr. Brewer on the essential character of daily Eucharist for the work done at Our Lady of Perpetual Help.

---

8. Braswell, "Death and Resurrection in Our Lady of Perpetual Help Home," 12.

[T]he resurrected Christ truly becomes present and alive to us . . . in the Eucharist. . . . [W]e claim even though the elements appear still to be bread and wine that it actually is Christ there. So when we receive it, Christ comes into our hearts and as such his power dwells in our hearts. To inspire us and to strengthen us to go out and to live the Catholic faith. To do the Christian work.[9]

Thus, the resurrected body of Christ is at the heart of caring for the dying in this hospice. Braswell also quotes a Sister: "So we see Christ in the patients and their families and we hope they see Christ in us. And so it's just like a continuous thing of going from Christ to Christ to Christ.[10]

Braswell notes that

Accepting the resurrection in the chapel leads the sisters to bring the resurrection to patients at the bedside. And yet, in a paradox, these patients themselves represent Christ to the sisters. This paradox is resolved by considering the dual nature of Jesus as both human and god [sic!]. The patients represent Jesus' dying human body, while the resurrected Christ in the chapel is his divinity. In this sense, the sisters are able to move from "Christ to Christ to Christ," because, by moving from the Chapel to the bedside, they move through the entire span of Christ's existence, from death to resurrection, to death and resurrection again. In this sense, Jesus' dual nature provides the sisters with both the energy and the empathy necessary to care for the dying.[11]

Setting aside Braswell's slightly misinformed theological interpretation, the resurrected body of Christ changes our understanding of Jesus's death, and it changes the sisters' understandings, not only of their own death, but of the deaths of those for whom they care. And it changes their understanding of the morally wounded and frail bodies of the dying, such that the bodies of the dying are not anticipatory corpses, but living bodies living toward the resurrected body. In this sense then, I think we can begin to understand the resurrected body as both the epistemological lens through which we interpret all living and dying bodies.

Yet, the work in which the sisters are engaged is not different by virtue of a simple change in orientation. Just as the Eucharistic prayers are performative, where the words of institution and epiclesis bring the Word made

9. Ibid., 185–86.
10. Braswell, "Death and Resurrection in US Hospice Care," 183.
11. Braswell, "Death and Resurrection in Our Lady of Perpetual Help Home," 11.

flesh into the present and the space of liturgy, so also that Word made flesh enables their bodies to do the performative work of care for the bodies of others.[12] Thus, the work in which they are engaged is not different by virtue of their attitude, understanding, motivation, or intention. It is ontologically a different kind of care being offered, a kind of care that originates in divine gift, returning to the divine Giver.

Rather than the corpse, the resurrected body of Christ is epistemologically normative for us. But the resurrected body is not merely an epistemological lens through which the living body is seen. The resurrected body of Christ is an ontological reality. The resurrected body of Christ that is ontologically foundational for the Christian, and it is also the teleological body toward which all bodies aim and by which they gain their bearings. In other words, for the Christian, the resurrected body is not only epistemologically normative, it is also the formal and final cause of our material bodies.

I would need more time and space to begin flesh this out. At his death, as pointed out by John Behr, Christ says, "it is finished." Behr takes this to mean that all of creation is completed on the cross.[13] But I also think it means that Christ's resurrected body is the pinnacle of all creation. I think that these insights need to be brought to the forefront of theological scholarship, but I also think we need only turn to the work of the church to see these realities playing themselves out in the way that the church cares for the frailties of humanity. What would it mean for a Christian medicine to have the resurrected body of Christ as the source and consummation of a Christian medicine? How might a Christian medicine grounded in the resurrected body of Christ look different from a medicine grounded in the corpse as an ideal type? I suspect that there are marginal communities within the mainstream West that are deploying this sort of care, including health care, in their local communities. I also suspect that in non-Western contexts these theologically grounded medicines are enacted. And I would contend that the dominant strand of Western medicine has much to learn from the margins.

12. Pickstock, *After Writing*, 167–273.

13. Behr, *Mystery of Christ*.

Bibliography

Amaral, P. P., M. E. Dinger, T. R. Mercer, and J. S. Mattick. "The Eukaryotic Genome as an RNA Machine." *Science* 319 (2008) 1787–89.

Atran, Scott. *In Gods We Trust: The Evolutionary Landscape of Religion.* Oxford: Oxford University Press, 2002.

Auden, W. H. *Collected Poems.* Edited E. Mendelson. New York: Modern Library, 2007.

Auletta, G., G. F. Ellis, and L. Jaeger. "Top-Down Causation by Information Control: From a Philosophical Problem to a Scientific Research Programme." *Journal of the Royal Society Interface* 5 (2008) 1159–72.

Badiou, Alain. "The Event of Trans-Being." In *Theoretical Writings*, translated by Ray Brassier and Alberto Toscano, 97–102. London: Continuum, 2004.

Baker, Lynne Rudder. "Cognitive Suicide." In *Contents of Thought*, edited by Robert H. Grimm and Daniel Davy Merrill, 1–18. Tuscon, AZ: University of Arizona Press, 1988.

———. *The Metaphysics of Everyday Life.* Cambridge: Cambridge University Press, 2007

Balthasar, Hans Urs von. *Dare We Hope "That All Men be Saved"?* Translated by David Kipp and Lothar Krauth. San Francisco: Ignatius, 1988.

———. *Does Jesus Know Us? Do We Know Him?* Translated by Graham Harrison. San Francisco: Ignatius, 1983.

———. *La Foi du Christ.* Paris: Cerf, 1994.

———. *Heart of the World.* Translated by Erasmo S. Leiva. San Francisco: Ignatius, 1979.

———. *Life Out of Death.* Translated by Davis Perkins. Philadelphia: Fortress, 1985.

———. *Mysterium Paschale.* Grand Rapids: Eerdmans, 1993.

———. *Theo-Drama*, vol. V, *The Last Act.* San Francisco: Ignatius, 1998.

Barth, Karl. *Church Dogmatics* 3.2, *The Doctrine of Creation: Part Two.* Edited by G. W. Bromiley and T. F. Torrance. Edinburgh: T. & T. Clark, 1960.

Behr, John. *Becoming Human.* Crestwood, NY: St. Vladimir's Seminary Press, 2013.

———. *The Mystery of Christ.* Crestwood, NY: St. Vladimir's Seminary Press, 2006.

Benner, S. A., H. J. Kim, and M. A. Carrigan. "Asphalt, Water, and the Prebiotic Synthesis of Ribose, Ribonucleosides, and RNA." *Accounts of Chemical Research* 45 (2012) 2025–34.

Benner, S. A., H. J. Kim, and Z. Yang. "Setting the Stage: The History, Chemistry, and Geobiology behind RNA." *Cold Spring Harbor Perspectives in Biology* 4 (2012) a003541.

Bernard, Claude. *An Introduction to the Study of Experimental Medicine.* Translated by Henry Copley Greene. 1865. Reprint. New York: Dover, 1957.

Bichat, Marie Francois Xavier. *Physiological Researches on Life and Death.* Translated by F. Gold, edited by Daniel N Robinson. Physiological Psychology Series (Significant

Contributions to the History of Psychology). 1805 Reprint. Washington, DC: University Publications of America, 1978.

Bishop, J. P. *The Anticipatory Corpse: Medicine, Power and the Care of the Dying.* South Bend, IN: University of Notre Dame Press, 2011.

Bitbol, Michel. "Materialism, Stances and Open-Mindedness." In *Images of Empiricism: Essays on Science and Stances, with a Reply from Bas van Fraassen,* edited by Bradley Monton, 229–70. Oxford: Oxford University Press, 2007.

Bloch, Maurice. *Prey into Hunter: The Politics of Religious Experience.* Cambridge: Cambridge University Press, 1992.

Blosser, Benjamin. *Become Like Angels: Origen's Doctrine of the Soul* Washington, DC: Catholic University of America Press, 2012.

The Book of Concord. Translated and edited by Theodore G. Tappert. Philadelphia: Fortress, 1959.

Bowker, John. *The Religious Imagination and the Sense of God.* Oxford: Oxford University Press: 1978.

———. *The Sense of God: Sociological, Anthropological, and Psychological Approaches to the Origin of the Sense of God.* Oxford: Clarendon, 1973.

Bowler, F. R., et al. "Prebiotically Plausible Oligoribonucleotide Ligation Facilitated by Chemoselective Acetylation." *Nature Chemistry* 5 (2013) 383–89.

Boyer, Pascal. *Religion Explained: The Human Instincts That Fashion Gods, Spirits and Ancestors.* London: Heinemann, 2001.

Braine, David. *The Human Person: Animal and Spirit.* London: Duckworth, 1993.

Braswell, Harold. "Death and Resurrection in Our Lady of Perpetual Help Home." Presentation at ASBH Meeting, 2013, Washington, DC.

Brosius, J. "The Persistent Contributions of RNA to Eukaryotic Gen(om)e Architecture and Cellular Function." *Cold Spring Harbor Perspectives in Biology* (2014) Doi: 10.1101/cshperspect.a016089.

Bulgakov, Sergei. *The Lamb of God.* Translated by Boris Jakim. Grand Rapids: Eerdmans, 2008.

———. *Philosophy of Economy: The World as Household.* Translated by Catherine Evtuhov. New Haven, CT: Yale University Press, 2000.

Bunge, Mario, and Martin Mahner. *Foundations of Biophilosophy.* Berlin: Springer, 1997.

Burtt, E. A. *The Metaphysical Foundations of Modern Physical Science.* Amherst, NY: Humanity Books, 1999.

Cabasilas, Nicholas. *Life in Christ.* Edited and translated into French by M.-H. Congourdeau, SC 361. Paris: Cerf, 1990; English translation by C. J. deCatanzaro. Crestwood, NY: St Vladimir's Seminary Press, 1974.

Calcagno, Antonio. "The Incarnation, Michel Henry, and the Possibility of an Husserlian-Inspired Transcendental Life." *Heythrop Journal* 45.3 (2004) 290–304.

Carroll, B. W., and D. A. Ostlie. *An Introduction to Modern Astrophysics.* 2nd ed. Boston: Addison-Wesley, 2006.

Cassell, E. J. "The Nature of Suffering and the Goals of Medicine." *New England Journal of Medicine* 306 (1982) 639–45.

Cavarnos, John. *St. Gregory of Nyssa on the Human Soul.* Belmont, MA: Institute for Byzantine Studies, 2000.

Cech, T. R. "The RNA Worlds in Context." *Cold Spring Harbor Perspectives in Biology* 4 (2012) a006742.

Chang, R. *Chemistry.* 9th ed. Columbus, OH: McGraw-Hill, 2007.

Chesterton, G. K. *Orthodoxy.* London: Fontana, 1961.

Chomsky, Noam. *Rules and Representations.* New York: Columbia University Press, 1980.

Costanzo, G., S. et al. "May Cyclic Nucleotides be a Source for Abiotic RNA Synthesis?" *Origins of Life and Evolution of Biospheres* 41 (2011) 559–62.

Counts, D. R., and D. A. Counts, eds. *Coping with the Final Tragedy: Cultural Variation in Dying and Grieving.* Amityville, NY: Baywood, 1991.

Cowan, R. *History of Life.* 5th ed. Oxford: Wiley-Blackwell, 2013.

Crane, Tim, and D. H. Mellor. "There is No Question of Physicalism." In *Contemporary Materialism: A Reader*, edited by Paul K. Moser and J. D. Trout, 65–89. London: Routledge, 1995.

Cunningham, Conor. *Darwin's Pious Idea.* Grand Rapids: Eerdmans, 2010.

———. "The End of Death?" In *Yearbook of the Irish Philosophical Society*, edited by James McGluick, 19–42. Maynooth, Ireland: Irish Philosophical Society, 2005.

———. *Genealogy of Nihilism.* London: Routledge, 2002.

———. "Lacan, Philosophy's Difference, and Creation from No-One." *American Catholic Philosophical Quarterly* 78.3 (2004) 445–80.

———. "Natura Pura: Invention of the Antichrist?" *Communio: International Catholic Review* 37.2 (December 2010) 242–55.

———. "Nihilism and Theology: Who Stands at the Door?" In *Oxford Handbook to Theology and Modern European Thought*, edited by G. Ward and G. Pattison, 325–44. Oxford: Oxford University Press, 2012.

Damiano, L., and P. L. Luisi. "Towards an Autopoietic Redefinition of Life." *Origins of Life and Evolution of Biospheres* 40 (2010) 145–49.

Danchin, A., "Bacteria as Computers Making Computers." *FEMS Microbiology Review* 33 (2009) 3–26.

———. "Natural Selection and Immortality." *Biogerontology* 10 (2009) 503–16.

Davies, Douglas J. *Death, Ritual, and Belief: The Rhetoric of Funerary Rites.* London: Cassell, 1997.

———. *Emotion, Identity, and Religion: Hope, Reciprocity, and Otherness.* Oxford: Oxford University Press, 2011.

———. *Meaning and Salvation in Religious Studies.* Leiden: Brill, 1984.

———. *The Theology of Death.* London: T. & T. Clark, 2008.

Davies, Douglas J., and Alastair Shaw. *Reusing Old Graves: A Report of Popular British Attitudes.* Dartford, UK: Shaw & Sons, 1995.

Davies, P. C. W. *The Origin of Life.* Penguin Science. London: Penguin, 2003.

Dawkins, R. "Darwin's Five Bridges." Lecture delivered at the University of California, Santa Barbara, UCSB. April 2012. Online: http://www.youtube.com/watch?v=t1nuEbFvZ-8.

Denzinger, Henry, ed. *Enchiridion symbolorum*, 36th ed. Rome: Herder, 1976.

Derobert J. *Padre Pio: Transparent de Dieu.* Tournai, Belgium: Marquain Hovine, 1987.

Derrida, Jacques. "Faith and Knowledge: The Two Sources of 'Religion' at the Limits of Reason Alone." In *Acts of Religion*, edited by Gil Anidjar, 42–101. London: Routledge, 2002.

Dickens, Charles. *Hard Times.* Harmondsworth: Penguin, 1969.

Dinger, M. E., et al. "Pervasive Transcription of the Eukaryotic Genome: Functional Indices and Conceptual Implications." *Briefings in Functional Genomics and Proteomics* 8 (2009) 407–23.

Durkheim, Emile. *The Elementary Forms of the Religious Life.* 1912. Reprint. London: Allan Lane, 1976.

———. *The Rules of the Sociological Method.* 1895. Reprint. London: The Free Press, 1982.

———. *Suicide: A Study in Sociology.* 1897. Reprint. London: Routledge, 1970.

Engelhart, A. E., M. W. Powner, and J. W. Szostak. "Functional RNAs Exhibit Tolerance for Non-Heritable 2'-5' versus 3'-5' Backbone Heterogeneity." *Nature Chemistry* 5 (2013) 390–94.

Fabro, Corenlio. *Participation et causalité selon s. Thomas d'Aquin.* Louvain: Publications Universitaires, 1961.

Falque, Emmanuel. *Métamorphose de la finitude: Essai philosophique sur naissance et la résurrection.* Paris: Cerf, 2004; English translation by George Hughes, *Metamorphosis of Finitude: An Essay on Birth and Resurrection.* New York: Fordham University Press, 2012.

———. *Les noces de l'agneau: Essai philosophique sur le corps et l'eucharistie.* Paris: Cerf, 2011.

———. *Le passeur de Gethsémani: Angoisse, souffrance et mort. Lecture existentielle et phénoménologique.* Paris: Cerf, 1999.

———. "Y a-t-il une chair sans corps?" In *Phénoménologie et christianisme chez Michel Henry: Les derniers écrits de Michel Henry en débate,* edited by Philippe Capell, 95–133. Paris: Cerf, 2004.

Fearon, K, J. Arends, and V. Baracos. "Understanding the Mechanisms and Treatment Options in Cancer Cachexia." *Nature Reviews Clinical Oncology* 10 (2013) 90–99.

Filippenko, A. *Understanding the Universe: An Introduction to Astronomy.* 2nd ed. Chantilly, VA: The Great Courses, 2006.

Fodor, Jerry. "Making Mind Matter More." *Philosophical Topics* 17.1 (1989) 59–79.

Foucault, Michel. *The Order of Things: An Archaeology of the Human Sciences.* New York: Vintage, 1994.

Fox, E. "Predominance of the Curative Model of Medical Care: A Residual Problem." *Journal of the American Medical Association,* 278 (1997) 761–63.

Fraassen, Bas C. van, *The Empirical Stance.* The Terry Lecture Series. New Haven: Yale University Press, 2004.

Frankl, V. *Man's Search for Meaning.* Translated by I. Lasch. Boston: Beacon, 2006.

Freud, Sigmund. "Beyond the Pleasure Principle." In *The Freud Reader,* edited by Peter Gay, 594–625. New York: Norton , 1989.

Fuchs, Joseph. *On the Soul and Memory and Recollection.* Santa Fe: Green Lon, 2001.

Garbedian, H. G. "The Star Stuff That Is Man." *New York Times Magazine,* August 11, 1929 page SM1.

Gelfert, A., "Synthetic Biology between Technoscience and Thing Knowledge." *Studies in the History and Philosophy of Biological and Biomedical Sciences* 44 (2013) 141–49.

Ghiselin, Michael T. *Metaphysics and the Origin of Species.* New York: State University of New York Press, 1997.

Gilson, Etienne. *The Unity of Philosophical Experience.* San Francisco: Ignatius, 1937.

Glaser, Barney G., and Anselm L. Strauss. *Awareness of Dying.* Chicago: Aldine, 1965.

Grabow, W., and L. Jaeger. "RNA Modularity for Synthetic Biology." *F1000Prime Reports* 5 (2013) 46.

Gschwandtner, Christina M., "Can We Hear the Voice of God? Michel Henry and the Words of Christ." In *Words of Life: New Theological Turns in French Phenomenology,* edited by Bruce Ellis Benson and Norman Wirzba, 147–57. New York: Fordham University Press, 2010.

———. "What About Non-Human Life? An 'Ecological' Reading of Michel Henry's Critique of Technology." *Journal of French and Francophone Philosophy* XX.2 (2012) 116–38.

Hadot, Pierre. *Philosophy as a Way of Life: Spiritual Exercises from Socrates to Foucault.* Oxford: Wiley-Blackwell, 1995.

———. *What is Ancient Philosophy?* Cambridge: Belknap, 2004.

Haldane, John. "Common Sense, Metaphysics, and the Existence of God." *American Catholic Philosophical Quarterly* 77.3 (2003) 381–98.

Hanson, Jeffrey, and Michael R. Kelly, eds. *Michel Henry: The Affects of Thought.* New York: Continuum, 2012.

Heidegger, Martin. *Being and Time.* Translated by Joan Stambaugh. Albany NY: SUNY Press, 2010.

———. "Memorial Address" (for composer Conradin Kreutzer) in his *Discourse on Thinking,* translated by John M. Anderson and E. Hans Freund, 43–57. New York: Harper & Row, 1966.

———. "What is Metaphysics?" In *Pathmarks,* edited by William McNeill, 82–96. Cambridge: Cambridge University Press, 1998.

Hein, J. E., and D. G. Blackmond. "On the Origin of Single Chirality of Amino Acids and Sugars in Biogenesis." *Accounts of Chemical Research* 45 (2012) 2045–54.

Henry, Michel. *Barbarism.* Translated by Scott Davidson. London: Continuum, 2012.

———. "La critique du sujet." In *Phénoménologie de la vie. II. De la subjectivité,* 9–23. Paris: PUF, 2003.

———. *The Essence of Manifestation.* Translated by Girard Etzkorn. The Hague: Nijhoff, 1973.

———. *I am the Truth: Toward a Philosophy of Christianity.* Translated by Susan Emanuel. Stanford University Press: Stanford, California, 2003.

———. *Incarnation: Une philosophie de la chair.* Paris: Seuil, 2000.

———. "L'incarnation dans une phénoménologie radicale." In *Phénoménologie de la vie. IV. Sur l'éthique et la religion,* 146–54 Paris: PUF, 2004.

———. *Material Phenomenology.* Translated by Scott Davidson. New York: Fordham University Press, 2008.

———. "La métamorphose de Daphné." In *Phénoménologie de la vie. III. De l'art et du politique,* 185–202. Paris: PUF, 2004.

———. *Paroles du Christ.* Paris: Seuil, 2002.

———. "Phenomenology of Life." Translated by Nick Hanlon, in *Transcendence and Phenomenology* (Veritas), edited by Peter M. Candler, Jr. and Conor Cunningham, 241–59. London: SCM, 2007.

———. *Seeing the Invisible.* Translated by Scott Davidson. London: Continuum, 2009.

Hertz, Robert. "A Contribution to the Study of the Collective Representation of Death." In *Death and the Right Hand,* edited by Rodney Needham and Claudia Needham, 27–86. New York: Free Press, 1960.

Hinde, Robert A. *Why Gods Persist: A Scientific Approach to Religion.* London: Routledge, 1999.

Hinshaw, D. B. *Suffering and the Nature of Healing.* Yonkers, NY: St. Vladimir's Seminary Press, 2013.

Hobbes, Thomas. *Leviathan*. Vol. 3 of the Collected Works, edited by William Molesworth. London: John Bohn, 1839.

Huang, W., and J. P. Ferris. "One-step, Regioselective Synthesis of up to 50-mers of RNA Oligomers by Montmorillonite Catalysis." *Journal of the American Chemical Society* 128 (2006) 8914–19.

Human Rights Watch. "Please, Do Not Make Us Suffer Any More . . ." Access to Pain Treatment as a Human Right. Online: http://www.hrw.org/en/reports/2009/03/02/please-do-not-make-us-suffer-any-more-0 (accessed on 14 March 2013).

Husserl, Edmund. *The Crisis of European Sciences and Transcendental Phenomenology*. Translated by David Carr. Evanston, IL: Northwesting University Press, 1970.

Inwagen, Peter van. *Ontology, Identity, and Modality: Essays in Metaphysics*. Cambridge: Cambridge University Press, 2001.

Jacob, François. *The Logic of Life: A History of Heredity*. Translated by Betty Spillman. New York: Pantheon, 1973.

Jaeger, L., and E. R. Calkins. "Downward Causation by Information Control in Micro-Organisms." *Interface Focus* 2 (2012) 26–41.

Jogalekar, A. "How a college student can derive the RNA world hypothesis from scratch." Online: http://wavefunction.fieldofscience.com/2011/03/how-college-student-can-derive-rna.html (2011).

Jonas, Hans. *The Phenomenon of Life: Toward a Philosophical Biology*. Evanston, IL: Northwestern University Press, 2001.

Jones, Richard. *Reductionism: Analysis and the Fullness of Reality*. Lewisberg, PA: Bucknell University Press, 2000.

Joshi, P. C., et al. "Progress in Studies on the RNA World." *Origins of Life and Evolution of Biospheres* 41 (2011) 575–79.

Joshi, P. C., et al. "Homochiral Selectivity in RNA Synthesis: Montmorillonite-Catalyzed Quaternary Reactions of D, L-purine with D, L-pyrimidine Nucleotides." *Origins of Life and Evolution of Biospheres* 41 (2011) 213–36.

Joyce, G. F. "RNA Evolution and the Origins of Life." *Nature* 338 (1989) 217–24.

Jüngel, Eberhard. *Death: The Riddle and the Mystery*. Philadelphia: Westminster, 1974.

———. *God as the Mystery of the World*. Grand Rapids: Eerdmans, 1983.

———. *God's Being Is in Becoming*. Edinburgh: T. & T. Clark, 2001.

Juvin, Hervé. *The Coming of the Body*. Translated by John Howe. London: Verso, 2010.

Kahane, Ernest. *La vie n'existe pas!* Paris: Éditions Rationalistes, 1962.

Kerr J. F., et al. "Apoptosis: A Basic Biological Phenomenon with Wide-Ranging Implications in Tissue Kinetics." *British Journal of Cancer* 26.4 (1972) 239–57.

Kim, Jaegwon. *Mind in the Physical World*. Cambridge: MIT, 1998.

Lacan, Jacques. *The Seminar of Jacques Lacan, II: The Ego in Freud's Theory and in the Technique of Psychoanalysis, 1954–1955*. Edited by Jacques Alain-Miller; translated by Sylvana Tomaselli. New York: Norton, 1991.

Lazcano, A., and S. L. Miller. "The Origin and Early Evolution of Life: Prebiotic Chemistry, the Pre-RNA World, and Time." *Cell* 85 (1996) 793–98.

Lee, G. N., and J. Na. "The Impact of Synthetic Biology." *ACS Synthetic Biology* 2 (2013) 210–12.

Lewis, David. "Reduction in Mind." In *A Companion to the Philosophy of Mind*, edited by Samuel Guttenplan, 412–31. Oxford: Blackwell, 1994.

Lienhard, Marc. *Luther: Witness to Jesus Christ*. Minneapolis: Augsburg, 1982.

Liddell, H. G., and R. Scott. *A Greek-English Lexicon*. Revised by H. S. Jones and R. McKenzie. Oxford: Oxford University Press, 1968.

Linoli, O. "Histological, Immunological and Biochemical Studies on the Flesh and Blood of the Eucharistic Miracle of Lanciano (8th century)." *Quaderni Sclavo di diagnostica clinica e di laboratorio* 7 (1971) 661–74.

Louth, Andrew. *Maximus the Confessor*. The Early Church Fathers. London : Routledge, 1996.

Lubac, Henry de. *Theology and History*. Translated by Anne Nash. San Francisco: Ignatius, 1996.

Luisi, P. L. "About Various Definitions of Life." *Origins of Life and Evolution of Biospheres* 28 (1998) 613–22.

MacDorman, Karl F., and Hiroshi Ishiguro. "The Uncanny Advantage of Using Androids in Cognitive and Social Science Research." *Interaction Studies* 7.3 (2006) 297–337.

Maddell, Geoffrey. *The Essence of the Self: In Defense of the Simple View of Personal Identity*. London: Routledge, 2015.

Mannermaa, Tuomo. "Why Is Luther So Fascinating? Modern Finnish Luther Research." In *Union with Christ: The New Finnish Interpretation of Luther*, edited by Carl E. Braaten and Robert W. Jensen, 1–21. Grand Rapids: Eerdmans, 1998.

Mansy, S. S., et al. "Template-Directed Synthesis of a Genetic Polymer in a Model Protocell." *Nature* 454 (2008) 122–25.

Martin, Dale B. *Inventing Superstition: From the Hippocratics to the Christians*. Cambridge: Harvard University Press, 2004.

Matthews, C. N., and R. D. Minard. "Hydrogen Cyanide Polymers, Comets and the Origin of Life." *Faraday Discussions* 133 (2006) 393–401; discussion 427–52.

Mautner, M. N. "Directed Panspermia. 3. Strategies and Motivation for Seeding Star-forming Clouds." *Journal of the British Interplanetary Society* 50 (1997) 93–102.

Mercer, T. R., and J. S. Mattick. "Structure and Function of Long Noncoding RNAs in Epigenetic Regulation." *Nature Structural & Molecular Biology* 20 (2013) 300–307.

Metzinger, Thomas. *Being No One: The Self-Model Theory of Subjectivity*. Cambridge: MIT Press, 2003.

Meyer, A. J., J. W. Ellefson, and A. D. Ellington. "Abiotic Self-Replication." *Accounts of Chemical Research* 45 (2012) 2097–2105.

Miller, Franklin G., and Robert D. Truog. *Death, Dying, and Organ Transplantation: Reconstructing Medical Ethics at the End of Life*. New York: Oxford University Press, 2012.

Moltmann, Jürgen. *The Coming of God*. London: SCM, 1996.

Mori, Masahiro. "Bukimi no tani [the uncanny valley]." *Energy* 7 (1970) 33–35.

Naas, Michael. *Miracle and Machine: Jacques Derrida and the Two Sources of Religion, Science, and the Media*. New York: Fordham University Press, 2012.

Nagel, Norman. "Martinus: Heresy, Doctor Luther, Heresy! The Person and Work of Christ." In *Seven-Headed Luther: Essays in Commemoration of a Quincentenary 1483–1983*, edited by Peter Newman Brooks, 25–49. Oxford: Clarendon, 1983.

Nesteruk, Alexei V. *Universe as Communion: Towards a Neo-patristic Synthesis of Theology and Science*. London: T. & T. Clark, 2008.

Novello, Henry. "Death as Privilege." *Gregorianum* 84.4 (2003) 779–827.

———. *Death as Transformation: A Contemporary Theology of Death*. Aldershot, UK: Ashgate, 2011.

————. "Heaven in Evolutionary Perspective: The New Creation in Process." *Irish Theological Quarterly* 76.2 (2011) 128–49.

————. "Integral Salvation in the Risen Christ: the New Emergent Whole." *Pacifica* 17.1 (2004) 34–54.

————. "Jesus' Cry of Lament: Towards a True Apophaticism." *Irish Theological Quarterly* 78.1 (2013) 38–60.

————. "Lack of Personal, Social and Cosmic Integration: Original Sin from an Eschatological Perspective." *Pacifica: Australasian Theological Studies* 22.2 (2009) 172–97.

————. "The Nature of Evil in Jewish Apocalyptic: The Need for Integral Salvation." *Colloquium* 35.1 (2003) 47–63.

O'Callaghan, John. *Thomist Realism and the Linguistic Turn: Toward a More Perfect Form of Existence.* Notre Dame, IN: University of Notre Dame Press, 2003.

Onofrio, F. D. *Joseph Moscati: As Seen by a Medical Doctor.* Messina, Italy: ESUR Ignatium, 1991.

Otto, Rudolph. *The Idea of the Holy.* 1917. Translated by John W. Harvey. Oxford: Oxford University Press, 1924.

Parker, E. T., et al. "Primordial Synthesis of Amines and Amino Acids in a 1958 Miller H2S-rich Spark Discharge Experiment." *Proceedings of the Natural Academy of Sciences USA* 108 (2011) 5526–31.

Parrella sj, D. *St. Joseph Moscati: The Holy Doctor of Naples.* Napoli, Itali: Padri Gesuiti Chiesa del Gesù Nuovo, 1987.

Pasachoff, J. M., and A. Filippenko. *The Cosmos: Astronomy in the New Millennium.* 4th ed. Cambridge: Cambridge University Press, 2014.

Pedersen, Johannes. *Israel: Its Life and Culture.* London: Oxford University Press, 1926.

Péguy, Charles. *Dialogue de l'histoire et de l'âme charnelle.* Paris: Pléiade, 1957.

Peirce, Charles Sanders. *Reasoning and the Logic of Things: The Cambridge Conferences Lectures of 1898.* Edited by Kenneth Laine Ketner; introduction and commentary by Hilary Putnam. Cambridge: Harvard University Press, 1992.

Pickstock, Catherine. *After Writing: On the Liturgical Consummation of Philosophy.* Challenges in Contemporary Theology. Oxford: Blackwells, 1998.

Pieper, Joseph. *Living the Truth: The Truth of all Things and Reality and the Good.* Translated by Lothar Krauth and Stella Lange. San Francisco: Ignatius, 1989.

Pino, S., et al. "On the Observable Transition to Living Matter." *Genomics Proteomics Bioinformatics* 9 (2011) 7–14.

Powner, M. W., et al. "Synthesis of Activated Pyrimidine Ribonucleotides in Prebiotically Plausible Conditions." *Nature* 459 (2009) 239–42.

Pross, A. "On the Emergence of Biological Complexity: Life as a Kinetic State of Matter." *Origins of Life and Evolution of Biospheres* 35 (2005) 151–66.

Putnam, Hilary. *The Threefold Cord: Mind, Body, and World.* New York: Columbia University Press, 1999.

Quine, W. V. "Two Dogmas of Empiricism." In *From a Logical Point of View: Nine Logico-Philosophical Essays,* 20–46. New York: Harper and Row, 1951.

Rahner, Karl. "Anonymous Christians." In *Theological Investigations,* vol. 6, 390-98. London: Darton, Longman & Todd, 1969.

————. "Christian Dying." In *Theological Investigations* 18, 226–56. London: Darton, Longman & Todd, 1983.

————. *On the Theology of Death.* London: Burns & Oats, 1965.

——. *Traité fondamental de la foi*. Paris: Centurion, 1983.

Ratzinger, Joseph. *Dogma and Preaching*. Translated by M. Miller and M. O'Connell. San Francisco: Ignatius, 2011.

——. *The God of Jesus Christ: Meditations on the Triune God*. San Francisco: Ignatius, 2008.

——. *Introduction to Christianity*. San Francisco: Ignatius, 1990.

Riches, Aaron. *Ecce Homo*. Grand Rapids: Eerdmans, 2016.

Ricoeur, Paul. *Oneself as Another*. Translated by K. Blamey. Chicago: University of Chicago, 1995.

Ritson, D. J., and J. D. Sutherland. "Synthesis of Aldehydic Ribonucleotide and Amino Acid Precursors by Photoredox Chemistry." *Angewandte Chemie International Edition (English)* 52 (2013) 5845–47.

Rizzolatti, Giacomo, and Laila Craighero. "The Mirror-Neuron System." *Annual Review of Neuroscience* 27 (2004) 169–92.

Robertson, M. P., and G. F. Joyce. "The Origins of the RNA World." *Cold Spring Harbor Perspectives in Biology* (2012) 22 pages. Online: http://cshperspectives.cshlp.org/content/early/2010/04/26/cshperspect.a003608.full.pdf+html.

Ruse, Michael. *Taking Darwin Seriously: A Naturalistic Approach to Philosophy*. Oxford: Blackwell, 1986.

Ruse, Michael, and Edward O. Wilson. "The Evolution of Ethics." In *Religion and the Natural Sciences: The Range of Engagement*, edited by James Huchingson, 308–12. San Diego: Harcourt Brace, 1993.

Russell, Bertrand. *An Outline of Philosophy*. London: Routledge, 1927.

Russell, Norman. *Cyril of Alexandria*. London: Routledge, 2000.

——. *The Doctrine of Deification in the Greek Patristic Tradition*. Oxford: Oxford University, 2004.

Russell, Robert J. "Bodily Resurrection, Eschatology, and Scientific Cosmology." In *Resurrection: Theological and Scientific Assessment,* edited by Ted Peters, Robert John Russell, and Michael Welker, 3–30. Grand Rapids: Eerdmans, 2002.

Sagan, C. *The Cosmic Connection: An Extraterrestrial Perspective*. Garden City, NY: Anchor Press/Doubleday, 1973.

Saladino, R., et al. "Formamide and the Origin of Life." *Physics of Life Review* 9 (2012) 84–104.

Saladino, R., et al. "From the One-Carbon Amide Formamide to RNA All the Steps are Prebiotically Possible." *Biochimie* 94 (2012) 1451–56.

Saunders, C., and N. Sykes. *The Management of Terminal Malignant Disease*. 3rd ed. London: Hodder and Stoughton, 1993.

Schmemann, Alexander. *O Death Where is Thy Sting?* Translated by Alexis Vinogradov. Crestwood, NY: St. Vladimir's Seminary Press, 2003.

——. *The World as Sacrament*. London: Darton, Longman and Todd, 1966.

Schönburn, Chrisoph Cardinal. *Man, The Image of God*. Translated by Henry Taylor and Michael Miller. San Francisco: Igantius, 2011.

Schrum, J. P., et al. "The Origins of Cellular Life." *Cold Spring Harbor Perspectives in Biology* 2 (2010) a002212.

Searle, John. *The Mystery of Consciousness*. London: Granta, 1997.

Sebbah, François-David. *Testing the Limit: Derrida, Henry, Levinas, and the Phenomenological Tradition*. Stanford: Stanford University Press, 2012.

Seybold, Kevin S. *Explorations in Neuroscience, Psychology and Religion*. Aldershot, UK: Ashgate, 2007.

Shostak, Stanley. *Death of Life: The Legacy of Molecular Biology.* London: Macmillan, 1998.

Shu, F. H. *The Physical Universe.* Mill Valley, CA: University Science Books, 1982.

Somerhoff, Gerd. "The Abstract Characteristics of Living Systems." In *Systems Thinking: Selected Readings,* edited by F. E. Emery, 147–48. Hamnondsworth, UK: Penguin, 1969.

Souletie, Jean-Louis. "Incarnation et théologie." In *Phénoménologie et christianisme chez Michel Henry: Les derniers écrits de Michel Henry en débat,* edited by Philippe Capelle, 135–51. Paris: Cerf, 2004.

Smart, John Jamieson Carswell. *Essays Metaphysical and Moral: Selected Philosophical Papers.* Oxford: Blackwell, 1987.

Smith, William Robertson. *Lectures on the Religion of the Semites.* New York: Appelton, 1889.

Spaemann, Robert. *Essays in Anthropology: Variations on a Theme.* Translated by Guido de Graaff and James Mumford. Eugene, OR: Cascade, 2010.

———. *Persons: The Difference between "Someone" and "Something."* Translated by Oliver O'Donovan. Oxford: Oxford University Press, 2006.

Spradlin, Wilford, and Patricia Porterfield. *The Search for Certainty.* New York: Springer, 1984.

Stroud, Barry. "The Charm of Naturalism." In *Naturalism in Question,* edited by Mario De Caro and David Macarthur, 21–35. Cambridge: Harvard University Press, 2004.

Szostak, J. W. "Attempts to Define Life Do Not Help to Understand the Origin of Life." *Journal of Biomolecular Structure and Dynamics* 29 (2012) 599–600.

Tesoriero, R. *Reason to Believe: A Personal Story.* No loc: Ron Tesoriero, 2007.

Tesoriero, R., and L. Han. *Unseen.* No loc: Ron Tesoriero, 2014.

Thomas à Kempis. *The Imitation of Christ.* London: Fontana, 1963.

Turner, Stevie. *Up to Date Poems, 1968–1982.* London: Hodder and Stoughton, 1987.

Tylor, Edward B. *Primitive Culture.* 1871. Reprint. New York: Harper, 1958.

United Nations. "World Aging Report 2009." Online: http://www.un.org/esa/population/publications/WPA2009/WPA2009_WorkingPaper.pdf (accessed 12 March 2013).

Updike, John. "Seven Stanzas at Easter." In *Telephone Poles and Other Poems.* London: Andre Deutsch, 1961.

Vagaggini, Cipriano. *The Flesh: Instrument of Salvation.* Translated by Charles Underhill Quinn. New York: Society of St Paul, 1969.

Vishnevskaya, Elena. "Divinization as Perichoretic Embrace in Maximus the Confessor." In *Partakers of the Divine Nature,* edited by Michael J. Christensen and Jeffrey A. Wittung, 132–45. Grand Rapids: Baker Academic, 2008.

Wagner, N., et al. "Selection Advantage of Metabolic over Non-Metabolic Replicators: A Kinetic Analysis." *Biosystems* 99 (2010) 126–29.

Wallace, A. R. *My Life: A Record of Events and Opinions.* London: Chapman and Hall, 1905.

Watson, A. D. "Astronomy: A Cultural Avocation." *The Journal of the Royal Astronomical Society of Canada* 12.3 (1918) 81–91.

Whitehouse, Harvey. *Modes of Religiosity: A Cognitive Theory of Religious Transmission.* New York: Altamira, 2004.

Wippel, John. *The Metaphysical Thought of Thomas Aquinas: From Finite Being to Uncreated Being.* Washington, DC: Catholic University of America Press, 2000.

Wolfenden, R., and M. J. Snider. "The Depth of Chemical Time and the Power of Enzymes as Catalysts." *Accounts of Chemical Research* 34 (2001) 938–45.

World Health Organization. *National Cancer Control Programs: Policies and Managerial Guidelines.* 2nd ed. Geneva: World Health Organization, 2002. Online: https://apps. who.int/dsa/justpub/cpl.htm (accessed on 23 June 2011).

———. "Global Status Report on Noncommunicable Diseases 2010." Online: http://www. who.int/nmh/publications/ncd_report2010/en/ (accessed 14 March, 2013).

Wright, N. T. *The Resurrection of the Son of God.* London: SPCK, 2003.

Young, J. Z. *An Introduction to the Study of Man.* Oxford: Clarendon, 1971.

Zizioulas, John D. "Human Capacity and Incapacity: A Theological Exploration of Personhood." *Scottish Journal of Theology* 28.5 (1975) 401–47.

Zubay, G. *Origins of Life on the Earth and in the Cosmos.* 2nd ed. Waltham, MA: Academic Press, 2000.

Made in the USA
Coppell, TX
11 January 2020